I0795264

Corners of Texas

Corners of Texas

Publication of the Texas Folklore Society LII

Francis Edward Abernethy
Editor

Carolyn Fiedler Satterwhite
Assistant Editor

University of North Texas Press
Denton, Texas

Copyright © 1993 by the Texas Folklore Society
All rights reserved
Printed in the United States of America

First Edition 1993
Requests for permission to reproduce material from this work should be sent to:

Permissions
Texas Folklore Society
Stephen F. Austin State University
P. O. Box 13007, SFA Station
Nacogdoches, Texas 75962

The paper used in this book meets the minimum requirements of the American National Standard for Permanence of Paper for Printed Library materials, Z39.48.1984. Binding materials have been chosen for durability.

Library of Congress Cataloging-in-Publication Data

Corners of Texas / edited by Francis Edward Abernethy. — 1st ed.
p. cm. — (Publications of the Texas Folklore Society ; 52)
Includes bibliographical references and index.
ISBN 0-929398-57-2 : $29.95
1. Folklore—Texas. 2. Texas—Social life and customs.
I. Abernethy, Francis Edward. II. Series: Publications of the Texas Folklore Society ; no. 52.
GR110.T5C67 1993 93—7447
398'.09764—dc20 CIP

Contents

Preface ix

Acknowledgements xxiii

PART ONE HISTORY

1. **Richard A. Holland**
   A Corner Forever Texas: The Southwestern Writers Collection 3
2. **Nolan Porterfield**
   John Lomax and Texas: Roots of a Career 31
3. **Paul Stone**
   J. Frank Dobie and the American Folklore Society 47
4. **Al Lowman**
   Beautifully Printed and Expressive of Texas: Carl Hertzog and the Texas Folklore Society 67

PART TWO FOLKLORE

5. **Joyce Roach**
   Pistol Packin' Mamas: Gun Code for Western Women 87
6. **Phyllis Bridges**
   "First Thing We Do, Let's Kill All the Lawyers" 95
7. **George Ewing**
   Forked Stick Folkcraft 105

8. **Tom E. Breedlove**
No-Eared Joe: Oil Field Folk Hero 115

9. **Fernando Garza Quirós**
The Boat Called *"El Pato"* 123

10. **Richard Graham**
From African Spirit Catcher to American Folk Art Emblem: The Trans-Atlantic Odyssey of the Bottle Tree 131

11. **Bill Brett**
A Hog Race 139

12. **Mark Busby**
An East Texas Lynching: The Humphries/Wilkinson-Greenhaw Feud 147

13. **Jean Granberry Schnitz**
Hammered Dulcimers and Folk Songs: The Musical Heritage of the C. A. Lee Family 159

14. **Patrick B. Mullen**
The Rabbit, The Lion, and The Man: Race Relations in Folklore Fieldwork 175

15. **F. E. Abernethy**
Longino Guerrero's Corrido on J. Frank Dobie 197

16. **Julia Whitsitt**
Peripatetic Proselytizing 201

17. **Janet K. Jeffery**
The Sunbonnet as Folk Costume 209

18. **Sylvia Gann Mahoney**
College Creates a New Breed of Cowboy 221

19. **Rana K. Williamson**
Laughing at the Clouds: Texas Drought Humor 231

20. **Alan Govenar**
The Blues and Jives of Dr. Hepcat 239

21. **Rollo K. Newsom**
Motorcycles and Majorettes: Grave Markers for Youth in Central Texas 247

22. **Richard J. Mason**
Singing People Are Happy People: A Brief Look at Convention Gospel Music 267

Contributors 279

Index 285

Dyak shaman blessing the house in Tanjung Isui, East Kalimantan, Borneo (Courtesy of F. E. Abernethy)

Preface: In which the editor slyly slips in a travelogue under the guise of folklore

This preface is not your simple foist. I am not asking you to come over and look at the slides of my vacation. The fact of the matter is I took a trip through islands of Indonesian folklore, and this is my official report. I received an award last year that carried with it some funds for professional improvement. Needing which, I wrote an inspired travel request for the study of Indonesian folklore, sent it in to the university's vice president, the president, and the governor of the State of Texas, and they all were generous enough to sign it. The result was that I did take a folklore tour, and because you are folklorists I want to tell you about some of it.

"And gladly would he learn—and gladly teach."

I am not long back from Indonesia, but the trip has already achieved a metaphysical status. I see it romantically, the fatigue and frustrations becoming amusing interludes in an adventure in another dimension. I traveled by myself, and being the center of one's concerns does tighten the focus on one's experiences.

I traveled thirty-eight hours, counting layovers, from Houston to Medan, North Sumatra.

The sidewalks in Medan are broken and canted. On one I encountered a street vendor with a pole on which were strung, heads down, a half dozen flying foxes. I asked and he said, "For food. Very good." He also had young monkeys tied about. I did not ask.

I made a trip out of Medan to Bukit Lawan and the orang-utan rehabilitation center. This is an area of untouched mountain jungle where biologists condition young captive orang-utans for a return to life in the wild.

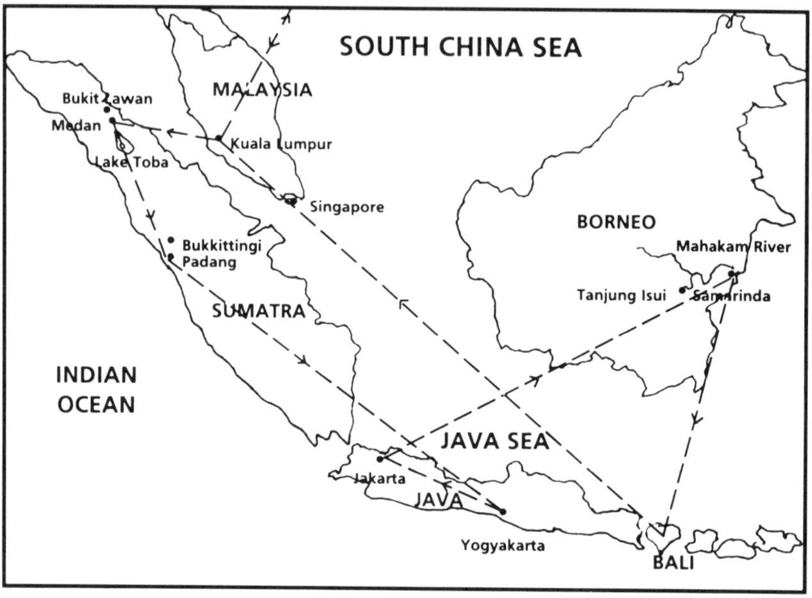

Indonesia

We had been climbing for an hour or more, as close to vertical as one can without falling over backwards, and I stopped on a reasonably flat surface to ease my quivering knees and gasp some air into my aching lungs. The others—the guide and an athletically constructed Dutch couple who had been bicycling around northern Sumatra—had gone on at my request. As I leaned over, semiconscious, hands on knees, I heard a swooshing through the tree tops some distance off and above. With some difficulty I stood erect, turned, and looked up—and saw that God was coming down to me in the form of a large orangutan swinging through the trees. I watched as this grand old man of the forest—he who abducted young maidens to satisfy his hairy passions and he who could speak but does not for fear of being made to do humans' work—came closer. I dropped down and leaned against a tree trunk and sat and watched him as he proceeded in his leisurely swing through the jungle, coming directly toward me. I was struck with wonder at the ease and beauty of this animal and his movement, and I was blessed that he had come down to share himself with me. He slowed as he got over me. He stopped and looked down—a sweet and gentle and trusting face—curious that this mortal should clutch the earth instead of the sky as he did. Then he moved swooshing along and soon was only a sound getting fainter and fainter.

I saw three more grown orang-utans that day, one female carrying her young, and saw several young ones when we reached Bukit Lawan, the village below, but nothing so thrilled and expanded me as the epiphany of that first sight. It was a metaphysical glimpse into The Mystery—assisted, of course, by intoxication brought on by oxygen deprivation.

Back in Medan, thirsting for a cold drink, I asked the porter to bring me a thermos of water. He brought a large thermos that had on it a picture of a child drinking and saying in English, "I love a warm water." Considering this an interesting custom but honored more in the breach than in the observance, I convinced the porter that I wanted *cold* water, whether it was bad for me or not.

The next day I struck a deal with Ucok, a street-wise driver-guide, to make a tour of the area of Lake Toba to the south, the largest lake, more like a sea, in Indonesia.

The Bataks, with a long-held reputation for ferocity and a taste for human flesh, had their origin on the island of Samosir in Lake Toba. Before the time of humans, the Bataks' special god Ompung lived on Samosir. One day he took his rest leaning against a great tall banyan tree. Ompung's movement shook this tree of life, and a branch fell into the water, and from the branch came all fishes and water life. He rocked again and the next branch created insects, and again and tigers and monkeys and jungle animals were formed. The fourth branch produced horses and water buffaloes and pigs, the domestic animals. Now that the world was populated with beasts of the sea and the air and the fields, human beings were needed to watch over them. Ompung commanded that a large bird lay many large eggs. Then he caused the earth to tremble, the eggs broke open, and the Batak people came forth to claim the jungles and rivers around Lake Toba as their territory, where they remain today.

"Ladies and gentlemen, we have received reports of terrible storms ahead, but our pilot is very brave and we will continue this flight." That announcement was made on another Asian flight, but flying Garuda had its moments too. As our plane descended to the runway on the flight from Medan to Padang I could feel the plane tilt, and I could look out the starboard window and see the tip of the wing almost scraping the runway, three feet off, at most. We straightened out and then went into a tilt the other way, almost dragging the port wing on the runway. The pilot finally got the plane trimmed and we landed, bouncing and yawing left and right until we came to a stop. Our landing was dramatic enough to draw a crowd out of the airport and the hangars. As we disembarked, wide-eyed and relieved, I saw the pilot sitting silently with both hands still on the steering wheel. I imagine that he was waiting for someone to pry them loose.

A couple of Dutchmen and I split the taxi fare, about seven dollars each, from the Padang airport to the beautiful mountain town of Bukkittingi, sixty miles uphill amidst forests and volcanos.

The Minangkabau of Bukkittingi live in longhouses built high off the ground with roofs that extend like horns of the tribe's totemic water buffalo. Although this roof design is now an urban architectural commonplace, the early roofs were extended and open to allow air currents to clear this house-of-many-hearths of the smoke from its cooking fires.

The Minangkabau women wear beautifully woven and folded headpieces that also resemble the horns of a buffalo. The women should dress splendidly. They own the houses and the land the houses are built on and all accoutrements therein and thereon—because the Minangkabau are a matrilineal, matriarchal society in spite of their being Islamic.

Minangkabau legends link their people to western culture through Alexander the Great of Macedonia. One of Alexander's three sons was sailing west from India searching for the Land of the Sunset when he came aground on an island. The water receded and the island became the volcanic Mount Merapi, the center of the world for the Minangkabau and the center of the tribe's territory. Iskander, The Son, descended from Mount Merapi, and he and his people took the surrounding land, West Sumatra, as their hunting and planting ground.

Royal Minangkabau house of many horns, near Bukkittingi (Courtesy Paul van Gaalen)

Centuries later the Minangkabau were engaged in a long and violent war with the Javanese to the south. The warring chiefs gathered, and they decided that rather than waste more men in battle they would stake victory on one contest between water buffaloes. If the Javanese buffalo won, the mountain tribe would submit to their rule; if the tribe's buffalo won, the Javanese would return to their island.

On the day set for the contest the Javanese came to the field with a huge male buffalo, hide slick and clean of mud, with horns heavy and sharply pointed. To the invaders' amusement, the tribe led in a young buffalo calf. Because it had only nubbins for horns, they had tied knives to the sides of its head. They had also held the young calf off its mother's milk for two days and it was frantic with hunger. The animals were turned into the field together. Javanese laughter ceased when the starved calf rushed at the bull, searching for a bag and teats with milk. As it lunged to nurse, the knives slashed the bull's belly and wounded it to its death.

The victorious hill tribesmen took their name from the victor: Minang (Winning) Kabau (Buffalo). For those who might wish to establish the historicity of this legend, one horn of the losing buffalo and the stone on which the knives were sharpened to adorn the calf's head are kept by the chieftain of the village of Minangkabau.

I rode a bus from Bukkittingi down the mountain to Padang on the coast. The incline is precipitous. The driver was fearless. He never touched the brake, never slowed as we plunged in a roller-coaster blur down the mountain through villages packed to the roadside with children playing, chickens wandering, broken-down ancients carrying loads twice their sizes, monkeys strolling, bicycles, cars, and other buses taking their halves out of the middle of the road. The miracle is that all things animate and inanimate on that incline were not flattened, smashed, ricocheted out of their early orbits, or sucked into our bus's vortex and carried with us down to the ocean.

I sat that evening on the black volcanic beach in Padang, dined on a roasted ear of corn, watched the sun set on the Indian Ocean, and for one of many times on that trip experienced euphoria.

I flew south out of Padang to Yogyakarta, Java. Tankers and freighters uncountable lay in wait off the north Java coast, waiting to go in to Jakarta for freight and oil. I have never seen so many ships together since World War II. Jakarta is trying to join Hong Kong, Singapore, and Bangkok as an Asian economic power.

The natives pronounce Yogyakarta "Jogja," even though the city's name is modernly spelled with a Y. Yogyakarta is large—three million people—has many sights for tourists to see, and I would take my wife there. The stoplight on Jalan Malioboro, the main downtown street, plays "I don't want to play in your yard" when it changes. The telephone at my hotel's desk, instead of ringing, chimed "Dixie" and "When the Saints Go Marching In." I exclaimed upon this musical phenomenon, and the clerk was amused that I thought these were American, not Javanese, songs. I did not pursue this topic.

The hand of the Hindu and the Indian *Ramayana* is everywhere in Yogya and environs. Episodes from this ancient

Sanscrit folk epic of Rama and Sita are carved and painted on walls, acted by shadow puppets, and danced at the theatre at Prambanan, an eighth century B. C. Hindu temple near Yogya.

The performance of the *Ramayana* at Prambanan begins with gamelan music. A gamelan band is percussive: lots of gongs and xylophone-looking instruments, and drums of all sizes. If a melody is needed it is supplied by a bamboo fife or two, sometimes by a stringed instrument called a rebab, and sometimes by a person chanting. Melody is minimal. Music is an art, and therefore has order and pattern, all of which is difficult to discern for one not schooled in that Javanese musical tradition. One does, however, accept it immediately as background to Javanese dancers acting the *Ramayana.*

Dance and drama are the same in Java, and Bali to the south. The traditional dress for dancers, particularly of the heroes and heroines, are beautifully, classically formal, with towering gold headpieces, extravagant oriental necklaces, bracelets, anklets, and sashes and sarongs in all the exotic colors. The dancers do not leap about nor do they touch one another. Some of their movements are as jerky as the gamelan music; some so fluid that the dancer changes position without noticeable movement. They dance and communicate with a bend of their fingers and toes, a tilt of the head, a movement of an eyebrow. I did not know that I had such an admiration of serenity and restraint and self control until I watched Javanese dancers.

The *Ramayana* dance-drama-ballet begins with Prince Rama, his wife Sita, and his brother Laksamana in exile in the forest, sent there by his evil stepmother. They are peacefully enjoying the forest. The evil giant-king Rawana, however, lusts after Sita and kidnaps her while Rama is hunting a golden deer. The complication of the story consists of Rama and Laksamana's adventures as they search to regain her. They encounter giants, demons, and wild animals. In one episode Rawana's equally evil brother shoots Rama with a magic arrow that turns into an encircling snake. He is rescued by the holy king of birds, Garuda, who pecks the snake to death. Eventually, with the help of the white monkey Hanuman, the brothers with an army of monkeys and bears attack Rawana's palace, kill Rawana, and rescue Sita. Most foreign audiences are ready to stop at this point, happy that the loving couple is reunited. Not so. Rama brings Sita home but decides that he must put her away because she *might have been* defiled by Rawana. Sita—dear beautiful girl that she is—calls on Agni, God of Fire, and goes into the flames to purify herself. Miraculously she escapes harm and Rama generously accepts her as his wife.

Yogya is blessed with palaces and theatres and markets. The solid line of market stalls along Jalan Malioboro is inspirational, almost the equal of the market square in Kathmandu for "stuff." Nearby Borobodur, an eighth-century Buddhist temple, rivals Angkor Wat in Cambodia, and beyond that is the beauty of the road to the Dieng Plateau, which was once a volcanic crater.

Garuda, the sacred bird, is now Indonesia's main airline, and its route from Yogya to Samarinda, East Kalimantan, in Borneo included a two-day layover in Jakarta.

We landed at the Jakarta airport in a downpour and miles from the city. The ride into Jakarta was a drownout with much wading and car pushing. I recovered my body and soul by ten that night and went to a restaurant that was the hangout for peripatetic hippies and others of the traveling demimonde. I sat with an architectural student from Idaho, and we ate mie goreng and drank great green bottles of Bintang beer and talked late into the night.

Jakarta is a messy town with much trash and mangy dogs and magnificent mosques and minarets on the skyline and international-looking buildings looking seedy. The National Museum is impressive and contains samples from the material traditions of all Java, as well as treasures looted from surrounding ruins.

Old Batavia, the flourishing Dutch seaport of the seventeenth to the nineteenth century, is still intact and leads out to the present port of Jakarta, with its rows of high-prowed wooden ships that ply the Java Sea.

The Wayang Museum in Batavia is the university for the school of puppetry. In lands where television, cinema, and stage plays are a rarity, puppet shows are an enduring tradition. I went to my first Asian puppet show in Pagan, Burma, and along with episodes from traditional stories the puppets portrayed hip-popping rock singers and cowboys. The tent was filled that evening, and the audience cheered and clapped and yelled its approval and disapproval of the antics of the puppet people.

The Burmese puppets were three dimensional, and twenty-four inches tall, more or less, and were operated from above by strings.

Javanese puppets, called *wayang,* were of three kinds: regular puppets controlled from above by strings, stick puppets controlled from below with sticks, and shadow puppets, which were flat and controlled by sticks.

The museum also had Batak puppets, which are life-size and are operated from below with sticks. A folktale relates that a woman of the island of Samosir in Lake Toba, Sumatra, lost her husband. To assuage her grief she had a wooden, mobile statue made in his image and dressed in his clothes. When she was very sad and lonely she called in a puppeteer to make the statue-puppet dance and sing and talk to her. These large puppets are still used in Batak funeral and wedding ceremonies. The more sophisticated ones can weep and blink their eyes, stick out their tongues, and smoke cigarettes.

Back stage at a shadow puppet performance at Wayang Museum, Batavia (Courtesy F. E. Abernethy)

Wayang kulit, the shadow puppets, are popular traditional entertainment in Java, and shows are presented regularly at the Wayang Museum. At first one does not know where to sit. A white sheet is stretched as a screen across the middle of the room. On the left and right sides of the screen are filed a large cast of shadow-puppet characters, ready for immediate use by the *dalang,* or puppeteer. A naked light bulb hanging from the ceiling illuminates the puppeteer and his shadow puppets as they act out the story. A gamelan band of many sounds and colors faces the screen, and many in the audience stand at the back of the gamelan band. That is not where the audience is supposed to be. They are supposed to be on the opposite side listening to the music and watching the shadow of the puppets as they act out more adventures of Rama and Laksamana in their never ending search for Sita. The shows go on for two or three hours, with some amusing slapstick. The members of the band laugh at the funny parts, but only the most dedicated of *wayang kulit* enthusiasts can last an entire show. Gringos are inclined to wish they would cut to the chase.

From Jakarta to Samarinda, East Kalimantan, we flew over miles of what had been the jungles of Borneo but was now cleared land or scrubby second growth. Samarinda was a logging town and a delightful surprise, with two well stocked market places, one modern and one traditional.

Chance delivered unto me a guide who became a friend. His name was Dian and he was slight and he looked very young. He was sitting in the lobby of the Sewarga Indah Hotel in Samarinda. I had been trying to arrange a trip north to the Kutai Game Preserve, but because no tourists were on hand to share expenses, the trip would have cost more than I was then ready to pay. Dian had heard that I was looking for a tour, so he suggested that we go up the Mahakam River toward the land of the Dyaks. On a sheet of graph paper he figured the schedule and costs very carefully, gave me a price, and we were off the following morning.

During our negotiations, in a splash of overstatement, I said, "My God, Dian, you're going to kill me." I was really only commenting on some late arrival times and early departures. He was hurt, and very literal, and said, "O Mister, I not kill you." I guess he was still carrying the ethnic guilt of the warlike Dyaks.

The Mahakam is larger than the Mississippi at its mouth near Samarinda. It is a swarm of ships and boats of all sizes and bells ringing and whistles blowing and buying and selling and drinking and whoring. Huge rafts of four-five-six-foot in diameter logs, a mile wide and too far to see, were chained into islands, after having been towed down from the scraped interior.

We caught a large river boat and bought space on the upper deck. We each had a six-by-three area, furnished with a much used straw-tick mattress and a pillow. It was quite comfortable and relatively exclusive. On the deck below, passengers were propped and stretched (no seats) in all sorts of positions in and out of the freight the boat was carrying. People read and smoked and played radios. Several family groups were gathered around little stoves where women cooked foods too foreign for a gringo's palate. Goats and pigs were tied loosely enough that they could make continual foot and mouth noises. The captain-helmsman steered from this deck. If he had a crew beyond his wife I never saw them.

We stopped at several villages along the Mahakam, and Dian bought foods from the docks and from the boat peddlers that came alongside, all sorts of cakes and strangely fried bananas, and rice and noodle dishes wrapped in banana leaves. He was educating me in the way of customary foods.

As I sat on a forward hatch cover that night, I could see the Big Dipper off the starboard bow and the Southern Cross off the port bow.

We left the river boat at two in the morning at Muara Muntai and slept a few hours in primitive quarters. The next morning we hired a fifteen-foot longboat with an extended outboard motor and left the Mahakam to journey up a tributary to Lake Jempang, which boasts a population of freshwater porpoises, which I did not see. On the far side of the lake was Tanjung Isuy, where we got a wooden bed and a mosquito net in a Dyak longhouse. Later by boat, through magic miles of water grass and water buffalo and scampering tribes of monkeys and my God the birds! we went to a Dyak chief's longhouse in the remote village of Moncong.

The most interesting monkeys on that golden voyage were the big red proboscis monkeys. We saw one huge old fellow with his long nose and head hanging forward over his bulging beer belly. He sat on a limb and leaned against the trunk. Dian the Dyak said his people called these monkeys Fat Dutchmen. He said that when the Dutch were finally driven from Borneo, those Dutchmen who could not get out changed themselves into proboscids so the Dyaks would not kill nor enslave them. One could definitely see the resemblance.

We were back at our longhouse by dark. I took a traditional Indonesian bath, dipping water out of a barrel with a saucepan and splashing it over my body. I gasped aloud on the first cold splash. It was a controlled gasp, but it was enough to bring one of the women of the house running to see if I was all right. I was on my mat and asleep by nine.

At one A.M. I exploded awake to the sound of a gamelan band next door playing fortissimo.

My curiosity overcame my indignation, and I wandered out in a fine misty rain to a light in the house next door. The house had one large room, no furniture, and a shed-roofed cooking area in back. The gamelan band was seated against the entrance wall. A large extended family was in the shadows at the far side. A pale, emaciated, and dying old man lay still and covered on the floor near the middle of the room. And a shaman, in a purple turban and a cabalistic sarong, danced and chanted as he clung to a holy cloth that hung from the rafters of the roof.

These were the old man's final rites, and the shaman swept him with long bundles of grass to brush away all the evil of his living days. He swept him, blessed him, and figuratively died with him and was resurrected as he lay on the floor beside the old man, still singing and swaying. Then he blessed the people and the things of the house and the food and water so that when the spirit finally left the old man it would not—out of envy of the living—harm the house and those who remained.

The musicians never missed a beat. If they tired or wished to smoke a cigarette, someone slipped in by them, and the rhythm of the ritual was never interrupted.

Dian and I discussed the ritual in detail the next morning. He explained the significance of the ceremony and said that it was very old among the Dyaks, the Long Ears, so called because the old folks stretched their earlobes with large ear decorations. Dian himself was a short-eared city Dyak, and he was a Muslim and therefore did not believe in such rituals and such superstitions. The dying man and his people, he said with some superiority, were Christians.

I was cannily taken in a trade with an ancient, sarong-skirted, barefooted Long Ears at Tanjung Isuy. He had a necklace of boar's teeth that I longed for. He gave me a price; I offered him half. He came down ten percent. We haggled, going up and coming down, for several minutes, neither speaking the other's language, and his single-toothed wife shuffled out of the shadows with two sets of Dyak earrings made from porcupine quills. She tossed in another figure—scratched it on the back of a board—for the necklace *and* the two ear jobs. I responded with laughter that she could ask such an outrageously high price. I offered her half. The old woman shook her head sorrowfully, implying that I was out to rob her of all that she held dear. The Long Ears low-talked his wife and added ten percent to my half offer, letting me know that he was taking a loss, but because he liked me he wanted me to have these works of art. That sounded good so I took the loot, gave him the agreed upon rupiahs, and we shook hands. I noticed his big grin at the same time that the cash register rang in my head. He had snookered me! I grabbed him by the shoulders and said, "You old rascal, you took me!" He died laughing and hugged me around the waist, as did his equally laughing wife. And the three of us jigged around, laughing and hugging each other at this great bit of world trade that we had engaged in. I left them still laughing and talking at me. I lost all of a dollar and a half on this deal, but I made their day—or month!

The Mahakam and the Dyaks, Dian and Tanjung Isuy, Samarinda: This was the climax of my trip. I flew to Bali but Borneo stayed on my mind.

In Bali, Sanur Beach slopes gently down to the clear easy waters of Badung Strait. Two hundred feet offshore, an easy wade and swim, lies a long flat reef that shoals at low tide and reveals all sorts of sea animals in the tidal pools. To the north rises red in the sunset Gunung Agung, the volcano that destroyed much of eastern Bali in 1963 and killed thousands of Balinese. Smoke still rises from its top.

Sanur Beach is a place to sit in the evenings and listen to the chirping of the gekkos and watch the outriggers walking like Jesus spiders on the blue-green water. It is a place to remember that Bali floats at the earth's center on the back of a huge sea turtle under a sky perfumed by great rushes of flowers. Bali is an island of flowers that decorate streets and buildings and cars, and every morning when one steps out of his room he finds fresh flowers arranged to delight the good spirits of the island, and fresh flowers scattered randomly to placate the evil spirits. Hindu temples are everywhere flower-decked to share some of their influence with the indigenous gods. Bali is the most religious of the islands; my driver said that he gave ninety percent of what he made to the temples. I am still working on that.

A Hindu temple in the Monkey Forest in Ubud, Bali's culture center, displayed a sign that said, "Entrence is for bidden to menstruating womens."

Balinese aristocracy perished in 1906. It committed *puputan*, a suicidal battle to the death with the Dutch. The Dutch, extending their control over southeast Asia, marched on Denpasar and the three reigning princes of southeastern Bali. Rather than surrender and be banished from their island, the princes and their followers marched out to meet the Dutch. The Dutch begged them to lay down their arms, but they would not. The Balinese charged the guns of the Dutch in waves, and four thousand, all of them, were dead on the ground when the battle was over.

The Dutch insisted that the Balinese women cover their bosoms. Some refused. They are now in their seventies and eighties, and they really should.

I flew homeward out of Bali at six A.M. As we rose and circled we could see the sun rising and walking westward along the beaches and chasing monkeys through the tree tops.

At a restaurant in Chinatown in Kuala Lumpur was a sign: "Pepper Pork Stomach—Mushroom Chicken Feet."

I doubt that ever again will I have such an experience.

Francis Edward Abernethy
Stephen F. Austin State University
Nacogdoches, Texas
Dry October, 1992

Acknowledgements

For the aforementioned exercise in professional development, I thank my good friend Archie McDonald, Professor of History and Director of the East Texas Historical Association, among his many other offices and accomplishments, past and present. Archie both takes me and sends me to foreign places and sees to it that I stay involved and included in his own energetic academic world. I truly appreciate his care and concern. For material support I thank University Past-Vice-President Jim Reese, University Past-President William R. Johnson, and the office of Texas' Past-Governor Bill Clements.

Corners of Texas, this fifty-second Publication of the Texas Folklore Society, was *relatively* easy to construct because we have had a spate of interesting papers in our past two or three meetings. Once again, the Texas Folklore Society thanks the contributors for their research and for their writing. Those who do not write for publication do not realize the amount of work that is involved in such labor. Nor do they understand the courage required to submit this written part of one's soul to the intimate examination of strangers.

The *Corners of Texas* title was taken from Frank Dobie and Dick Holland, who tell about library corners that contain writings that are forever Texas. The title seemed fitting since that is where this folklore comes from, various corners of Texas.

Related to this office's continued concern with the history of the Society, this book begins with a special section about the history of the Society itself and its sainted elders. These introductory historical essays can be considered as supplemental to whatever is forthcoming in the formal history of the Texas Folklore Society. Following that, *Corners* is a traditional TFS miscellany, the best of the Society's papers over the past three years and with as much variety as one could hope for.

This office, this book, and this editor are once again blessed with the expertise, care, and diligence of Assistant Editor Carolyn Satterwhite. She improves the quality of life considerably.

The Texas Folklore Society is annually thankful for the support of the administration of Stephen F. Austin State University and particularly of Patricia Russell, the head of the Department of English.

F. E. A.

PART ONE

★

HISTORY

Southwestern Writers Collection, Southwest Texas State University
(Courtesy Richard A. Holland)

1

A Corner Forever Texas: The Southwestern Writers Collection

Richard A. Holland

TEXAS FOLKLORISTS AND COLLECTORS ARE FULLY AWARE OF THE healthy market in materials related to the life and writings of J. Frank Dobie. Dobie's long career as a writer, his legendary generosity as an inscriber of books, the limited availability of the special editions of his works, and the large number of important association items on the market are some of the factors that have made Dobie much sought after in bookshops, dealer's catalogues, and in venues such as the annual Texas State Historical Association auction.

The state of Dobie's original material, i.e., his book manuscripts, research files, correspondence, diaries, and personal papers, was thought to be long settled. Everyone knew that Dobie's own library and manuscripts resided at "the University." Although that is largely true, the placement of Dobie's materials at the University of Texas is not a simple story, nor are the UT libraries the only repositories that should be visited in order to fully understand the shape of Dobie's life and career. In some respects the history of Dobie's papers reflects his long and ambivalent relationship with the University of Texas, but a deeper reason for the surprisingly wide distribution of his papers may lie in his instinctive distrust of institutions and a reluctance to be contained in one place. His research files, correspondence, and personal papers form a rich tapestry that combine his intellectual concerns and his personal life. In many ways they bring his published writings to life.

The assiduous researcher can profitably work not only at the Harry Ransom Humanities Research Center and the Barker Texas History Center at the University, but also in the special collections at Baylor, Southwestern University at Georgetown, Texas A&M, Texas Tech, the University of Texas at El Paso, UT San Antonio, and the Southwestern Writers Collection at Southwest Texas State University in San Marcos. The Southwestern Writers Collection is the newest of these special collections, having been founded by Southwest Texas State in 1986. Its creation is directly linked to the papers J. Frank Dobie held in his home until his death. The story of Dobie's own collection and its eventual move to San Marcos has never been told, and has some of the characteristics of a mystery story. The story features Texas's best known bird watcher, Mr. Dobie's long-time secretary, and one of his most talented proteges. There is no villain, but the passage of time and the nature of the Dobie estate created an uncertain outcome for an important part of Dobie's legacy. The story has a happy ending.

Dobie had left the University of Texas in 1947, after the refusal of his seemingly routine request for fall leave by University President Theophilus Painter. The ensuing uproar brought into bold relief Dobie's controversial place on the campus and the hostility with which he was viewed by the Texas board of regents. His leaving became a *cause célèbre* and was followed by the national press. Texas novelist George Sessions Perry's reaction when he heard the news was typical: "the University has finally turned its back on great, lovable, intractable Frank Dobie, who for so long a time has been the state's and university's ambassador to the world" (Lon Tinkle, *An American Original: The Life of J. Frank Dobie,* 204).

Ten years later the political and cultural climate on campus had changed, as evidenced by the rapid rise of Harry Ransom, a young professor of English who had visionary ideas for building a university of the first class. In 1957 Ransom approached Dobie through Walter Prescott Webb about returning to the University on an emeritus basis. Dobie emphatically turned Ransom down, but did agree to negotiate to sell his library to the University and told Ransom that his books could do his teaching. After a lengthy appraisal, Dobie's 8000 volume library, his western art collection, and boxes of papers were transferred to the University. By the time of his death in September, 1964, it appeared that University of Texas President

Harry Ransom had succeeded in bringing J. Frank Dobie back into the institutional fold on the Austin campus. Within weeks of Dobie's death the University dedicated Ransom's new Academic Center building that housed the Undergraduate Library and, on the fourth floor, a special Dobie room that housed his library and much of his western art. The curator for the room was Dobie's secretary, Willie Belle Coker.

In 1938 Dobie had written an eloquent plea for a "corner forever Texas" at the University in the form of a library furnished in native woods that would pull together the history, culture and art of the Southwest (*A Corner Forever Texas,* Austin: Whatley, 1938). Ironically, the University achieved this in 1950, three years after Dobie's angry dismissal, with the creation of the Eugene C. Barker Texas History Center that combined the Texas Collection and the University Archives. The Dobie room in the Academic Center was perhaps Ransom's idea of creating another corner, one that entirely captured the spirit of Dobie.

A few weeks before his death, in the late summer of 1964, Dobie wrote a letter to Humanities Research Center Director Dr. Warren Roberts summarizing the sale of his library and papers to the HRC. Almost as an afterthought, Dobie wrote: "There are still many papers here in this house. I still have in steel cabinets, in boxes, on shelves, and elsewhere in our house perhaps half a dozen manuscripts, some more than half written on rattle-snake lore, animal stories, character sketches, Charles M. Russell, autobiography, and perhaps one or two other subjects." It is clear in the letter that Dobie assumed that the remaining contents of the house would be passed on to the University at some point after his death.

After Dobie's death Bertha Dobie remained in their house, preparing five posthumous Dobie books for publication, largely from the materials in the house. After her death in 1974, the Dobie house passed to Edgar Kincaid, Mrs. Dobie's nephew, who had lived with both Dobies since he first came to Austin to attend the University in 1939. The Dobies were childless, and Mrs. Dobie and her nephew had a very close tie; according to their friends they were temperamentally very similar—meticulous and proper. The year of his aunt's death marked the publication of *The Bird Life of Texas,* edited by Kincaid. Likely the most ambitious book ever published in the state, *The Bird Life of Texas* was begun by Dr. Harry Oberholser in 1901 and was scheduled for publication in 1905. Still unpublished in 1941, Oberholser's manuscript was more than three million words long, over 11,000 typed pages. After Oberholser died in 1963 at the age of 93, Edgar Kincaid was brought in to edit and complete the book. During the next ten years, Kincaid and his assistants drove over 243 Texas counties, establishing hundreds of bird sightings where none had existed before. Partially funded by Kincaid's ranching family's wealth, *The Bird Life of Texas* was a definitive survey of the state with the largest number of birds on the continent and was considered an ornithological masterpiece.

Edgar Kincaid gave bird names to his friends if he liked them—feeling that birds were more noble than humans. He called himself the Cassowary, a huge flightless bird found in Australia, known for its dagger-like claws that could cut open a man's belly. A gentle soul who hated the urbanization of Texas, Kincaid liked the idea of a bird exercising revenge on man. He lived for eleven years after Bertha Dobie's death, slowly becoming more reclusive and frightened of the world. By the last year of his life, Kincaid relied on his young friends to help straighten the house—he piled up papers, including cash, all over the house and frequently slept on the floor in a down sleeping bag. The house was broken into and vandalized in the summer of 1985, and Kincaid was tied up and held at gunpoint. Two days later he died at the home of close friends.

Mr. Kincaid had remained close to Mr. Dobie's former secretary, Willie Belle Coker (who had left the Dobie Room and was not replaced), and it was to her that he left the house and its contents. The week after Edgar Kincaid's death, the house was broken into again—apparently word was out on the street that there might be money lying about. Pictures were taken down from the walls and ripped apart, and papers and books were strewn all over the floors of the two-story house. The bank trust department that served as the executor of the estate immediately pressured Mrs. Coker to act in a timely way to liquidate or protect the house, one of the estate's largest assets. After a tremendous amount of straightening work, she decided on the only course open to her.

On Friday, December 13, 1985, a prominently printed classified ad ran in the *Austin American Statesman* that sent a shock through the world of Texas rare book dealers, collectors, and friends of the Dobies:

> Estate Sale
> J. Frank Dobie Home
> 702 East 26th
> Saturday 9–5
> Sunday 1–5
>
> W. C. Attal, Jr. of the Southwest Gallery has been commissioned to sell the personal property of Mr. and Mrs. J. Frank Dobie and their nephew Edgar Kincaid. Items include Mr. and Mrs. Dobie's personal desks, Victorian walnut dining table and chairs, oval mahogany library table, raw hide chairs, glass fronted Victorian walnut bookcase, open-fronted bookcases, cedar chests, Mrs. Dobie's custom made china and display case, Mr. Dobie's and Mr. Kincaid's personal libraries, including many scarce Dobie pamphlets, books pertaining to Texas and the Southwest, many scarce Encino Press books, natural history books, art and literature, fine art—including original drawings by Bill Wittliff, sketch by Borgium, scarce Tom Lea lithograph of Mr. Dobie, plus many miscellaneous household items and appliances. Positively no sales before 9:00 a.m. Saturday.

By 7:00 A.M. on the morning of Saturday, December 14, a line had begun to form in front of the Dobie house even though the temperature was down in the 20s. For the next two days there was a brisk business, as buyers carried out kitchen chairs, tables, items of clothing, and many books. Individual sheets of Dobie's paisano stationery, designed by Carl Hertzog, sold for a dollar each. Some shoppers expressed their dismay with the sale even as they carried out furniture or personal items. It appeared that everything left of Edgar Kincaid and the Dobies was being scattered to the winds.

Negative reaction to the sale was quick to follow in the form of a column in the *Austin American Statesman* written by Texana columnist Mike Cox, who had attended the sale. Cox commented on several significant books that were sold from the house, including Mrs. Dobie's copy of *The Bird Life of Texas* inscribed to his aunt by Edgar Kincaid. A common sentiment was expressed by a book dealer quoted by Cox: "If Harry Ransom were still alive, he would have written one check for the house and all of the contents and this place would have been run by the university as a Dobie museum."

Unknown at the time was the fact that Mrs. Coker had telephoned a few Dobie family friends before the sale to inform them of it. One of these friends was Bill Wittliff, publisher of the Encino Press, who in the 1980s had become active as a television and motion picture writer and producer. Wittliff was scheduled to be out of town on the day of the sale and was invited to come over the day before to look at the mesquite desk in Mr. Dobie's upstairs study. He bought the desk and, while writing a check for it, noticed a large pile of books and papers in the corner of the room on the floor. Informed that this was what was left of Dobie's books and papers, Wittliff said, "Oh, those will be going to the University." He was told no, that the stack of material, stored in several crammed cardboard boxes, would be part of the public sale. After looking quickly at the top of the stack, he saw manuscript sheets, signed books, and personal papers, and, after calling his wife Sally, wrote another check for the entire pile. It was raining, and Wittliff loaded the archive in several heavy duty trash bags and drove his truck to his office.

Bill Wittliff was one of Mr. Dobie's most talented proteges. Growing up in South Texas and the Hill Country, Wittliff had been given *Tales of Old Time Texas* by an aunt who worked in the book department of Joske's and had been mesmerized by the story "The Wild Woman of the Navidad," having heard the same story growing up. He had wanted to meet Mr. Dobie when he was an undergraduate at Texas in the early sixties, but his girlfriend Sally was the first to knock on Dobie's door in January, 1961, to get some of Bill's Dobie books signed. Wittliff himself soon visited with Dobie, who discouraged him from majoring in journalism, remarking that he needed to learn something in college with a little substance.

In the summer of 1963, Dobie was living in the faculty club of the University of California in Berkeley writing his final book, *Cow People*. He was not in good health and part of the time was uncharacteristically gloomy. Dobie did take the time, however, to drop an encouraging note to his young friend Wittliff, who at that moment was in basic training in San Antonio. Somehow Dobie had found his correct military address, and in the conclusion of his note he wrote: "I believe in you!"—a sentiment that meant quite a lot to Wittliff, particularly since it was counter to much of what he had heard during basic training.

Just before Christmas of 1963, Dobie invited Wittliff to his house and presented him with two grocery bags full of books, pamphlets, and things from his desk, all signed and inscribed. By this time, Bill and Sally Wittliff were married and living in Dallas, Bill working for the SMU Press. His dream was to start a small press himself, and he soon asked Mr. Dobie if he could publish one of the Dobies' Christmas keepsakes, "Bob More, Man and Bird Man," as the first book published by the Encino Press. Dobie at first refused, saying that a writer "shouldn't spread his brand too thin." A month before his death Dobie relented, and late in 1964, the second Encino Press imprint, designed and printed by Bill, was published by the Wittliffs. The timing of the publication made *Bob More, Man and Bird Man* Dobie's first posthumous book and a cornerstone for the press that evolved into a distinguished American press during the next two decades.

After Christmas of 1985, Wittliff had time to begin going through the papers and books he had bought at the Willie Belle Coker sale and realized that it was a very rich archive. It was what Dobie had described to Warren Roberts in his 1964 letter as the unfinished projects left in the house, stored on shelves and in filing cabinets. What Wittliff found were the unfinished projects and much more, including diaries, letters, most of the books that Dobie had inscribed to Bertha Dobie, and many more research files than Dobie had indicated were left in the house in his letter to Roberts. When Wittliff realized the magnitude of what he had bought, he decided that it was too important to be in private hands and decided to place it in a library. His and Sally's Dobie collection could complement the materials from the Dobie house. Further, he knew that many of the writers he had published under the imprint of the Encino Press had literary papers that had not been collected. This included a mature generation of Texas writers—John Graves, Larry L. King, and Bud Shrake among others. Lastly, Wittliff also had an appreciation for the photography of the region because of his own *Vaquero* project that had been touring the country since the 1970s and because of his friendship with the great documentary photographer Russell Lee. He decided to pursue an idea to begin a University library collection devoted to the writers, artists, and musicians of the Southwest.

Seeking advice, Wittliff called the Director of the Humanities Research Center, Decherd Turner, who quickly and politely assured Wittliff that the University of Texas had no interest in a Southwestern collection. Wittliff preferred that the collection be close to Austin, and he eventually made an inquiry at Southwest Texas State University in San Marcos. As it happened, SWT, under University President Robert Hardesty, had been working hard on gaining approval from the state Coordinating Board for a new library building. The week of the first meeting that Hardesty had with Wittliff, the board approved plans for a new 31 million dollar library building for the SWT campus. The University Library's representative at the meeting was Bill Mears, who coordinated much of the campus planning for the building. Mears became more and more impressed with Wittliff's idea as Wittliff showed the group portions of the Dobie collection and told stories. After another meeting, the SWT group quickly agreed to begin a special collection devoted to Southwestern writers and artists that would have its own space in the new building, a corner forever Texas. Planning for the space and a search for a curator for the collection would begin immediately.

Six years later, the Southwestern Writers Collection is in place on the seventh floor of the Albert B. Alkek Library, yet another corner forever Texas. The writers collection is attractively situated behind doors of hand-carved first growth pine and features generously designed exhibit cases and a reading room in which scholars and students conduct research, Southwestern studies classes meet, and public events such as readings and book signings take place. Set into the wall at the end of the reading room is a capstone with a lone star taken by Dobie from the Bee County courthouse when it was remodeled.

Southwestern Writers Collection, Southwest Texas State University (Courtesy Richard A. Holland)

At the dedication of the writers collection in the fall of 1991, Bill and Sally Wittliff were honored with the President's Excellence Medal, and the speakers included John Graves, Larry L. King, and Governor Ann Richards, who reminisced about many of the Texas writers she had known. The collection's exhibits have been broad in focus, ranging from Billy Lee Brammer's heavily marked typescript for his 1960 novel *The Gay Place,* to a large display of costumes, drawings, scripts, and artifacts from the "Lonesome Dove" miniseries, to a collection of stunning photographs donated by Jean Lee, Russell Lee's widow.

Prominently featured are portions of the Wittliffs' Dobie Collection, the cornerstone of the collection. The collection reveals both the breadth of J. Frank Dobie's interests and the ways in which he conducted his research. His personal papers and artifacts are at least of equal interest and in some cases are revelatory. What follows is an outline of the major sections of the collection, focusing on what Wittliff bought at the Dobie estate sale.

Book Manuscripts

1. *Cow People:* Drafts of the Contents, Dedication, Introduction, Note on Sources, and ten chapters. Typed with handwritten additions and corrections.

2. ***Out of the Old Rock:*** Nine pages of preliminary notes by Bertha Dobie, including a list of possible Dobie essays and three typescripts of the book, the first and second containing essays later eliminated. All is the work of Mrs. Dobie; the third draft includes her instructions to the typesetter.

3. ***Prefaces:*** The production material for Dobie's 1975 collection published by Little, Brown. This file contains typescripts of the pieces, galley proofs with corrections, bound advance proofs with corrections, and Mrs. Dobie's typescript of her Introduction with handwritten corrections.

4. ***Tales of Old-Time Texas:*** Dobie's copies of the original manuscript materials of the stories used in his 1955 collection. The file contains typescripts of twenty-one different tales, all with handwritten changes. Many of them indicate Dobie's other uses for the stories, i.e., his Sunday newspaper column, *Ranch Romances,* the *Southern Agriculturist,* etc.

5. **"Story-Tellers I Have Known":** A fascinating file tracing Dobie's development as a stylist. One of his best autobiographical pieces, the file begins with Dobie's original manuscript, traces it through many changes to the SMU galley proofs used for the Texas Folklore Society version and the four newspaper columns that reworked the same material. The article ultimately became the final chapter of *Some Part of Myself.*

Books

1. **Books inscribed to Bertha Dobie by JFD:** The Willie Belle Coker sale included thirty-two books inscribed to Bertha Dobie, fifteen of them books written or edited by Dobie. A typical inscription is that in *Legends of Texas* (Texas Folklore Society, 1924):

Dear Burbie:

I have just come across this book on a foreign shelf and I turned to first two or three pages and saw their blankness. Then I was smitten with a kind of stupid wonder why I did not dedicate this book to you. I suppose I did not regard it as being sufficiently mine. As I look back now it seems to have been as much yours as mine. Often and often I think of how you corrected everything and helped me organize and rewrote some of the contributions. I was in Austin—having come down from Oklahoma to attend a meeting of the Texas Folk-Lore Society, you will remember—when the book was turned out of the press. This was the first copy finished and I brought it home to you. It and all other first copies belong to you.

J.F.D.
Austin, Tx
Feb. 26, 1932

Of the other books inscribed to Bertha, several are by naturalists, including Dobie's favorite, W. H. Hudson, and some are specifically related to horticulture or botany.

2. Other Books: Other inscribed books in the Dobie house included *The Mustangs, Tales of Old-Time Texas, A Texan In England,* and *The Voice of the Coyote,* all inscribed to Edgar Kincaid, and several that Dobie inscribed to point out something about the book that he thought either Bertha Dobie or Edgar Kincaid might need to know. An interesting example of his setting the record straight is the following paragraph written in Frederick Remington's *Pony Tracks,* with an introduction by Dobie:

Savoie Lottinville, director of the University of Oklahoma Press, did not pay me much for the Introduction herein. I, nevertheless, spent a deal of time writing it. Harold McCracken, whom I expose as a charlatan in the beginning of the Introduction, had a lawyer, former governor of Wyoming—McCracken directs a museum at Cody, Wyoming—threatened to sue me and University of Oklahoma Press for libel. I did not reply to the letter. Savoie

Lottinville did, telling McCracken and lawyer to look at themselves. The suit, groundless, was dropped.

Frank Dobie
Nov. 22, 1963

The remaining books bought by Wittliff include many uninscribed Dobie books in various editions, the five posthumous Dobie books presented to Mrs. Dobie by the publisher Little, Brown, in special half-leather bindings, and a number of books by friends or acquaintances, including a copy of Tinkle's biography *An American Original, the Life of J. Frank Dobie,* presented to Mrs. Dobie by Bill and Sally Wittliff. Inside the book, she kept a newspaper clipping announcing the birth of the Wittliff's son Reid.

Correspondence

1. Dobie's Letters to Bertha 1917–1918: Dobie regarded his World War I officer's training experience at Leon Springs as a transforming experience. Later, he remarked that his "refined sensibility" kept him separated from his fellows in the training camp and that he "had too long soaked [him]self in poetry and novels." Gradually his natural robustness asserted itself and "without losing sensibility I became a match for the hardiest soldier" (*Some Part of Myself,* 225). The Wittliff Dobie Collection at SWT includes 128 letters written from December 1917 through May 1918 documenting this experience. In February, 1918, Dobie transferred from Camp Stanley in Leon Springs to Camp Wheeler near Macon, Georgia. Perhaps indicative of Dobie's awareness of transforming himself was his good-humored attempt to grow a mustache that he reported to Bertha in January, 1918:

> I have started my mustache, but unless one can get off on an isolated island for six weeks, he has no business to grow one. All that interrum to nondescript growth upon his face hovers somewhere between contemptible, pitiful, and ludicrous. So, I may cut it off before I see you, and I would not forego seeing you for

six weeks for the bravest moustachios that a brigand ever brandished.

2. Dobie's Los Olmos Letters: These fourteen letters in the Wittliff Dobie Collection reflect the vitality and openness of spirit that Dobie found working on his Uncle Jim Dobie's ranch. They are all written to Bertha when she was in San Antonio and in poor health. Her inability to live on the ranch, because of its distance from doctors, was one of the factors in Dobie's decision to return to the University. In May, 1921, Dobie wrote a letter describing his learning about Mexican folklore from Santos the vaquero:

> I am making a collection of Mexican (or folk) signs of the weather. Santos is my chief source. He told me of another sign today. When the goats are kidding if the season is to be good, the goats take their kids with great alacrity no matter though they be poor at the time. On the other hand, if their prophetic souls foretell a hard, barren season, they take unkindly to their kids, reasoning, I suppose, that they had better let them die at once than struggle along and in the end both die. Santos and I have many interesting conversations. He says that he gets very tired of these people who can't talk about anything but the rain, the grass, the goats, etc. We talk about Immortality, Predestination, etc. . . . Santos used to be a Mexican soldier; he killed a man in the war and always carries a gun now, in case the dead man's relatives should appear. He is the best friend I have out here excepting Lee Keithley.

In a later letter, Dobie writes of his interest in the Mexican folk belief in ascribing to animals the gift of weather prophecy. He concludes, "I am beginning a list of such beliefs. I think that I might sometime easily make it—if I had enough material—into a good folklore proper."

3. Dobie's Letters to Bertha 1927–1931: This four year period was marked by Dobie's full commitment to systematically travelling and gathering folk stories and culminated in the publication of *The Vaquero of the Brush Country* and *Coronado's Children.* There are 121 letters written from south Texas, Dallas, New Mexico, Arizona, Atlanta, and New York. The last letters in this section are written on the road during February, 1931, and mention the many interviews he is giving and all of the editors he has met with in New York, all associated with the publication of *Coronado's Children.* It is clear reading this correspondence that by 1931 Dobie had become a professional writer in his own mind.

4. The Dobie-Bedichek Letters 1924–1959: This rich archive consists of 178 handwritten and typed notes and letters, as well as six Town and Gown Club announcements, two typed manuscripts by Dobie, and notes and a remembrance of Bedichek by Bertha Dobie. Three quarters of the letters are from Bedichek to Dobie, the bulk of them dating from the 1940s when Dobie was in England. Many of these letters were collected in the *Letters of Roy Bedichek,* edited by William Owens and Lyman Grant (Texas, 1985). Bedichek gave all of his papers to the Barker Center before he died; Owens was his literary executor and used Bedichek's carbon copies for the book. This collection in the Southwestern Writers Collection contains the originals that Dobie kept at the house. Copies of some of Dobie's replies are in the file, and in many cases Bedichek enclosed carbons of his own letters to John Lomax or John Henry Faulk or some other mutual friend for Dobie to read.

The deep affection between the two friends is manifest in the earliest letter from Bedichek to Dobie dated April 12, 1924, with the salutation "Hail, Cowboy, Folklorist, pedagogue." (SWT's Dobie/Bedichek file provides a correction to the *Letters of Roy Bedichek* that states Dobie and Bedichek first corresponded in 1937.)

Bedichek, as head of the University Interscholastic League, was an old hand at the University by the time Dobie came along, and immediately recognized Dobie's talents and got him involved in the Town and Gown organization that Bedichek chaired for many years. By the early 1940s, their friendship had matured so that they corresponded about more than just birds or folktales. During this period, Dobie's newspaper column was becoming syndicated widely and Dobie used it as a vehicle for expressing many of his current research interests. Several of Bedichek's notes comment on the column, like the following one dated April, 1943:

> It's sweetly reasonable, it's salty, sensible, and there are spots of sweet, rich earth in it like some of the disquisitions of Sancho Panza manured two seasons ago with proverbial wisdom. . . .

A year later Dobie was lecturing at Emmanuel College, Cambridge, and was enamored of England during war time. Bedichek quickly tried to bring his friend back down to earth:

> You are doubtless seeing England at its heroic best. War has cured unemployment and doubtless much of the caste atmosphere which I encountered there in 1907. I suppose that Picadilly Circus is not now thronged after nightfall with painted whores a-glitter with paste jewels like cat's eyes in the dark, as in 1907. If you turned a deaf ear to their solicitations, they cursed you with the foulest oaths. And there were beggars, pimps and homosexuals in high-heeled shoes and corsets.
>
> I strung along for a while with a young sleuth who was gathering statistics for the Yearbook of the London Daily Express, and his special assignment was to trail piece-workers to their lairs and get the lowdown on living conditions. We often found families of 4, 5, or 6 littered in a 16-foot square room two stories under ground. I shall never forget the terrible sights. Never, before or since, have I seen humanity so degraded, and I worked once in the West Virginia coal fields.

Dobie returned to Austin for Christmas, 1944, and the invitation to a homecoming party was made up of copies of notes between Bedichek, Walter Prescott Webb, Henry Nash Smith, and Dobie during his absence. Entitled "Formal Homecoming Informally Celebrated," the invitation read:

> The Time is set: December 9. The Place: Old Man Rancher Webb's hideout. The company: Walter Webb, Roy Bedichek, Henry Smith, John Faulk, Mody Boatright, and J. Frank Dobie (guest), and not another soul, damned or blessed. Follows in numbered order communications which have settled these details. *Herein fail not.*—R.B.

The two friends shared an earthy nature that was not easily expressed elsewhere, particularly with their wives. Dobie marked the first passage below in a July, 1940, Bedichek letter and the second five years later :

> There is no patriotism without love of your physical environment just as there is no romantic love without a love of the physical body of some individual woman.
>
> The squeamishness of the 19th century concerning words describing or suggesting sex was, in my opinion, one of the conditions which inspired Whitman to such vigorous onslaughts. . . . He planted the yeast which is only now causing a stir in the heart of the loaf. It will do its work and finally people can write and talk of sex as naturally as they do of other fundamental appetites. . . .

Ironically, it was Dobie's attempt to capture the earthy side of his dear friend after his death that almost caused a split with Bedichek's widow, Lillian. After Mr. Bedichek's death in May, 1959, Ronnie Dugger, the editor of *The Texas Observer,* planned a memorial issue with reminiscences contributed by Dobie, Webb, Edgar Kincaid, Virginia Conkle, William Owens, and John Henry Faulk, among others. Mrs. Bedichek wrote Dobie after the special issue came out berating him for using an "obscene expression" in his piece. Dobie's offending sentences were in a passage describing Bedichek as a man who preferred the country to the city:

> He favored several kinds of independence common to the country. It did him good, he said, to walk out and empty his bladder on the ground instead of having to go in the house and empty it into a mechanical contrivance. I've heard him say that sometimes in the obscurity of before-daylight he would dig a hole in the ground out in the yard near 'the shack'—his study—and excrete into it, covering the place with dirt like a cat. It gave him a satisfaction to fertilize the ground.

Dobie didn't make changes in his piece and Ronnie Dugger refused to republish the Bedichek issue in pamphlet form cutting Dobie's paragraph. A month later Mrs. Bedichek wrote a conciliatory note to Dobie, but became upset again in the fall of 1959 when Dobie used the same passage in his introduction to a Bedichek book to be published by Doubleday.

At the end of this remarkable record of their thirty-five year friendship, Dobie planned a fit memorial for Bedichek—on September 12, 1959, he sent an invitation to "Webb, Wardlaw, Boatright, Hudson, Fuermann, Evans, Faulk, and Hutto" to meet him on October 3 at Paisano where "we shall pour a libation to his ghost."

Diaries

1. The Columbia Diary: In the posthumously published *Some Part of Myself* (1967), Dobie describes his graduate work at Columbia University: "For a while I kept a kind of diary, but after looking it over a few years ago, I was so disgusted with the sentimentality in it that I destroyed it" (*Some Part of Myself,* 184–185). This diary, from January, 1913 through June, 1914, is

Southwestern Writers Collection, Southwest Texas State University (Courtesy Richard A. Holland)

the one he thought he had destroyed, and indeed it is full of his youthful impressions of New York City, whose theater and opera he avidly attended. His experience of the city was balanced by excursions into New England with his friends and family who came to visit. The following entry is typical of the diary in its emotional tone and poetic sensibility:

> Monday Night June 23, 1913
>
> One of the best days of my life. I went to Concord where there is peace, and the most secure nature in the world. I saw the tombs of New England's greatest—Emerson, Thoreau, Alcott & Hawthorne, and I roamed through Walden woods and by Walden Pond, where there is a cairn marking the site of Thoreau's hut. I wish to God I had a hut there now. . . .
>
> After coming home Milton and I walked in the dusk by a girl murmuring to her lover. I said that the murmur of a girl in the silence of evening and the awaking of a girl—as in Cabanel's Birth of Venus—were the most beautiful and poetic of human things.

At the end of the diary are a few pages where Dobie jotted down random thoughts and ideas. Some of these indicate that as early as 1914 he considered his southwestern heritage as a source for future work: "Thoughts & Subjects, 'Camping Along the Trail.'"

Other Columbia period material in the Wittliff collection includes Dobie's class notes from his 18th Century Prose class and his eighty-three page handwritten Master of Arts thesis titled "Thomas Heywood: the Golden Age."

2. 1927 Trip Diary: Part of an extensive cattle trade file, this is a journal of an automobile trip that Dobie took alone to West Texas, New Mexico, and Arizona to talk to old-time cattlemen and to view and photograph ruins of old ranches and forts. The entire file is remarkable for the energy with which Dobie approached his research. In the trip diary, he describes Harry Warren, formerly a historian, but by 1927 a "desert rat":

> Toothless, squalid, surrounded by greasers, "descended from Charlemagne & Alfred," his father an eminent physician, writing a history of the Creek War from photostats made at the

Univ. of Wisconsin, his stomach worn out, his occupation the lowest in his profession, what passes through that old man's mind? He knows the Rio Grande as few men on earth know it. "My brothers in Mississippi have told me that if I would come back they would give me a farm. I could not leave these beautiful sunsets."

3. Mexico Trip Log, 1929: A fifteen-page diary of a trip Dobie made to Mexico in February-March 1929, probably with J. Evetts Haley. Handwritten in a leather-covered log book, Dobie's entry on the first page is: "Mexico Trip—After Javelina and Mt. Sheep Feb.-Mar., 1929." In the diary, Dobie and his travelling companion "Haley" arrive on the border during an uprising in northern Mexico:

> March 3
>
> Came to Nogales. Arrived 30 minutes before Revolutionists took over port. Lots of gossip. No facts; no bullets or blood—and no immediate chance of getting into Mexico.
>
> March 7
>
> Night back in Nogales. Saw Duncan Arkanion (sp.) reporting revolution. Everything around Nogales still quiet.
>
> March 8
>
> With help of Scrofford got passports from revolutionary forces—without cost—no pictures required. Got Cummins broker to get a 15 day permit for entering car, also 15 day permit for entering 30-30 rifles & 150 rounds of ammunition

The remainder of the diary lists photographs taken, definitions of some Spanish words, directions to Agua Zorca, etc.

4. The Saltillo Diary: A sixty-page handwritten diary detailing Dobie's trip to Saltillo Mexico, kept in a 7" x 4 1/2" yellow U.S. Geological Survey Level Book. On the cover Dobie wrote: "Trip to Saltillo, into Zacatecas, and back by Sierra Mojada with Henry Smith, Aug.-Sept. 1933. J. Frank Dobie." At the time, Dobie's friend Henry Nash Smith was editor of *The Southwest Review*. Much of the diary concerns the physical arrangements for the trip—accommodations, guides, food, horses and mules.

Dobie's ear for stories is evidenced in his entries for August 28 and September 3:

> Manuel (of Tecolotes) despite the fact that he has some education is naturally alert, intelligent & *gente de razon* believes that coyotes "magnetize" chickens & dotiles and that the poor horned frog has a poison horn.
>
> [Felix Aholla] described an old Vaquero who as a magician could turn a quirt into a rattlesnake, etc. He spent a half hour telling me the adventures of Aladin with his lamp of 1000 & 1 nights; told another long fairy story out of a book. Did not believe in weather signs but thought it possible that Villa could turn himself into some animal in order to escape. . . .

Inside the front cover of this unique diary Dobie drew several different brands and has noted: "Brands on horses and mules belonging to Felix and used on trip to Sierra Mojada."

Research Files

Dobie's research files make up the biggest part of the Wittliff Dobie Collection, representing the majority of the unique material in the house at the time of the estate sale. Examining the files, it is possible to determine how Dobie worked, gathering material that he would use in a number of different ways—in books, in articles, in his Sunday newspaper column, or for speeches or his weekly radio show. The research files for most of his published books accompanied the book manuscripts to one of the repositories at the University of Texas. What was left in the house were active files on subjects Dobie was not finished with at the time of his death.

1. The Animal Files: The largest Dobie research files in the Wittliff Collection concern bears, panthers, and rattlesnakes. The rattlesnake file provided the research for the posthumous *Rattlesnakes,* but the sizable file on panthers and the very large grizzly bear file never made it into book form, although they stretch chronologically for over forty years and Dobie stated many times his intention of writing major books dealing with both animals.

An examination of the Bear File provides basic insights into how Dobie conducted his research. The file is made up of a combination of Dobie's research from published sources, his transcriptions of field interviews, correspondence with a wide variety of individuals with bear stories, and drafts of his own writing on the subject. Long before the era of photocopy machines, Dobie copied portions of books and articles by hand; later he or his secretary typed long passages from books or magazine articles. Dobie's broad ranging research is evident in the array of sources that he quotes from. These include everything from standard accounts by and about western hunters and mountain men to pages from the *American Anthropologist*, the *Journal of Mammology*, and stories from small town newspapers all over the Texas and the West. Dobie wrote descriptive titles on much of the copied material such as "Grizzly Lordliness in the Yellowstone in the early 70's," "Humanity of a Grizzly vs. Mere Shooting of Him," and "The Bear Who Wanted Somebody Else to Dance." He would also put copies of materials in folders that he categorized; these titles included "Fights With Bears," "Playing Possum," "Indians and Bears," and "Buffalo."

Dobie's interviews and correspondence in the Bear File reveal the intensity with which he gathered material. Most of the interviews are from the fall of 1940 through the summer of 1941. Many interviews were with Indians—sometimes with an interpreter. Some of these include interviews with Chief Yellowtail and The Bird Above, conducted at the Crow Agency in Montana, and a tale that Dobie called "Playing Dead With a Grizzly" told by Dr. Rodolphe Petter, author of the English-Cheyenne Dictionary. His correspondence gathering bear stories stretches from 1937 to 1959 and includes a sizable correspondence with the W.P.A. in New Mexico and Arizona and the Bureau of Indian Affairs to see if Apaches killed bears. In the book Dobie was planning, an important chapter was to be on Nat Straw, whom Dobie called "the last of the grizzly hunters" in a twenty-eight page *Saturday Evening Post* story that he wrote in 1937. Just prior to writing the piece, Dobie interviewed Nat Straw on the

Gila River in New Mexico. This interview is transcribed on twenty handwritten pages, two typed index cards, and three handwritten cards.

The bear book was developed to the point that Dobie had a tentative table of contents and an introduction to the book titled "The Humanity of Bears." The Panther File is similar to the Bear File in its organization. It is not as large, but Dobie's gathering of mountain lion stories matched his interest in the grizzly.

2. The Alamo Controversy File: In 1936 and 1937, Dobie conducted a public campaign against the appointment of sculptor Pompeo Coppini to design the Alamo Cenotaph in San Antonio. Dobie deplored the choice of Coppini, who had done work on the University of Texas campus. The file is a fascinating record of Dobie launching a publicity campaign and includes his extensive correspondence on the matter, including letters to and from Gutzon Borglum, sculptor of the Mount Rushmore monument. The file also includes the manuscript of his newspaper column on the subject, his seven-page radio script, and many newspaper clippings.

3. The Cattle Trade File: Dobie maintained a sizable file on "the cattle trade" that brought together interviews, diaries, and letters pertaining to old-time ranch life in Texas, New Mexico, and Arizona. It includes a 1926 interview Dobie conducted with D. F. Doan of Doan's Crossing, other stories about cattle drive days, and a wonderful letter dated July 10, 1935, from Jake English of Eagle Pass who passes on a story about Lafayeete Vivion, the first "white child" born in Goliad County.

It is Old Testament-like in the rhythm of its names:

> He was borned March 31, 1847, in old rock house built by his father Lloyd Vivion in year 1846. There were thirteen old pioneer women at his birth and each wanted to name him, so they commenced. The first called him Monroe. The second called him Jackson. And third called him Jasper. And fourth called him Eldredge. And fifth called him Augustus. And sixth called him Adolphus. And seventh called him Cicero. And eighth called him Brown. And ninth called him Dee. And tenth called him Charley. And eleventh called him Blue.

And twelfth called him Lloyd. But his mother called him Lafayeete and this is the name he went by. And cowmen called him fate.

4. The Pancho Villa File: This remarkable file reveals Dobie's lifelong interests in the Mexican Revolution and particularly in Pancho Villa, whom he described as "Villa the Unkillable & Uncapturable." Beginning with a newspaper clipping from 1916, the file extends to August 6, 1961, when Dobie used two Villa anecdotes in his Sunday newspaper column. The file contains Dobie's handwritten transcripts of Villa stories that he gathered beginning in 1923. At the top of a nine-page interview with Erasmo Barraza titled "The Killing of Pancho Villa," Dobie wrote "The truth." In the file Dobie recounts Villa's elaborate methods of trading clothes with his followers and eating off others' plates, all in order to protect himself. Other topics relating to Villa that Dobie concentrated on are Villa's superstitions, Villa's treasure, and, of course, what became of Villa's head after his death.

Other significant Dobie research files present in the Southwestern Writers Collection are the Judge Roy Bean File, the Battle of the Alamo File, the Jim Bowie File, the Southwestern Characters File, the Cow Dog File, the Treasure File, and "Handwritten Notes on Stephen F. Austin."

Speeches and Lectures

1. "Old Speeches": This is a collection of 77 speeches dating from 1924 to 1948. Representative titles are "Tales of the Texas Soil," "Culture and Coyotes," "The Adventures of a Story-Hunter in New Mexico," and "Brothers of the Soil, Animal Stories." Dobie addressed the Texas House and Senate in July, 1931, on "Longhorns with a Capital L," dedicated the Trail Driver's Monument at Doan's Crossing later in the same year, and delivered many talks in Colorado, New Mexico, and Oklahoma. The spontaneity of some of his talks is reflected in his jotting notes on the back of envelopes. His talk titled "The Preservation of the

Culture of the Southwest," delivered in the Senate Chamber in Austin to the Texas Round Table, was from an outline jotted on the back of the program.

2. Notes for Later Speeches: By the late 1940s and early 1950s, Dobie was speaking to more sophisticated audiences about more literary topics. From this period, the Wittliff Dobie Collection has notes for speeches Dobie delivered to the Caxton Club in Chicago, at Northwestern University, to the Illinois State Historical Society, and a talk to the Friends of the UCLA Library on "Books of the Southwest." Miscellaneous items in Dobie's speech file include quotations that he used in his talks from writers as disparate as Mark Twain, James Joyce, Virginia Woolf, and Lawrence Clark Powell.

3. The Cambridge Lectures, 1943–1944: In September 1943, Dobie left Austin to succeed Henry Steele Commager in the recently established Professorship of American History at Emmanuel College, Cambridge University. This collection contains twenty-three of his Cambridge lectures, some as notes, some written out verbatim, but all in their first draft form. Although Dobie wrote Bertha that never had he dreaded making a class appearance more, he was popular at the University and soon was in great demand as a speaker off campus as well. His University lectures considered major figures and events from Tom Paine to the TVA, but one of his lectures was titled "The Ebullient West," and he wrote Bertha the "it did not take me long to lug in Sam Houston and then I felt more or less at ease" (Tinkle, *An American Original,* 181).

Wills

The Wittliff Dobie Collection contains many personal and family materials, including Dobie's tax records, family Bibles, address books, World War I orders, foot locker, uniform, and several items of clothing, including a pair of handmade shoes, a white linen summer suit, and two hats. The personal effects include six versions of Dobie's last will and testament and one of Bertha Dobie's wills. Dobie's earliest will, dated August 12, 1937, is handwritten and reads in part:

> If I die before my mother dies, then let a Methodist preacher, for my mother's sake, preside at the funeral. If my mother dies before I die, then I wish no preacher to have anything to do with the services. I should like a good funeral oration by Evetts Haley or, if he is not available, by some Texas man who knows me and comprehends the work of my life. I'd like for the funeral to be a cheerful sort of occasion, with somebody to sing "Goodbye Old Paint, I'm a-Leaving Cheyenne." I don't want to be buried in any damned memorial park and I hope that friends instead of undertaker hirelings will throw dirt in on me. I would not mind being buried in the State Cemetery, somewhere in the vicinity of Bigfoot Wallace. Otherwise I'd just as soon have my body burned and the ashes scattered among the liveoaks and mesquites on my old ranch home, to which almost every day of my life I have returned in memory, in Live Oak County.

Six years later, the second will was written, apparently after Dobie's break with Haley: "Evetts Haley wouldn't want to preach my funeral sermon. Let that go. I'm not as much interested in my own funeral as I used to be."

There are indications that Dobie turned his attention away from his library's purchase by the Humanities Research Center even as the Dobie Room was being built. Lon Tinkle quotes a letter that he wrote to Bertha from Berkeley in the summer of 1963: "If I am to be remembered at all, it will be through my writing; what goes to the library is of little more significance than a graveyard monument" (*An American Original,* 233). It had been twenty-five years since Dobie had written "A Corner Forever Texas," and his greatest recognition had come after his firing from the University in 1947. Harry Ransom and Warren Roberts should be given credit for their efforts to bring his work back onto the campus, but Dobie's ambivalence towards the University and its libraries is clear.

Examining the Dobie material at the Southwestern Writers Collection, the researcher who is familiar with other Dobie collections is struck by their interrelatedness. Dobie, Mrs. Coker, and others who worked for Dobie over the years routinely typed two or three carbons of everything, and, as we have seen in the instance of the Dobie/Bedichek letters, the original may be located in San Marcos and the carbon of the same letter at the Barker Center, or another repository, or vice versa. Because Dobie's papers have been dispersed to their different locations over a fifty-year period, it is probably inevitable that directly related material is found in different places. For instance, Dobie's Columbia class notes can be found both at the Ransom Center and at the Southwestern Writers Collection.

The Wittliff Dobie Collection for the most part contains what was in the Dobie home at the time of the estate sale in 1985, and as we have seen it ranges throughout Dobie's life from his college days to the years after his death when Bertha Dobie was editing his posthumous works. Given the difficult circumstances of the Dobie estate sale, the result of one person buying everything and that one person being Bill Wittliff was serendipity of a high order. Wittliff's knowledge of Dobie's life and work and his friendship with both Dobies guided him when he examined the papers from the sale. His instincts as a collector and creator made him a persuasive advocate for beginning a new special collection—a corner forever Texas at a state university in 1986, in itself a startling accomplishment.

Endnote

This guide to the Dobie manuscript collections was made possible by a notable group of librarians, collectors, and book people, all involved in Dobie's life and work in some way. The librarians whose help was indispensable are Norma Assadourian at Southwestern University; Sally Leach, Cathy Henderson, and Jennifer Patterson at the Ransom Center; Kate Adams, Don Carleton, and Ralph Elder at the Barker Center; Don Dial at Texas A&M; Kent Keeth at Baylor; and Dora Guerra at UT San Antonio. Other important help was provided by Harold Billings, Dudley Dobie, Jr., Franklin Gilliam, Al Lowman, Bill Mears, Anne Norman, Warren Roberts, and Bill Wittliff. Wittliff's office, in the person of Connie Todd, is responsible for the beautifully produced inventories of the Dobie Collection at SWT. René LeBlanc's editorial advice was timely and wise. Finally, two remarkable women, Willie Belle Coker and Isabel Gaddis, were generous both with their reminiscences and their time.

J. Frank Dobie, Secretary-Editor 1923–1943. Fellow of the Texas Folklore Society (Courtesy Texas Folklore Society)

The four Lomax boys: Front row, L to R: *George* and Robert; back row, L to R: John and *Jesse* (Courtesy Nolan Porterfield)

2

John Lomax and Texas: Roots of a Career

Nolan Porterfield

JOHN AVERY LOMAX WAS NOT A NATIVE TEXAN, BUT HE MIGHT AS well have been. The eyes of Texas were on him early, and the course of the Lone Star fixed his direction for most of his eighty years. He was never a cowboy either, although he was forever carrying on about "my father's ranch beside the old Chisholm Trail," and as a youth he had spent considerable time on the back of a pony, herding milk cows and the occasional family beef. As soon as he could, he took himself off to the city in earnest pursuit of the refinements of civilization and polite society—books and ideas, the Rotary Club, indoor plumbing. But it was Texas and its cowboy lore that set him on the path to fame and fulfillment, and the image or mirage of "Texas" in its epic sense—rough and sprawling, dynamic, discordant, paradoxical, and glorious—governed his life and shaped his achievement.

Like Texas, like its cowboys, Lomax had some distinctly rough qualities. He was in many ways an American primitive, raw, bumptious, xenophobic, yet it was his very faith in traditional values, his love of things native and national, that first pointed him toward his life's work. In another paradoxical sense, he was the true pioneer—true American, true Texan—in his eagerness to break new ground, to go where others had not, and do what they had not. He was, in short, like most accomplished human beings, a mass of contradictions. But as in the case of "Texas" and "cowboy," it is the extravagant character and unique mix of oppositions in "John Avery Lomax" which give his life the force of legend.

When the Lomax family migrated to Texas from Mississippi in the late fall of 1869, the Lone Star State was, strictly speaking, not even a state. Four troubled years after the Civil War, it was still under military occupation, in chaos and turmoil, suspended between conquered territory and provisional statehood. A fiercely contested and probably fraudulent election in November gave dictatorial control to carpetbagger Radical Republicans, who won the statehouse by a small majority of some eight hundred votes. But with an administration now aligned to the policies of the Reconstruction Congress in Washington, way had been made for readmission to the Union the following spring. Yet political and economic turbulence continued to boil, even after southern Democrats regained power in the mid-1870s, when the newly-arrived Lomaxes were struggling to make a new home for themselves. These years constituted, in the words of historian T. R. Fehrenbach, "the most disastrous period in Texas history," worse even than the terrible days of the war itself (408).

But conditions had been no better in the wartime home of the Lomax clan. Years afterward, John Lomax's father recorded his reasons for leaving his "old home" in Mississippi near Goodman in Holmes County, where he had farmed and operated a small tanyard. His motive, said James Lomax, was "to get away from the wreck of the war, and take my young family out of a state of society that can only be expressed by the word 'chaos'" (144). Westward migration was in the air, and James Lomax was caught up in popular notions of wide open spaces and fresh opportunities in Texas. He was anxious, he said, "to give my boys room to expand" (John Lomax, *Adventures* 2), and he was sure the wholesome climate he had heard about from exuberant land agents would ease the miseries of age and help him recover from poor health caused by the war.

He was less open about family problems that weighed on the move to Texas. For some time there had been ill feelings between him and his younger, more prosperous brother, Tillman (who, James felt, owed his wealth and social position to his wife's inheritance). During the war, Tillman Lomax had been elected captain of a company of Home Guard into which James was conscripted as a middle-aged private. When higher authorities relieved James from soldiering and set him to work tanning leather and making shoes for the army, Tillman, out of envy and malice, entered his brother on the company roll as a deserter.

Years later, young John Lomax and his brother Richard spent considerable time and money turning up evidence to clear their father's name, but the official record was never corrected.

There was another, even less presentable reason for leaving Mississippi, a reason also rooted in feelings of prejudice and social inferiority. "I did not want my family raised in contact with the negro either as slave or as 'freedman,'" said James Lomax later (144). It was an attitude only to be understood in the context of its time, and highly ironic in light of the career of his son John, who would one day gain a national reputation from close association with blacks and his efforts to record and popularize their culture.

If James Lomax was something of a bigot, however, he was no ordinary run-of-the-mill-lower-class-Southern bigot, despite the fact that, many years later, son John would relish the term "po' white trash" in describing his family origins. To be sure, John's phrase was "*upper crust* of the po' white trash," but as commonly used by those closest to it, "po' white trash" does not denote economic level so much as it describes a state of mind and a condition of the spirit. Whatever his financial ups and downs, and despite the racist cast of his social attitudes, James Lomax was not a man without culture, or cultural aspiration. Among his complaints against *antebellum* Mississippi was his view that "the ruling classes possessed all the culture and intelligence," clearly indicating that one reason for the move to Texas was his hope—poor doomed hope—of finding those qualities of life which had been denied him in Mississippi. His notions about racial separation must also be considered in light of his declaration that "slavery was a curse to the South"; in almost the same breath that he excluded himself and his family from the society of blacks, he spoke out vigorously against injustices suffered by "ignorant negroes" in the aftermath of the war (144).

James Lomax was a native of South Carolina, born in Abbeville County in 1816 to a family rumored to have been prosperous landowners until a land title dispute took most of their wealth. He married in his early thirties and migrated to central Mississippi, where he worked as a tanner and occasional farm hand. By 1850 he owned his own small farm in

Holmes County and later built a tanyard there. His first wife, who bore him five children, died in 1854, when the oldest was only fifteen. Three years later, aged 41, he married Susan Frances Cooper, twenty years his junior, who lived nearby and had helped the widower's mother with household chores and tutored his small children. She was a plump, gentle, religious young woman, with more schooling than most girls of that time and place, including one year at a "Female Institute."

The marriage between James Avery Lomax and Susan Frances Cooper was typical of many alliances in those days, as much a matter of convenience as of romance. James valued her strength of character as wife and homemaker; for her part, "I respected him," she said, "and I felt sorry for him" ("A Trip to Texas" 254). In time they were to become the parents of eleven children. Six (two of whom died in infancy) were born in Mississippi prior to the move to Texas. John Avery Lomax was the last of these six, born September 23, 1867. He was just past his second birthday when the Lomax family arrived in Texas in December, 1869.

"Oh, how sorry I was to leave our Mississippi home," said Susan Lomax ("A Trip to Texas" 255). Despite the ravages of war and reconstruction, Mississippi was a place familiar to her, settled and civilized. Going to Texas meant a perilous journey of five hundred miles by mule-drawn wagon, ending somewhere far from relatives and friends in a wild, unknown land. Moreover, she was seven months pregnant—a circumstance apparently so ordinary that she made no mention of it in the otherwise detailed account of the arduous trip which she wrote later. As much as anything else, "I dreaded the Indians," she said—and with good reason, in light of reports that bands of savages still roamed the frontier region where James planned to homestead. She had fretted long and hard over the matter, but finally rationalized her decision to go on the ground that "my husband had better judgment than I did." There was true grit in her going; sadly, there was in it also the dutiful submission demanded of a wife in that time and place.

Whatever worries Susan Lomax had about the wild and woolly nature of Texas were well founded. As a popular expression among Texans had it, "the bottom rail was on top"—the

James Avery Lomax and Susan Frances Cooper Lomax (Courtesy Nolan Porterfield)

entire political, economic, and social order had been overturned by war and the ensuing "reconstruction." Yet civil harmony is a relative matter; it seems unlikely that the larger turmoil had much bearing on the daily lives of the Lomaxes as they set about tending to more basic matters: finding a home, a roof, food for the table.

In fact, one effect of the general upheaval was to create a circumstance that James Lomax found quite favorable: cheap land prices. With cotton depressed to less than twenty cents a pound, rich prairie lands could be bought for as little as fifty cents an acre. But James Lomax was accustomed to water and trees, and he preferred to pay six dollars an acre for slightly more than a quarter section of timbered bottom land on the Bosque (off the Texan tongue, "Bosky") River a few miles north of the hamlet of Meridian in Bosque County. While it lay along the very edge of the frontier, geographically and culturally it was in those days about as close as one could get to deep in the heart of Texas. In the 1870s and '80s its geographical features made Bosque County a nexus of socio-economic frontiers and gave it a heightened, if not unique, sense of cultural contrasts (McNutt 19–20).

Meridian, which John Lomax came to call home, is practically at the center of the valley and halfway along the river's course. The town's name, however, comes from the fact that it sits almost astride the 98th meridian—which in 1870 marked the farthest reach of the Texas frontier. The 98th meridian was—and remains—an important dividing line in other respects. Just beyond it lay an unsettled, incredibly harsh land where savage Comanches and Kiowa raiding bands still roamed, where the annual rainfall was never more than thirty inches and often less, where all life was subject to frequent and violent change: drouth, then flood; blazing sun, then high chill winds and blowing snow. Feast, then famine.

In the ensuing hundred years, the land beyond the 98th meridian has, of course, been settled, in one fashion or another, and the Indians "disappeared." But the weather and topography remain essentially unchanged, and they dictate to a large extent the nature of human existence there—not merely the day-to-day life of people, but their ideas and values and attitudes. The historian Walter Prescott Webb, a contemporary of John Lomax, coined the term "institutional fault" to describe the process of social and cultural alteration that took place in the movement from lush timbered areas to treeless plains. "Fault" has moral and spiritual dimensions that seem not to have occurred to Webb, although he did point to evidence that "the plain gives man new and novel sensations of elation, of vastness, of romance, of awe, and often of nauseating loneliness" (8, 489).

Other historians and sociologists have dealt with the 98th meridian primarily in agricultural terms, as a division between what is "farmable" and "unfarmable"—but farmers speak of cultivating the land, and it is the question of "cultivation" in broader terms that devolves on the homeland of John Lomax as the dividing line between the civilized and the primitive. Growing up in Bosque County, Texas, in the 1870s, he absorbed a little of both, and a curious mix of refinement and coarseness shows up in almost everything he did.

Meridian, Texas, unlike many small towns in America, today seems a lively and thriving place, no doubt due in part to its climate and location, nestled among rolling cedar hills and high-topped mesas. Although change has come to the Bosque Valley in the past century, it is not hard to see the land as it was when John Lomax was a boy there. In many respects, the vista is that transmitted to the rest of the world—to non-Texans—by the words "Texas" and "cowboy." It is an almost Ur-western-movie landscape, rivaled in the state only by the Big Bend canyons and Kerrville's Hill Country as a place where one might reasonably expect to see Gene or Roy or Hopalong riding after the bad guys. One has to remember, of course—and then perhaps ought to forget—that most of the movies which taught us (even us Texans) what Texas looked like were filmed in Southern California.

Among the first of the old Texians to leave the protection of Stephen Austin's colony on the Brazos and go "outside the line of posts" in the 1840s were those who settled in what is now Bosque County (Ford 445). More concentrated settlement began in the 1850s, leading to the organization of the county in 1854. When the Lomaxes arrived there fifteen years later and settled about eight miles north of Meridian, their neighbors were mostly fellow Southerners—Tennesseans, Alabamans, and Missourians (who were Southern by culture if not by geography). Some settlers before the war had brought in slaves, who as freedmen remained to work the river bottom cotton lands. In 1865 blacks in Texas had numbered about one out of three residents in a population of roughly 600,000, but they were largely concentrated in the east and in plantation areas along the lower Colorado and Brazos (Hogan 22; Fehrenbach 683). The ratio was considerably smaller in areas like Bosque County along the frontier. Still, blacks were sufficient in number to create a distinctly black subculture—and to serve as a catalyst for bitter, often violent racial prejudice. Among John Lomax's stark childhood memories—recalled frequently in later years—was the lynching of a Negro accused of raping a white woman.

At another extreme, the cultural pluralism of the region was further heightened by the presence of a number of Norwegian families, whose opposition to slavery, secession, and the war had set them quite apart from the rest of the community. In time still another minority formed, as small numbers of Hispanics made their way into the region, adding to its ethnic diversity. The heterogeneous strains of Bosque County were to blend in various patterns to shape the outlook of young John Lomax, but that part of Texas was an ironic destination for a man like his father, who claimed he wanted to live only among his own kind.

In addition to his wagons and teams and household goods shipped by rail, James Lomax came to Texas with about $4,000 in gold, mostly acquired from the sale of his tanyard and farm in Mississippi. Four thousand dollars was a considerable sum in those days, but not quite the substantial bankroll it might seem. Texas at the time was essentially a moneyless society. The only cash crop was cotton—fragile, uncertain, and labor-intensive—and it was at that time a risky one, because of severely depressed prices. But in the winter of 1869–70 the Lomaxes were months away from any crop whatever. In the meantime necessities had to be bartered. Money was useful mostly for paying taxes and, as John wrote later, to buy "clothes, sugar, coffee, tobacco and a gallon jug of whiskey hid behind the kitchen door for morning drams for my father" ("John A. Lomax Tells").

The purchase of 183 acres of Bosque County land had taken about one fourth of James Lomax's capital. Soon after the first of the new year—1870—he finished a small two-room cabin "at the bottom of the second bluff that marked the Bosque river" ("John A. Lomax Tells") and set out to clear enough land by spring to plant cotton and corn. He began to raise horses and cattle, both for private use and as an investment, and he went after spare cash by putting his older sons to work cutting timber to sell in town for stove wood. Later, as the boy John grew to it, chopping and hauling firewood became one of his major chores. There were many other tasks as well, more than enough for even a large family. By the time he was six, John was working alongside his brothers in the field, planting corn, hoeing and picking cotton. He herded the family's work stock, tended the beef cattle, and helped clear new ground, a terrible job that required literally grubbing the trees out by their roots with pick and mattock. "Broken to work" is a country phrase used of both horses and boys; by the time he was in his teens, John Lomax was qualified. Soon he would find a way to escape the drudgery of the farm, but a distinguishing mark of his character throughout life was his awesome capacity for labor, an almost compulsive need for it, and a seemingly tireless energy that only increased with the passing years.

Lomax complained of the narrowness and toil of his frontier youth. Those early years were no doubt a drab and often difficult time. Yet life was not without its diversions, and in old age he looked more kindly on his childhood. In his autobiography he recounted with considerable feeling the pleasures of roaming the "cedar-clad hills" and lush valleys of the Bosque in the days when the river still ran swift and clear, its banks overhung with willows and cottonwoods, elm, sycamore, and hackberry. "The beauty of the region grew in my soul," he wrote, reliving the sensations of riding his favorite pony, Selim, at a gallop across the rolling pasture lands thick and vivid with native flowers. "I hunted and fished, went in swimming, and lived with my kind," he said (*Adventures* 4, 5). His "kind" were the common run of country boys, Texas Huck Finns who, left together unattended, romped and wrestled and tumbled like pups, played risky pranks, dodged work whenever they could (which was not often), and generally behaved as boys always have. One or two were town boys—notably his best friend,

Johnny Cochran, who was also an in-law, related to the husband of John's older sister, Mary. In his teens young Cochran learned to set type for the weekly *Meridian Blade,* and in so doing became for John Lomax one avenue of escape from the harshness and tedium of life in the back country.

Whenever he brought a load of firewood to town, John would stop at the newspaper office to see his friend, and eventually he became acquainted with the editor, William Fields, who had served in the Confederate army and later became, in Lomax's words, "a distinguished member of the Texas legislature." From time to time, Captain Fields (as he was known to John) would give the boy an armful of "exchanges"—newspapers from other towns, sent to the *Blade* in trade for a complimentary subscription. "In those days 'patent sides' [syndicated material] of country newspapers carried columns of general world news," said Lomax. "Reading those papers was the real start of my education—a powerful influence on my mental growth" ("John A. Lomax Tells"). Headed home in the empty lumber wagon with his cache of newspapers, young John would give the mules, Jack and Fan, full rein to find their own way, while he slipped from the seat and settled himself on the floor of the wagon box with his papers, braced his feet against the front corners, and lost himself in boilerplate reports of the outside world. The eight-mile journey often took two or three hours; passersby grew accustomed to the sight of an apparently driverless wagon drawn by two plodding mules—and occasionally the top of John Lomax's sandy head, fixed on the newspaper before him, bouncing up momentarily above the sideboards as the procession rolled along over bumps and ruts.

Later his father subscribed to out-of-state papers, including the *Louisville Courier* and the weekly *New York Sun,* with its visions of a faraway, magic metropolis which the Texas farm boy could scarcely believe existed. (In time he would become a casual visitor to its fine hotels and clubs, warmly received, even lionized.) Together with the "patent sides" of the county seat weeklies, these papers became, as Lomax said later, "the real start of my education," supplanting the meager and sporadic learning offered by the school system.

By the mid-1870s, when John Lomax was old enough to start to school, old-line Democrats had retaken control of the state.

Passionately opposed to "centralized government" (in a fashion the older John Lomax would affirm), they made drastic cuts in state expenditures and essentially wrecked the fledgling state educational system (Ramsdell 312; Fehrenbach 433–434). While these actions constituted, historically, real setbacks for the intellectual climate in Texas, it is unlikely that they seriously altered the course of public education in rural Bosque County, which even under state supervision had been rudimentary. The important thing for John Lomax was that his parents respected education and were determined that their children have as much schooling as possible. Neighboring families, in the face of incessant demands for laboring hands and backs on the farm, were quick to take their offspring out of school to plant and harvest. Sometimes James Lomax had to do the same, but he tried to see that his children, boys and girls alike, attended every session they could. His own education had been brief and spotty, but he served as trustee for the Meridian community school and steadfastly asserted the values of "book learning." John's father was a stolid, straight-ahead man, at times a stern taskmaster, but he was no ordinary frontier yeoman, this James Lomax, who in a stronghold of tea-total Methodism kept a jug of whiskey behind the kitchen door, subscribed to national newspapers at considerable expense, and urged books and education on his children.

In any event, schooling of some sort was a natural part of life for John Lomax from an early age. Even before he was old enough for the first grade, he was frequently taken to visit by his older brothers and sister. The old Bosque cowboy, Ed Nichols, writing his memoirs, remembered seeing the Meridian school children on their way in the mornings, "two and two, some of them barefoot, laughing, talking, a book satchel over one shoulder, a dinner bucket in one hand." Often Richard Lomax and "his redhaired sister Mollie" (Mary) led the way and "sometimes their little brother Johnny came along to spend the day."

> He was a pretty, fat little fellow four or five year old, and I can see him now as he ran along by their side, sometimes holding his sister's hand, sometimes holding Richard's. On these days when Johnny came to school, the pupils studied something like

> half the time and watched him the other half. The little rascal was full of mischief. (56–57)

The mischief lasted, but it soon took more subtle, subdued forms; by the time he was going to school regularly, nobody had to "watch" Johnny Lomax. Sobermindedness grew in him like an extra organ. It was probably true, as he later asserted, that he was never a discontented or dissatisfied boy, but in later years he spoke of the loneliness and isolation he suffered as a child and of his feeling that he had inherited his father's stern and stubborn nature. The picture that emerges is one of an outwardly normal boy, sometimes rowdy, yet governable, industrious, always dutiful—but also a child solemn and self-contained, often shy, moody, given to daydreams, filled with the vague but gnawing sense that there was another, better life for him to find. In American culture, it is a familiar, almost legendary image: the sensitive, intelligent youth of the provinces, whose ideas and aspirations find little understanding or encouragement in a crude, hostile environment.

Religion—the "hellfire and damnation of frontier Methodism"—contributed to this temperament, sometimes in paradoxical ways. The Lomaxes were irregular church-goers (despite Susan Cooper Lomax's religiosity and, in large part, because of James's indifference to it), but fundamentalist Christian doctrine was a strong and pervasive influence in their daily lives. Good and evil were clearly delineated according to the Old Testament. Hard work was a testing ground for the elect; retribution to the fallen was swift and certain. "We were earnest folk," said John, "and we worked hard at our religion (*Adventures* 6). Church might keep or not, but on Sundays the Lomax children were forbidden to play games, go fishing, or swim in the river. In later years a more secular, unbuttoned John Lomax regretted the "rigid rules of conduct" imposed by his parents, but he also prided himself in having obeyed them—"I cannot remember . . . that I ever felt rebellious," he said with a certain sadness, even regret (*Adventures* 13–14).

The rural church of Lomax's time served, on the one hand, to foster this attitude of willing submission, just as it contributed mightily to the drab tedium of life by seeking to impose a single, absolute religious belief, puritanical standards of behavior, and harsh punishments for those who strayed. Ironically, at the heart of such strict fundamentalism was a fiery emotionalism always in danger of erupting—at worst into reactionary rebellion, at best into passionate brotherhood: frontier religion in Texas was as much a force for social cohesion, an occasion for tribal gathering, as it was for the dissemination of ideology. Young John Lomax shrank from the dark, terrible doctrines of primitive Methodism, which literally caused him nightmares ("dreaming that I myself was immersed in a pool of blood, oceans of blood"), but the social aspects of the church—especially its annual camp meetings—appealed to him as welcome relief from the loneliness and dull routine in his life, a source of the fellowship and comradery he always hungered for.

At one such camp meeting, when he was thirteen, he succumbed to "the emotional appeal of Brother Levi Harris' singing" and, to put an end to his mother's embarrassing prayers for his conversion, stood to announce himself "saved." Later he remembered mostly his discomfort and anxiety at being the center of public attention. His real motivation for joining the church, he clearly indicated, was to end his "agony of self-consciousness," make his mother happy, and thereafter be spared the vexation of the mourner's bench.

In his mind the mourner's bench was also linked to an innocently amorous but troubling encounter with a young belle of the congregation, "several years older than I," who had sat down beside him on a back pew during the mourning period and rubbed her cheek against his. That was hardly sin enough for repentance, he felt, but years later he enjoyed equating it with the "carnal desires of the flesh" which the church required him to renounce. Of his snuggle with the Older Woman, he said simply, "I found the sensation pleasant" (*Adventures* 12). It was not the only time he would connect some key circumstance in his youth to the romantic or erotic. Remarking on the books he had read as a boy, he noted that his family bought from a traveling book agent two popular tracts of the day, *Golden Gems of Thought* and a treatise on phrenology by Dr. O. S. Fowler. The former he found "stupid and dull reading," but "Dr. Fowler's comments and the sexy illustrations appealed powerfully to my imagination. I wanted to get off to myself whenever I read that book" ("John A. Lomax Tells").

The rare few books which came his way were at once treasured and consumed. Later he told Lincoln-esque stories of toilsome days in the fields and of nights spent reading by a tiny brass lamp in his garret room after the family was asleep. Following Fowler, a powerful literary influence in these early years was *Pilgrim's Progress*, "the first book I read completely through." Like many another unlettered country youth, he was largely unaware of its moral and theological allegory and read it simply as "a thrilling adventure." At sixteen he fell under the spell of Eugene Sue's grand melodrama, *The Wandering Jew*, a popular sensation when published forty years earlier. Once more he was immune to the author's weightier intentions. Only later did he learn that *The Wandering Jew* was, among other things, an attack on Catholicism; at the time it was "only a moving drama" which burned in his consciousness with such intensity that for days he went about his chores in a daze. "One more Wandering Jew," said his father derisively, "and you'll be a candidate to the Austin lunatic asylum" ("John A. Lomax Tells").

There were other diversions. As an older John Lomax was fond of pointing out, over and over, the family farm was situated "beside a branch of the old Chisholm Trail" (*Adventures* 19). In the early years there was a steady procession of covered wagon caravans, trail herds, and riders on horseback. Cowboys and other wayfaring strangers often spent the night in the Lomax house, bringing, said John, "the big, outside world [to] our door" (*Adventures* 4). These visitors, he felt, first awakened him to the realization that there were important people and ideas beyond the Bosque Valley.

Cowboys were the focus of other compelling events. The rodeo as we know it was yet to be invented, but the so-called "cowboy tournaments" served a similar function. These were riding contests patterned on anachronistic frontier notions of knights' jousts, as filtered through Sir Walter Scott, Sidney Lanier, and other creaky bastions of "honor" and "chivalry" in the Old South. The contests themselves were merely the raison d'etre for a whole panoply of related rituals, displays, and ceremonies. Like similar events in our time—tractor pulls, demolition derbies, road rallies—the cowboy tournaments were social as well as competitive occasions, often the centerpiece for county picnics, political debates, and school celebrations. The proceedings were highly ritualized, with a parade before and a dance afterward, featuring a variety of promenades and jigs accompanied by songs and calls in cowboy vernacular.

Young John Lomax was drawn to the music as well as to the derring-do of these pageants—he credited tournament heroes like Bob Hanna and Ed Nichols with having "deepened my love for cowboy songs" (*Adventures* 19)—but it is not clear just when and how the interest surfaced. In a recollection more than a little tinged with romantic hindsight, he supposedly remembered hearing, at the precocious age of four, a cowboy somewhere in the night, crooning "Git Along, Little Dogies" and yodeling to his restless cattle (see *Adventures* 19–20). There is little historical evidence of a true "cattle call" yodel until well into the twentieth century. When Lomax's autobiography appeared in 1947 with this recollection, J. Frank Dobie wrote to their mutual friend, Roy Bedichek: "I meant to jump [Lomax] about his yodeling cowboys away back there 65 years ago or more. I feel sure that at that time there was no yodeling among people of the soil anywhere in America" (*Three Friends* 263).

Books and camp meetings, cowboys, occasional trips to town—all these brought release from the daily grind at home. But their pleasures were fleeting, and always at his back Johnny Lomax heard not only Time's winged chariot but the wrenching creak of a Georgia stock and single-row planter. At the same time, recurring bouts of imagination—an ancient affliction of bright farm boys—were rendering him less and less fit for the dull, routine tasks of frontier agriculture. Perversely, as he grew aware of the world beyond Bosque County, his own existence there seemed all the more narrowed and confined, his choices limited, the passage through life already booked and confirmed. He was nearly twenty years old before an alternate route presented itself.

Works Cited

Dugger, Ronnie, ed. *Three Friends in Texas: Roy Bedichek, J. Frank Dobie, Walter Prescott Webb.* Austin: University of Texas Press, 1967.

Fehrenbach, T. R. *Lone Star: A History of Texas and the Texans.* New York: Macmillan Co., 1968.

Ford, John Salmon. *Rip Ford's Texas.* Ed. Stephen B. Oates. Austin: University of Texas Press, 1963.

Hogan, William Ransom. *The Texas Republic: A Social and Economic History.* Norman: University of Oklahoma Press, 1949.

Lomax, James A. "Reflections of J. A. Lomax, as Dictated to W. F. Graves." *Genealogical and Historical Sketches of the Lomax Family.* Grand Rapids: Rookus Printing House, 1894.

Lomax, John A. *Adventures of a Ballad Hunter.* New York: Macmillan Co., 1947.

Lomax, John A. "John A. Lomax Tells of the Reading that Influenced Him in His Early Life; A Tribute to the Newspapers." *Dallas Times Herald,* Aug. 19, 1945.

Lomax, Susan Frances. "A Trip to Texas." *The Southwestern Historical Quarterly,* XLVIII (Oct. 1944): 254–261.

McNutt, James. *Beyond Regionalism: Texas Folklorists and the Emergence of a Post-Regional Consciousness.* Unpublished Ph. D. dissertation, University of Texas, 1982.

Nichols, Edwin Seymour. *Ed Nichols Rode a Horse.* Dallas: Texas Folklore Society and the University Press of Dallas, 1943.

Ramsdell, Charles William. *Reconstruction In Texas.* New York: Columbia UP, 1910.

3

J. Frank Dobie and the American Folklore Society

Paul Stone

THE J. FRANK DOBIE WHO RETURNED TO THE UNIVERSITY OF Texas from his uncle's South Texas ranch in the fall of 1921 was not the same man who left a year earlier. Put simply, while ranching full-time Dobie heard something which changed his outlook about place and inner knowledge. He experienced a revelation about the significance of folklore to his part of the state, a "ranch country, arid and covered with thorned brush and prickly pear, as extraordinary in character as the maquis of Corsica or the Everglades. . . . " Dobie was later to write, "This brush hides old, old secrets . . . " (*Some Part of Myself* 231).

Rancho Los Olmos vaquero Santos Cortez, a master storyteller, his uncle and Los Olmos "patron" Jim Dobie, and others who "talked or stayed silent," had, in 1920–21, unleashed in Frank a primitivist intuitive sense, and, in doing so, made him even more a Romantic than he already was. Dobie's biographer Lon Tinkle called this transformation an "epiphany," and drew the analogy that he was, at that moment, like "young Goethe at the University of Strasbourg, when Herder persuaded [him] that the fountainhead for his writing lay, not in . . . neo-classicism, but in German folklore" (*Makings of an Ample Mind* 6).

Even though Dobie had been a member of the Texas Folklore Society since 1914, his professional folkloric impulse grew from his Los Olmos "epiphany." Within a year, this sudden recognition of cultural significance as a key component of personal identity, propelled him simultaneously into a position of preeminence in the Texas Folklore Society as well as the inner leadership circle of the American Folk-Lore Society.

Once Dobie was back in Austin, Texas Folklore Society co-founder L. W. Payne easily convinced him to take over the largely defunct regional organization, which, as he saw it, *was* technically a branch of the AFS.[1] The national organization had been founded at Harvard in 1888, the year of Dobie's birth. Before Dobie, the TFS direction had been in the hands of Leonidas Payne and John Lomax. Another leader was Stith Thompson, who brought Dobie into the Society and who edited its first book-length publication in 1916.[2] In this volume Thompson plainly stated what he saw as the relationship between the Texas society and the AFS:

> The Folk-Lore Society of Texas is the state branch of The American Folk-Lore Society. The purpose of the Society is in the exploration of the great field of folk-lore in Texas and the Southwest, and it invites into its membership all who are interested in promoting this end. It holds annual meetings, at which papers on folk-lore are read and discussed.[3]

John A. Lomax, the other co-founder of the TFS, might not have seen the Texas organization exactly as a "branch" of the AFS, but clearly thought of the two as sister societies with appropriately overlapping memberships. Lomax recalled:

> George Lyman Kittredge . . . suggested I . . . organize a Texas Folk-Lore Society . . . (which) started-off with quite a number of members who belonged to both the American Folklore Society and the Texas Folk-Lore Society (*When the Woods Were Burnt* 17–18).

As the new secretary/editor for 1922, Dobie matched Thompson in energy, but surpassed him in personal enthusiasm for the subject. This passion quickly led to a schism with the AFS. This rift between the TFS and the AFS, which became apparent in 1925 and widened in the years to come, was an important episode in the history of American folkloristics as well as in Dobie's early career. It was a source of frustration to Lomax, who, as Kittredge's student and long-time friend, saw the rupture as a blow to both organizations.[4]

J. Frank Dobie as the new Secretary-Editor of the Texas Folklore Society, early 1920s (Courtesy Barker Texas History Center, The University of Texas)

The particulars of this breakup have long been something of a mystery, but solid evidence of its causes, which appear to be multiple, can be found in several sources. Dobie's correspondence with the AFS *Journal* editors Franz Boas and his successor Ruth Benedict, documents in the Archives of the American Folklore Society, and extant *Journal* copies in the original dark paper bindings, contain the best clues to this serious rupture between the parent North American folklore organization and its largest branch.[5]

Dobie did not start out as an enemy of the national organization but as a member of its governing body. In December of 1922 he attended the Thirty-fourth Annual American Folk-Lore Society meeting at the Massachusetts Institute of Technology in Cambridge, read a paper entitled "Weather Lore of the Texas-Mexican Border," and was elected to the organization's executive council. He presented a paper on Texas legends the following year and also had two papers accepted for publication in the JAF. Dobie was definitely involved in the AFS.

He was in grand company and knew it. Officers elected for 1923 included Colorado's Hispanic folklorist/linguist, Aurelio M. Espinosa (president), anthropologist Alfred M. Tozzer (1st vice-president), naturalist/anthropologist J. Walter Fewkes (2nd vice-president), Pliny Earle Goddard, director of the Museum of Natural History in New York (treasurer), archaeologist Charles Peabody (secretary), and the father of modern anthropology, Franz Boas of Columbia University (publications editor).[6]

Associate editors were Harvard's George Lyman Kittredge, the greatest Shakespeare authority of the time, Canadian folklorist C. Marium Barbeau and anthropologist Elsie Clews Parsons, a student of Boas.

Dobie's fellow councilors were anthropologists Edward Sapir and Alfred L. Kroeber, ballad collectors Phillips Barry and C. M. Barbeau, Native American lexicographer John Reed Swanton, archaeologist Edward K. Putnam, and finally, his old friend from U.T., Stith Thompson, by then professor of English at Indiana University.

Back in Austin, Dobie wrote Boas on January 5, 1923, about a small, but to him, troubling detail. Dobie felt the national

Franz Boas (1858–1942) Columbia professor of anthropology, editor of the *Journal of American Folklore* in early Twenties (Courtesy American Philosophical Society Library)

society was not getting the full story about what was happening in Texas.

> At the meeting in Cambridge, I spoke to you about there being another set of officers of the Texas Folk-Lore Society other than those whose names are now printed in the *Journal.* At the last election (1922) I sent this information to Dr. Peabody, but he was absent from this country, as I now know. The officers are as follows. . . . [5]

Dobie's notes state that Boas did respond, but that reply is not available.

On March 1, Dobie wrote Boas again complaining about the January-March number of the *Journal:* "The names of the officers of the Texas Folk-Lore Society *have never been changed.* The officers whose names you print *were elected in 1915–16* . . . . This makes the third correct list I have sent."

Next, without missing a beat, Dobie noted that the TFS had just published a volume of its own, Number II, which he was sending along to Boas.[7]

Dobie concluded the letter by bringing up another matter:

> When I saw you at Cambridge, you spoke of the need for more subscribers to the *Journal* . . . . I have secured two or three new members and feel I could secure a number of others, for our own society is increasing rapidly, having now close to two hundred members—a result of our publication. But . . . people who can't speak or read Spanish find a great deal of the material (in the *Journal* . . .) closed to them . . . (Would) there be any loss in having the Spanish material, at least the prose, published in translation? . . . If the policy of the *Journal* is to publish only for scholars, then there is perhaps no debate on the matter . . . nor would I have essayed to mention the matter had it not been that you mentioned . . . the matter of subscribers.

On March 5, Boas responded to Dobie's complaint with the explanation that the recently-published number *was still for 1921* and not for the past year, 1922. In other words, it was backdated for *one* year. "Therefore," he wrote, "the change has not been made."

Dobie, in turn, responded to Boas three days later, but that piece of correspondence is also missing. Boas, however, rallied again on March 13, advising Dobie that "current issues (in progress) are *still for 1922*," adding "I am not certain in regard to the list of officers for the Texas Society for that year. Will you please let me know?"

This exchange was the tip of an iceberg, having to do with the *Journal*'s publication dates, and Dobie was not the only one who spotted it. Problems with the *Journal*'s publication schedule began during the War and were exacerbated in 1921 due to a printers' strike in the Lancaster, Pennsylvania, plant where the volume went to press. Boas himself complained to Charles Peabody on March 6, 1917, about incorrect "list(s) of the Presidents of Local Branches . . . " and chronological inconsistencies including the listing of "branches which do not exist" (American Folklore Society Archives, Utah State University). From that point on, the *Journal* was printed with backdated dates and organizational information geared to match the intentional backdating.

By 1921 the problem had gotten worse. Libraries began to inquire. Charles Peabody responded on December 23, 1921, to a complaint from the periodicals librarian at Dartmouth College, Elizabeth Skolfield saying, "I regret . . . the Journal . . . is considerably in arrears—the number for October-December 1920 is the last . . . strikes and other troubles . . . caused the delay" (AFS Archives, Utah State University).

The tardiness issue came to a head on December 27, 1923, when the Council of the AFS, consisting of Franz Boas, P. E. Goddard, Elsie Clews Parsons, archaeologist A. V. Kidder, and J. Frank Dobie, now chairman of the English department at Oklahoma A&M, met for its annual business meeting at the Explorers' Club in New York.[8] In his "Editor's Report" at the same meeting Boas sounded a hopeful note as he outlined the current discrepancies between actual publication dates and the idealized year numbers:

> The affairs of the Journal have improved somewhat during the past year. We started 1923 more than a year behind in publication. . . . During 1923 five numbers were issued, so we

> have advanced one number and are starting the volume for 1923. . . .

Boas recommended "that the whole number for 1924 be printed abroad . . . and mailed out from there."

"Abroad" meant the firm of J. J. Augustin of Gluckstadt, Denmark, and Hamburg, Germany. Augustin had earlier quoted Boas a combined printing, binding, and distribution cost for the *Journal* one quarter of what past costs had been. The suggestion was approved by the council and overseas publication of the AFS *Journal* began. This practice continued until U.S. entry into World War II. Finally, Boas' motion that "an assistant editor be appointed to do the actual work of the Journal . . . " was also approved.

Here the story gets even more complicated. Prior to the 1923 meeting in New York, the AFS published two book-length "Memoirs" on folklore: one from the Cape Verde Islands and the other from the Sea Islands of South Carolina. One of these memoirs (though which one is not clear) was printed in and shipped back from Europe at a significant cost savings. Furthermore, the South Carolina memoir, which grew from a graduate student ethnographic project by Elsie Clews Parsons and was underwritten by society member John B. Stetson, Jr. (!), was a great critical success among anthropologists.

In addition, work on a third "Memoir" on Jamaican folklore was also underway. Boas hoped to see this volume (again, one he knew would be of interest to anthropologists) completed within a year and in print a year later—likely in 1926 or 1927.

For Boas the AFS "Memoirs" were a godsend. If everyone, himself included, was frustrated with the lack of the *Journal's* timeliness, the enthusiastic reception accorded the "Memoir" series meant there was still reason to be proud of the society's publications.

Moreover, it appears that an unexpected possibility may have presented itself to Boas at the 1923 meeting when he learned Dobie was editing a collection of Texas legends—a collection which might conceivably become the next American Folklore Society "Memoir," even before completion of the Jamaican volume.

On January 7, 1924, Dobie wrote Boas renewing his efforts to see a correct list of TFS officers in the forthcoming *Journal* number. However, the text and the tone of his letter make it clear he had other things in mind as well:

> Now, I do not know what to say about the American Folklore Society's publishing the volume of Texas Legends. There will be anywhere from 200 to 250 pages . . . . I hope to have [it] ready by February 1, but my teaching interferes with any outside work . . . . I have to have the volume for distribution by the middle of April. The University of Texas Press is subsidizing . . . to the extent of $100. . . and is to print it at cost. It would be an immense advantage to me personally and to the Texas Folk-Lore Society in general to have the legends come out under your supervision.
>
> Could your press get them out in two months? If so, what would 800 copies of 250 pages each cost? How much extra would it cost to bind 200 copies? Would it be possible to get credit on half or a third of the printing until September 1?

Dobie closed by thanking Boas "and other members of *our organization* in New York" for the "courtesies shown . . . a visiting folklorist" while he was there weeks earlier.

Boas responded on January 11, telling Dobie flatly, "you should take care of it yourself if out by April 1." He added, "If we want to save money on our printing we send it abroad, and that always takes some time."

While Boas was severe, Dobie's inquiry is also puzzling. The minutes clearly state he was at the AFS Council meeting in New York when the problems with the *Journal* were discussed and the decision made to print it in Europe. He was especially aware of the tardiness of past AFS publications and of Boas' thrift, both of which had led to the decision to publish in Europe.

Dobie wanted the *Legends of Texas* to receive serious academic attention as well as to have popular appeal. The project had already benefited from Herbert E. Bolton's role as a contributor. Sometime in the spring of 1923 Dobie contacted Bolton, by that time a senior professor in the history department at the University of California, Berkeley, and the foremost American authority on the history of the Spanish borderlands. He asked

Bolton to submit something to the legends volume.[9] On April 10, Bolton replied saying that he would be pleased to do so, adding, "I run across a good many Texas legends and someday mean to . . . [submit] them for publication."

Bolton concluded with encouragement of Dobie's "good work" and enclosed a check for his membership renewal in the TFS.

Dobie responded to Bolton on April 16:

> I am delighted that you are going to contribute to . . . the Legends number . . . . There are more legends than I thought. . . . [The] great old legends of El Dorado, the Gran Quivira, etc. . . . have perpetuated themselves often in curious twists. . . . Looking forward to your legends with much interest. . . . [10]

With *Legends of Texas* now in print as a Texas Folklore Society "Publication" rather than an American Folklore Society "Memoir," Dobie wrote Boas again on June 7, 1924:

> You may recall a conversation we had last Christmas respecting the volume of Texas legends that I was then engaged in editing. It is now out and I have asked that a copy be sent to you. There is something in this *Legends of Texas* that will, I think, interest you. It is the immense effect of Spanish upon the imaginations of the English speaking people of the Southwest. *Incidentally, if you should see fit I should be glad if you would have a slight review made of this publication in the Journal* (author's italics).
>
> I notice that the Journal for 1923 is running in the masthead names of officers in the Texas Folklore Society for 1922. . . . I am sending you a correct list for the year 1923–4. Also . . . a copy of our program at Austin for last month.

Later in the month, on June 22, Dobie wrote to Pliny E. Goddard, Treasurer of the AFS:

> I have your letter, per "H.K.,"[11] of June 17 offering to allow me your list of members of the American Folklore Society for copying. Thank you very much. If you will send me the list, I shall have it copied and get it back to you within two weeks.

Dobie may have already come to the conclusion that there was little reason for the Texas society to have an official relationship with the AFS. He had battled unsuccessfully for nearly two years to see an accurate list of officers printed in the *Journal* instead of one as much as eight years out of date. Without question, Dobie wanted to inform the general membership of the AFS about what he and other members of the Texas Folklore Society were doing, but there is more to it than that.[12]

This was the period Dobie began to sense an audience of his own in the popular press. I believe he also sensed that a large number of educated readers would have an interest in folklore that overlapped similar interests in anthropology and even natural history. Goddard surely knew that popular questions about cultural development of folkloric characteristics of particular peoples were often linked to interest in dinosaur bones or stuffed wildlife specimens. The visitors to the Museum of Natural History would have amply demonstrated this fact. There is every possibility that Dobie observed the same thing. If readers of *Country Gentlemen* would be interested in his subjects, why not those of *National Geographic* or *Natural History?* This confidence in a new audience became clear when Dobie addressed the Southwestern Library Association's annual meeting in Santa Fe in August, 1924, on the topic of Southwestern folklore:

> A quarter of a century ago . . . the American Folk-Lore Society depended . . . upon the support of men and women whose interests were more or less literary, or at least humanistic; today it draws its support largely from men and women whose interests are purely scientific, particularly anthropological. The result is something of a hiatus in the investigation and preservation of the lore of what politicians delight to call "the common people" of this country.
>
> The shift of emphasis has been due rather *to the pedantic aloofness from modern life and literature on the part of trained scholars in English and other modern languages than to any negligence of confessed scientists* (author's emphasis). It appears now that the pendulum is about to swing back. But however that may be, in any consideration of what is being done to preserve the folk-lore of the Southwest, cognizance must be taken first of the scientific institutions and of the large body of efficiently trained and eager

> scientists who have for half a century conducted their explorations and researches among the peoples and places of the Southwest . . . . [13]

Dobie referenced the Southwestern investigations of archaeologists William H. Holmes, Adolph Bandelier, J. Walter Fewkes, and Edgar Hewett, then praised the first anthropological folklorists to work in the Southwest and lower Great Plains: John G. Bourke, Frank Hamilton Cushing, Matilda Coxe Stevenson, James Owen Dorsey, and John Wesley Powell. He then added:

> Today, such scholars as Dr. Franz Boas, Dr. P. E. Goddard, and Dr. Elsie Clews Parsons are carrying on the work of collecting and preserving folk-lore of the Indians of the Southwest . . . and their findings are to be found recorded in the *Journal of American Folk-Lore* and in the *Memoirs* of the American Folk-Lore Society. . . . [14]

He was not ashamed to send this address to George Lyman Kittredge, despite its slap at the "aloofness" of literary folklorists.

On February 13, 1925, Kittredge wrote Dobie:

> Dear Mr. Dobie,
>
> Thank you very much for your essay on the Folk-Lore of the Southwest. I have read it with much interest, and I am glad to note that there is so much activity in this regard in your part of the country. Please continue to send me your papers, large or small, particularly such as may happen to be printed in newspapers or other places that might escape my notice.

Just before this, at the end of the year, on December 29, 1924, Boas wrote Elsie Clews Parsons. Boas had noticed something about the demographics of the AFS membership as well:

> I shall not be able to stay in Washington after 3 p.m. Friday. For this reason I am sending you the enclosed letters and the Editor's report. I do not know when the business meeting of the Folk-Lore Society is going to be held, and so I think I had better send you all this material. There will presumably be an invitation from the

> University of Chicago to meet with the Modern Language Association next year. Considering that we have received more than sixty new members from the MLA while they have received hardly any from us, I think it would be a good plan to elect one of the Modern Language people, perhaps Miss Pound of Nebraska, president [of the AFS . . .] and to meet with the Modern Language people and try at the same time to arrange the time that members may also attend the Anthropological Association meeting. . . .

Boas wrote to Dobie in Stillwater on March 9, 1925, apparently in response to a previous question:

> I am no longer the Editor of the *Journal of American Folklore.* The editor is Dr. Ruth Benedict, whom you will find at this address. I think I still have the right to give permission to reprint [John G.] Bourke's paper from the 7th Vol. of the *Journal.* If you reprint your paper on the Rancho de Los Olmos, be sure to print "*La* Cancion." I do not know how it happened that this error was not noticed in the *Journal.*

This appears to have been the last direct exchange of correspondence between Dobie and Boas. In one sense it seems an ironic parting. Just seven months earlier Dobie had publicly praised the anthropological folklorists who worked in the Southwest while, at the same time, slapping the "literary" ones for their "pedantic aloofness." Dobie praised Boas and his students in particular.

On April 30, 1925, the Recording Secretary and Treasurer of the TFS, Ethel Burch, wrote to Pliny Goddard:

> Enclosed you will find a check for $13.00 for which please enroll the following names as members of the American Folk-Lore Society for the year 1925.
>
> Dr. M. S. Handman, University of Texas, Austin
> Mr. Edward W. Huisinger, Beaumont
> Prof. J. E. Pearce, University of Texas, Austin
> Mrs. Ethel L. Drought, San Antonio

On May 18, 1925, Gladys A. Reichard, Secretary of Barnard College, and assistant to Benedict as AFS Editor, wrote Ethel Burch:

> Hereafter we are planning to publish in the *Journal* . . . a list of all the officers for the year of the local societies which send us their up-to-date list. Will you kindly keep this request on file and send us your list whenever your elections take place.
>
> The Editor is working hard on the *Journal* and we are all trying hard to bring the numbers up to date. It seems as if we shall be able to . . . by the end of this year or at least by the beginning of next.

Fannie E. Ratchford of Austin, the new recording secretary and treasurer of the TFS, responded to Reichard (no date) with the names of R. C. Harrison of Lubbock (president), Adina de Zavala of San Antonio (first vice president), Mayme W. Cox of Dallas (second vice-president), and J. Victor Smith of Alpine, as Councilor. Dobie was not mentioned.

Volume V of the Publications of the Texas Folk-Lore Society appeared in the Spring of 1926. Dobie wrote the following TFS description, which was printed on the inside of the back cover of the paperback first edition. He made no mention of the AFS whatsoever:

> Anybody interested in the exploration and preservation of the folklore of Texas and the Southwest is invited to become a member. It is not necessary to contribute to the proceedings of the Society. . . . All that is necessary is to pay the dues. . . .
>
> Once a year [the Society] meets in public session at which papers . . . are read; sometimes old songs are sung and old dances danced. In its programs and publications the Society aspires to be "solid" and, at the same time, interesting. Anybody who has anything definite in the way of folk-lore to contribute is invited to contribute it to the Society. . . .

This description stands in marked contrast to the one written by Stith Thompson a decade earlier in his PTFS I. The TFS was no longer a solely academic body but a public one as well.

On June 20, 1927, over two years since the last apparent AFS correspondence to Dobie, Ruth Benedict wrote him. Dobie had apparently sent her some information:

> Thank you so much for the data you forwarded to me on the Texas Folklore Society. It is certainly the most flourishing and

successful of the folklore organizations of the country, and I wonder if you could not prepare a writeup of its activities for either 1925–6 or 1926–7 and send it for publication in the *notes and queries* Department of the *Journal?* Or perhaps your modesty would make it difficult, in which case you will know best whom to ask.

The list of officers in the last *Journal* about which you complain is due to the behind handedness of the *Journal* issues. The last number is dated July–October, 1925, and the list is supposed to be that of the 1924 officers. I trust that next year will see this disgraceful tardiness remedied; we have now more than a year's issues in press.

A review of *Legends of Texas* is now in press, but the Publication No. 4, *Folksongs of the Mexican Border,* was by some mistake not received for review and had been unintentionally overlooked. Or perhaps when Miss Reichard returns from her year in Europe I will find that she sent it away for review and forgot to notify me of it. Your publications should all be reviewed in the *Journal* as they appear for they are of the greatest interest and encouragement to other ambitious but less flourishing societies.

It is hard to determine just when the Journal number 39, containing the review of *Legends of Texas,* did appear. It was not before the last half of 1927—over three years after its publication. To add insult, the review was halfheartedly positive, stressing its interest to local historians more than to "folklorists," and, it was unsigned.

Nearly two years later, on February 13, 1929, Gladys Reichard wrote to Dobie:

> We have had no word from the Texas Folklore Society in the past year. Inasmuch as only seven members are in good standing—none paid in 1928—and we require a membership of ten for a branch, I suggest that members who so desire become members at large. If you think the activities of the branch might be renewed we shall of course be glad . . . .

American Folk-Lore Society membership ledgers from 1925 on omit Dobie's name, and that year only four individuals opted for new AFS membership and Journal privileges. At the beginning of 1929, according to its own rolls, only seven TFS members were listed as members in the AFS, and none of these had paid

AFS dues during 1928. The parting of the water which began with some conversations and an exchange of letters in 1922–3 was now complete.

Ostensibly, this rift was triggered by Dobie's mounting frustration in the mid-twenties with *Journal of American Folklore* editor Franz Boas' failure to publish a correct listing of the officers of the Texas Folklore Society between 1922 and 1927, as well as from bitterness over the *Journal's* long-delayed then lukewarm review of *Legends of Texas.* However, indications are it that grew from other issues as well.

It might have escaped Dobie's notice in the spring of 1923 that the most volatile organizational issue in the history of the American Folklore Society since its founding in 1888 had been a membership one—that of "scholar/professional" versus "amateur/popularizer." In its first years Boas and AFS founder William Wells Newell had even raised questions about the appropriateness of Mark Twain's membership in the Society. Furthermore, Dobie might have also been ignorant of the otherwise well-known fact that Boas, the most powerful personality in the AFS, had battled quite successfully for thirty-five years to discourage participation in "amateur" activities, such as the "World Folk-Lore Congress" at the Chicago World's Fair in 1893. Consequently Dobie's query as to whether the *Journal* was "to publish only for scholars" could not have escaped Boas' scowl. In Boas' own mind, he had fought and won that battle thirty years earlier.

Likewise, Dobie's 1923 claim, possibly considered a boast, of a Texas membership in excess of two hundred dues-paying souls overlapping AFS membership only in part, doubtless also drew Boas' concerned attention. The AFS Secretary's report at the 1922 MIT meeting listed six honorary members, twelve life members and 394 annual members, for a total membership of 412 in its four Boston, Cambridge, Texas, and Canadian "branches."

Several questions come to mind. Had Dobie, in his enthusiasm about the practical independence of the TFS from the AFS, arbitrarily created a new classification of AFS membership (or non-membership) without the approval of the governing body of the national organization? Had Dobie appeared to Boas as both temperamental and opportunistic—an officer of the AFS with little or no degree of loyalty to it? Or was Dobie, perhaps like others such as Goddard, justifiably fed up with the inexactness of AFS communications and lateness of its publications? Or, finally, was Dobie merely outraged by the long-delayed, lukewarm review of what he knew was an important folkloric volume?

All of these seem to be possibilities. However, viewed against the larger context of Boas' long standing emphasis on strict academic professionalism within folklore studies and Dobie's emerging democratic, vitalist, and anti-modernist sentiments, the fracture seems almost inevitable—a fated break between organizations headed by strong-willed individuals of different generations who, as products of markedly different cultures placed decidedly opposing values on the activities of such "learned societies" as the American Folk-Lore Society and the Texas Folklore Society.

Notes

Editor: The preceding article is an excerpt from Stone's dissertation, *J. Frank Dobie and the American Folklore Movement: A Reappraisal.*

1. Payne wrote: "(Lomax) said that . . . Kittredge . . . had suggested to him that it might be a good thing to found a Texas branch of the American Folklore Society in order to facilitate the collection of the native songs and ballads as well as other forms of folklore . . . " (*When the Woods Were Burnt* 9–10).

2. Thompson completed a Ph.D. in Literature at Harvard in 1914, the year he, like Dobie, joined the U.T. faculty. Thompson's doctoral thesis, on Native American folktales showing influences from European literature, was directed by George Lyman Kittredge and was dedicated to Franz Boas!

3. Thompson significantly described the membership and dues structure thus: "The dues for national membership, including a subscription to the *Journal of American Folk-Lore* and to publications of the state society, are $3.00 a year. A national member is also a member of the state society through which he joins. *For membership in the state society alone (including a subscription to the publication of the state*

society) the dues are one dollar for the first year and fifty cents a year thereafter . . . " (emphasis added) (PTFS I, inside back cover).

4. Lomax wrote: "Dobie . . . early acquired a prejudice against the American Folklore Society with the result that [it] has maintained no connection with the national organization. In my judgement this . . . lack of relationship has been unfortunate. Some good might have been done with the close connection of the two Societies and certainly no harm would have resulted" (*When the Woods Were Burnt* 18).

5. Dobie's cited correspondence is located at the Harry Ransom Humanities Research Center, Austin. Other American Folklore Society correspondence, minutes, and records, are located on the AFS Archives at the University of Utah, Logan, Utah.

Most hard-bound library editions of the *Journal of American Folklore* lack these original covers for the individual numbers. They were likely removed prior to binding. However, it was on these paper covers the branch officers information in question was printed. Fortunately, the early JAF volumes in Harvard's Widener Library were not so altered during binding.

6. Boas was born in German Westphalia in 1858 and took a doctorate in physics in 1891 at the University of Kiel. He began his work as an ethnographer on an expedition to Greenland and Baffin Island, and later initiated anthropological researches in northern Canada and the Pacific coast. He taught at Clark University and worked on the staffs of the Museum of Natural History and the Field Museum in Chicago. Boas joined the faculty of Columbia University in 1896, and remained there until his death in 1942. His students, including Margaret Mead, Robert Lowie, Edward Sapir, and Elsie Parsons, defined the field of American anthropology in the early twentieth century.

7. When Boas received the Texas volume he may have noticed for the first time a developing sense of independence in Dobie's description of the Texas society and its membership categories and dues structure—one which significantly departed from the stance held by Thompson. Dobie wrote:

> *Theoretically,* the Texas Folk-Lore Society is the state branch of the American Folk-Lore Society. Practically, in its workings it is independent. It invites into its membership all people who are interested in the exploration and preservation of the folk-lore of Texas and the Southwest. Once a year the Society meets in public session, at which papers on folk-lore are read and discussed. . . .

Annual Members . . . pay fifty cents a year for dues, plus an initiation fee of fifty cents.

Annual Members With American Folk-Lore Journal Privileges . . . belong directly to the American Folk-Lore Society, as well as to the Texas Folk-Lore Society, and receive the Journal of American Folk-Lore, a quarterly. The dues are four dollars per year, seventy-five cents of which is kept by the Texas Folk-Lore Society, the remainder being sent to The American Folk-Lore Society.

All members of the Texas Folk-Lore Society have equal voice in the organization, and . . . receive free whatever publications are issued by it.

8. In the summer of 1923, after only two years back at the University of Texas, Dobie hastily accepted an offer of a professorship at Oklahoma A&M in Stillwater. Bertha was not pleased, and neither was the English department at Texas. Dobie, however, had no intention of giving up his TFS post. If anything, he saw it as an even greater responsibility.

9. Bolton (1870–1953), a native of Wisconsin, had previously taught medieval history at the University of Texas and had introduced there a course in the Spanish colonization of North America. He joined the Stanford faculty in 1909 and moved from there to Berkeley in 1911. He authored such works as *Texas in the Middle Eighteenth Century, Coronado,* and *Rim of Christendom.* He was also a charter member of the Texas Folklore Society.

10. It is worth noting that Dobie was thinking about treasure legends in particular at this time. Bolton's declared intention to produce a book of his own may well have sparked Dobie's imagination that he would do so as well.

11. This was possibly the historian Henry Kittredge—George Lyman Kittredge's son.

12. He likely also perceived a shift in emphasis within the folkloristic community toward the cultural fields which the leadership of the Society in the 1920s viewed as the proper ones for research. While this leadership—Boas, Benedict, Peabody, Goddard, and others—was "anthropological" and not "literary" in its leanings, Dobie was not publicly critical of this vantage, even if he was at odds with Boas. In fact, as a teacher of literature, he was remarkably complimentary of the present leadership of anthropological folklorists and critical of the "literary" ones.

13. This address was reprinted in *Chronicles of Oklahoma,* Vol. II, No. 3, Oklahoma City, September, 1924 (McVicker "D3"). Copy from the

Dobie collection in the Bancroft Library, University of California, Berkeley.

14. This address, one of Dobie's most obscure writings (not widely known, and never cited) was remarkable in a number of ways. Predictably, it contained praise for the folksong and ballad collections of John Lomax and Louise Pound of the University of Nebraska. However, it revealed what many of his critics and admirers, past and present, have not even suspected: a confident familiarity with the history of American ethnographic and anthropological folkloristics. His assessments of the value of the individual ethnographic researches, especially those of Cushing and Dorsey, are knowing and conceptually sophisticated. In fact, there is a striking similarity between Dobie's style here and that in the more popular essays of anthropologist Clifford Geertz from the last twenty years. Dobie's judgments on the stylistic and informational qualities of reports submitted to and published in various forms by the Bureau of American Ethnography show him as a more than able commentator on the value of this intellectual field. One is led to conclude that Dobie not only read widely, but must have undertaken direct research in the Bureau's archives sometime during the early 1920s.

Bibliography

Dobie, J. Frank. *Some Part of Myself.* Bertha Dobie, ed. Boston: Little, Brown and Company, 1967.

Tinkle, Lon. *J. Frank Dobie: The Makings of an Ample Mind.* Austin: Encino Press, 1968.

Lomax, John A., ed. *When the Woods Were Burnt,* Austin: The Texas Folk-Lore Society, 1946.

4

Beautifully Printed and Expressive of Texas: Carl Hertzog and the Texas Folklore Society

Al Lowman

WHO IN THE TEXAS FOLKLORE SOCIETY DOES NOT LOVE THE printed word? And when it is brought forth with typographical splendor, in the tradition of a Carl Hertzog, for example, we respond with enhanced pleasure even if we do not fathom all the subtleties that inspire such pleasure.

The book collectors among us—and there are several—are mindful that Carl Hertzog once served the Texas Folklore Society. Hertzog's affiliation with the Society came through his friendship with J. Frank Dobie, the Society's long-time secretary-editor. Dobie was a frequent El Paso visitor, having discovered the town to be a storyteller's haven while preparing such books as *Coronado's Children, Tongues of the Monte,* and *Apache Gold and Yaqui Silver.* Dobie's principal contact in El Paso was Maud Durlin Sullivan, director of the El Paso Public Library. She had been the catalyst for bringing together Hertzog and Tom Lea in 1937. Dobie was then promoting young Lea as illustrator of his forthcoming book, *Apache Gold and Yaqui Silver*.

By the time the Texas Folklore Society came to El Paso in the spring of 1938, all three men were well-acquainted, and it was natural enough that collaboration would evolve on the program for the annual meeting. To assure that local arrangements would be properly executed, the Society had cleverly selected a debonair Harvard PhD in English philology who had been retooled as a Southwest folklore specialist at the College of Mines and Metallurgy. His name, of course, was Professor Charles Leland Sonnichsen. Following the 1938 meeting the groundwork had been laid, albeit unwittingly, for future endeavors by Hertzog on behalf of the Society. With the outbreak of World

Carl Hertzog, Printer, in the 1940s (Courtesy Al Lowman)

War II, Stanley Marcus elected to close the Book Club of Texas and turn over its assets to the Texas Folklore Society for liquidation. Dobie then signaled his intention in a letter to Marcus dated May 10, 1941: "It is our plan to sell the books you are conveying as soon as possible, and with the money to publish a volume that will be in the tradition of the Book Club of Texas. With a little encouragement, we should be able to bring out an extra book every year—something beautifully printed and also expressive of the Texas scene" (CAH).

Alas the Society was unable to sell Book Club titles at the inventoried prices, but enough money was earned to begin its high-spirited Range Life Series. The first to be launched as war clouds gathered was *My Rambles as East Texas Cowboy, Hunter, Fisherman, Tie-Cutter* by Sol Wright. Admitted Dobie in the prospectus, "It does not make thrilling reading," but was nonetheless an honest, utterly unpretentious story. To T.F.S. member Ed Crane of Dallas, Dobie explained that "the old timer sent me his reminiscences several years ago and then died before they could be copied. They are certainly worth printing" (13 May 1942 CAH).

In a flush of enthusiasm Dobie admonished Hertzog that "we have simply got to get [the book] out by December" (5 June 1942 UTEP). Hertzog promptly responded, ". . . don't be worried because we will handle your job right straight through. One month for composition, one month for presswork, one month for binding—gives us plenty of time. . . ." Hertzog continued, "I planned to use very ordinary material—eggshell paper which will bulk to make [the] book look thicker, and

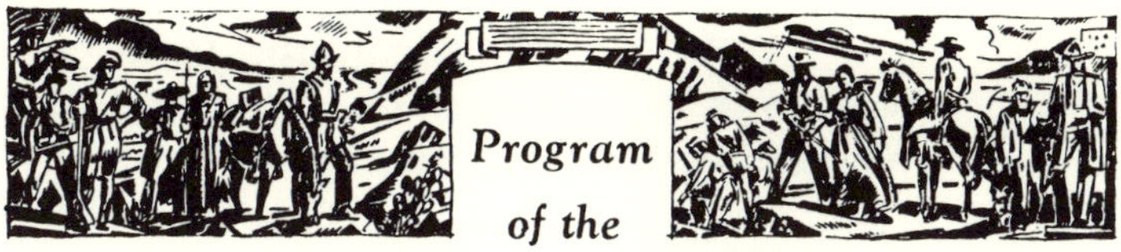

Program of the

Twenty-Fourth Annual Fiestacita

TEXAS FOLK-LORE SOCIETY

★

IN JOINT SESSION WITH THE

Hispanic Institute of New Mexico

APRIL 15 and 16, 1938

AT EL PASO, TEXAS

Headquarters: HOTEL PASO DEL NORTE

The public is cordially invited to attend all meetings and to inspect the exhibition of water colors by Elizabeth Keefer-Boatright, the specimens of Mexican craft work by Mela Sedillo, and Mrs. Ina Sizer Cassidy's collection of water colors by Indian students. The exhibits may be seen at the Centennial museum of the College of Mines free of charge by all who are interested. The banquet Saturday night is also open to all. Tickets cost a dollar and ten cents and reservations should be made not later than noon Saturday at the information desk in the lobby of the Hotel Paso del Norte or with any officer of the Folk-Lore society.

Shall Arizona woo me
Where the meek Apache bides,
Or New Mexico where natives grow
With arrow proof insides?

"Don't I have fleas?" says Pecos Bill.
"Shore ye do," says the old prospector. "But all Texians has fleas."

Hertzog's first endeavor for the Texas Folklore Society was this 1938 program using Lea's "pass of the north" sketch as a headpiece. Dobie selected the quotations that appear in the margins. Years later Hertzog commented, "I was present and remember J.F.D. in [a] white suit, going around shaking hand[s] with everybody *during the banquet!*

plain cloth. Even so we can use good spacing, good type, and make a better than average looking book" (10 June 1942 DRD).

Meanwhile Dobie had cooled toward the endeavor. When he submitted the manuscript in July he declared, "This book is not as interesting as I thought it would be. I cut it by a third nearly—and it is still too long" (24 July 1942 UTEP). It was not that Wright's spelling and grammar bothered Dobie. "The older I grow," he commented later, "the less importance I attach to either—I have been associated with too many blockheads who are perfect in both" (Wright xii).

Hertzog lost no time preparing a dummy for Dobie's consideration. The typeface was 10-point Medieval, which was—in Hertzog's words—"about the best I have to offer here." There was no expectation of making this a profitable venture. "Frankly the figures I gave you were rock-bottom with not much in it for anybody. What would be perfect for me would be to have you set a price per book and then let me give you all I can for the money," wrote Hertzog (28 July 1942 DRD).

Dobie held fond hope that Tom Lea would be able to prepare pen-and-ink sketches for the publication, but Lea's wartime assignment as artist-correspondent for Time-Life, Inc., precluded his involvement in this initial project. Hertzog chose to work instead with Barney Lewis, a fellow El Pasoan, who had been a cowhand in Arizona and Wyoming before studying art in Chicago. Hertzog debated for a time whether to set the chapter- and running-heads in Roman or italic face. "Italic is sometimes effeminate, but I finally decided it fits better than the Roman and has a little more class" (CH to JFD, 24 August 1942 DRD). Hertzog also had Lewis the illustrator to draw a longhorn steer skull set against a Texas star as the series trademark. In its final form the star was dropped, and the steer skull was set within a circling title.

Dobie now addressed two letters to Hertzog, both dated September 10, 1942. In the first letter Dobie said he did not like certain of the illustrations: "I won't read, except under duress, a book that lies about life. I don't like pictures that misrepresent it any better." By the time he wrote the second letter of the day Dobie had finished reading galleys and was having grave doubts about his choice of *My Rambles* as a series opener. He now characterized it as "the dullest reading I ever tried almost. I should have started the series off with something more interesting—but it is too late now." Moreover the mercurial Mr. Dobie had decided that he liked the artist and his artwork. "This boy has vitality—the one essential element to all artistic expression, no matter in what medium. Put his name on the title page." He was less pleased about the typeface. "The commas look like periods. I think the footnotes are too small . . . but do not reset" (UTEP).

Dobie's belated approval of the artwork now stimulated second thoughts on Hertzog's part. "Looks I made a bust on selecting the artist," he said in a letter dated September 11. "Of course, we are both spoiled by Tom [Lea] and his excellent work, which we can't afford in this instance. If we can get the subject matter . . . correct, I don't think the style is bad at all. In fact I like the heavy effect" (DRD).

Dobie concurred in his next letter of September 13. "I meant it when I said he has vitality plus sense of humor. By all means and emphatically, let us keep him." Dobie invited Hertzog to rewrite chapter titles to fit the typographical scheme. "Make the titles fit the type," he urged. "Furthermore, if when you come to make up a page proof, you should find that typographical looks would benefit by shortening a chapter, then shorten it by cutting out a paragraph or two" (UTEP).

On the 28th Hertzog complained to Dobie, "I have never experienced so many 'bad breaks' in making up pages." Specifically, the problems were leftover lines at the ends of chapters and leftover words at the end of paragraphs. "On proofs I have noted where I changed copy to get better fitting and cure these bad breaks . . ." (DRD). Part of this tampering was necessitated by his desire to have each chapter begin on a right hand page. For appearance's sake, he fudged some more by double leading (i.e. double spacing) Dobie's introduction "to make it come out two full pages." The author's foreword was still a little short and couldn't be aligned at the bottom, "but all the headings in that section will be uniform in position," Hertzog explained (CH to JFD, 1 October 1942 UTEP).

Dobie approved all of Hertzog's changes in an October 2 letter. "Do as you please about everything. I like the way you have added and subtracted when you thought desirable. There is nothing sacred about this chronicle." He even went so far as to tell Hertzog, "If for sake of looks you had rather leave out author's foreword, do so." How's that for carte blanche? At this time Dobie also told Hertzog that he was preparing copy for a special insert to be laid in between the front cover and the first flyleaf, advising T.F.S. members that this book was being sent in lieu of the usual numbered publication (UTEP).

The next day, October 3, Dobie posted another letter containing some extra verbiage that could be used to pad the author's foreword. "I have written a few words," Dobie claimed, "that are essentially Sol Wright's own. If you want to set them up to make the page come out even, do so. And feel at liberty to cut out or change sentences to fit your space." Dobie's remaining concern was to get the books out as quickly as possible in order to capitalize on the Christmas market (UTEP).

Ten days later Hertzog was lamenting that no good type fonts were available in El Paso. "I sub-let all my linotype work. It seems strange to me that out of 1000 fonts here, not one is good for book work. Printers have no sense of design. They get a hodge podge of type for catalogs and commercial work that is not suitable for good book work, whereas any good book type is also usable on commercial work. Would the Folklore Society want to own a font of very special mats?"

And then Hertzog concluded with a summary of his own private anguish. "*My Rambles* is hardly in the deluxe class. First, I figured the cost down as low as possible; second, war-time workmanship leaves many things to be desired. The work that I did with my own hands is in the deluxe class (page make-up and general design) but when I failed to sit on the lid, the presswork, alignment, etc. suffered and there were many times when I couldn't watch everything because I am harassed continuously by senseless interruptions. This crazy maelstrom in which I exist is not exactly ideal for doing careful work" (CH to JFD, 13 October 1942 HRC).

On the 19th Hertzog had further observations:

> Dear Frank:
>
> If I was going to start over again, I would say let's cut out about half the text. What we would have left would be damned good—I like old Wright and I think a good part of his story is very interesting.
>
> With half as much copy to set and half as many pages to print, we could buy paper twice as good, import special type, spend twice as much time in make-ready per page—and at the same or less cost we would have a deluxe job. No use crying over spilt milk, but this is something to think of when we get to the next book (HRC).

And by October 28 the next book was in sight. Dobie promised: "I will be getting the McCauley manuscript to you right away. You will just have to stop thinking about hand-pressed work for us. My ideal is distribution. I have never cared much for deluxe people." Dobie certainly seemed to have changed his tune since May 10, 1941, when he assured Stanley Marcus of his desire to bring out "something beautifully printed and expressive of Texas."

By December 23, it was obvious that sales of *My Rambles* had been disappointing, and Dobie again was in an economizing mood. "A small book, no matter how well printed, simply will not move off the counter at $3.00. I am thinking of putting a price of $2.00 on this next one and not printing more than 750 copies" (JFD to CH, HRC). It was a good move. There were 1200 copies of *My Rambles* and it would be two decades before it sold out, even after the price was cut from three dollars to two. J. F. "Bliss" Albright, manager of the Cokesbury Book Store in Dallas, reported that "all we sold came back on us. Before sending us the next book in the series . . . I would like to take a look at it before we place an order" (JFA to JFD, 23 February 1943 CAH). In reply Dobie expressed hope that the second book in the Range Life Series would help the first one to sell. "It is going to be mighty good," he promised (26 February 1943 CAH).

The story behind *A Stove-Up Cowboy's Story* is worth noting. Back in 1910, when John A. Lomax was gathering cowboy songs

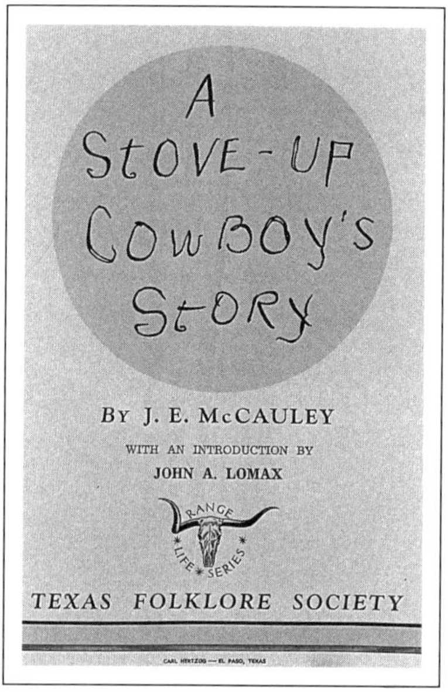

Dust jacket calligraphy for *Stove-Up Cowboy* was painstakingly rendered by Tom Lea's father. It is shown here on a rare version of the book's announcement. (Courtesy Al Lowman)

for his famous book on the subject, James Emmitt McCauley sent him some, including the classic "Buffalo Skinners." In appreciation Lomax sent McCauley one of the first copies of his new book. At this juncture, McCauley decided to write his autobiography; when completed in 1912, he entrusted it to Lomax, who held onto it for three decades until it appeared as the second title in the Range Life Series. McCauley had died in 1924.

Dobie sent the manuscript with a letter dated November 6: "Here it is. . . . We are printing her as the old cowboy writ her—and it is bully stuff." Dobie gave further opinions: "I think this series of homely books should be printed in a kind of plain, bold type" and "Damn any type that you can't tell a comma from a period in. If you need to buy $150 worth of font to get the right type, go ahead and buy it and we'll pay for it." In the next paragraph Dobie asserted, "Let's make chapter numbers of this book arabic. McCauley would not have used any other form of numbering." And he wishfully hoped that Tom Lea might find time to "do a few black and whites" (UTEP). Although Hertzog never denied that it was Dobie who first insisted on simplicity, neither did he credit Dobie. Thus arose a long-held assumption that Hertzog was solely responsible for the book's appearance. Realizing Hertzog's propensity for tinkering with text to avoid bad page breaks, Dobie now instructed Hertzog: "Don't you change a word, not even a comma" (McCauley 1965 facsimile edition 75).

McCauley's tale began: "On the 14th day of August, 1873, I came prancing into this world. I was found in Anderson County, Lone Star State, close to Palestine. . . . My first memory was to ride a stick horse [and] my first wishes and desires was to be a wild and woolly cowboy. My parents be poor like Job's turkey. But my first memory was to ride a stick horse and my first wishes and desires was to be a wild and woolly cowboy" (1).

By New Year's Day 1943 McCauley's book was in production. On January 4 Hertzog addressed

> Dear Frank.
>
> You have changed some of my ideas. I used to think only a classic type with a pedigree could be used for a good book, but Stove-Up Cowboy is being set and in a type that is not pretty, has no pedigree, but was designed scientifically to be EASY TO READ. I have access to an unlimited supply of "Ionic" type in various sizes. It is common looking but it is most legible. With chapter headings of unusual character (what I call Cowboy Script) and proper handling of spacing, we will have good looking pages (not classic but practical.) (CAH).

Dobie was glad to know of Hertzog's progress on the typesetting and then reiterated, "I never had the Book Club of Texas idea of exclusiveness. If a thing is worth printing, it should be worth reading. My idea is to give as wide a distribution as possible to whatever I attempt to put in print, at the same time trying to make a print look beautiful. Legibility is a primary desideratum" (7 January 1943 UTEP).

Dobie had cut a deal with Donald Day of the Southern Methodist University Press to aid in the marketing of the Range Life Series. Consequently he sent revised copy for the title page, the corrected galley proofs, and a sepia-toned photograph of the nineteen-year-old McCauley. Dobie was pleased with the galleys. "I think these rusty, rangy, gutcutting, alkali-swallering, mescal-drinking, horsesweating, devil-riding old cow hands want a bolder, more open type" (JFD to CH, 21 January 1943 UTEP). Dobie had further comment about McCauley's photograph: "Carl—I have just looked at this man's features under a magnifying glass. God he has a face. This will make a great frontispiece."

Hertzog recalled that "the picture was so faded and scratched that I couldn't figure out any way to use it so that it wouldn't make an ugly page in the book. I didn't dare to ask Tom Lea to make a pen-and-ink portrait because Tom had just returned from the South Pacific and was busy making his 'Hornet' drawings for the Navy with a scheduled date in *Life* magazine. But one day Tom walked into the shop, and because I was busy, he picked up some galley proofs and began reading *A Stove-Up Cowboy's Story*. When I was free to talk, he looked up from his reading, black eyes sparkling and said, 'Jeezis, this is so damn good I want to do something for it'" (McCauley 75). And one of the things he did was a pen-and-ink portrait from the McCauley photograph. He also redrew the steer skull emblem of the Range Life Series.

So Hertzog now proposed, "Allow me to print 100 extra books for Tom and me, and Tom will make the drawings, and I'll pay for the cuts and also the difference on a better grade paper." Actually the Society got 620 books, while Hertzog and Lea split one hundred. Hertzog's letter continued, "In a short book like this I don't see any need of running heads on every page. Why not just a plain page number centered at the top of every page? McCauley was so real and unpretentious that we must make his book simple but good. Tom says this is from the soil—no cowhand will be able to criticize the facts and language" (CH to JFD, 6 February 1943 HRC).

Before the book was shipped off to the Becktold Bindery in Saint Louis, an innovative dust jacket was conceived by Hertzog and Lea. As Hertzog recounted,

> Tom tried to do some crude lettering like McCauley might have done, but the result looked "faked" because Tom is an expert letterer. Then he remembered how his Dad struggled over addressing a package for mailing. Tom Sr. is a lawyer, not a letterer, but he obligingly agreed to do his very best printing for our dust jacket. The result a natural (McCauley 75–76).

No doubt Hertzog felt good about his newest contribution to the Range Life Series. To Dobie on April 26 he wrote: "Although the printing is far from perfect and the paper has wartime specks, we feel that the McCauley book is the best yet from this end of the line. It seems to fit McCauley—plain type, average quality material, no ornaments, but strong in appearance and easy to read" (HRC).

Now interestingly, in November 1945, Fannie Ratchford, a former treasurer of the Texas Folklore Society and then empress of the Rare Book Collection at the University of Texas, had expressed her own disappointment in the format of *A Stove-Up Cowboy's Story.* Hertzog chided her in a letter dated November 19.

> Dear Miss Ratchford,
>
> I was surprised at what you said about our Stove-Up Cowboy book, because Tom Lea thinks it is our best product, but you probably didn't read the book, or wouldn't be particularly interested in cowboys anyway. [Hertzog did not know, but promptly learned, that Fannie Ratchford was raised on a west Texas ranch.]
>
> The most important idea to me in designing a book is to have a reason for selecting certain type, paper and colors—to make the choice appropriate to the subject of the book. Most expensively made books are just pretty, and the dominating factors of design have no relationship to the subject matter.
>
> McCauley (the stove-up cowboy) was a simple man of the soil, unpretentious but vigorous, strong and honest. He would not know anything about deckle edges or Roman numerals, so I wouldn't use them. Simple paper, newspaper type, rough but strong chapter titles, no ornaments, no pretentions—seem just right.
>
> Please forgive me for "lecturing," but I like McCauley personally and think "I done right by him" (HRC).

A touching piece of correspondence was received at the Southern Methodist University Press in April 1944, and it reads as follows:

Dear Sirs,

Do you have any [copies] of A Stove-Up Cowboy's Life by J. E. McCauley. I would like to get one. The Author J. E. McCauley is my Father. One of the boys is in the South pacific and his ship was shot out from under him and his book was damaged badly. He has asked if I could get him another one.

Please send me one or let me know and I will mail money for one. Thanks.

Mrs. W. E. Jennings
Rt. 1, Box 59
Kilgore, Texas

The record indicates that Mrs. Jennings was sent the book on April 25, 1944, and billed $2.04, which she remitted on May 5th (11 April 1944 CAH).

Hertzog's next and last contribution to the Range Life Series was *A Tenderfoot Kid on Gyp Water* by Carl Peters Benedict, a west Texas rancher. His late brother, H. Y. Benedict, had been University of Texas president, and their mother was a daughter of the English Peters family whose members colonized north Texas and published music in Cincinnati. Carl P. Benedict had declined to publish his memoir during H. Y. Benedict's lifetime because he did not wish to embarrass his great brother, but upon H. Y.'s death he took his manuscript to the newspaper office in Odessa, where the editor suggested it be forwarded to Dobie (R. Henderson Shuffler to Al Lowman, undated memo in the Lowman collection, San Marcos, Texas). Dobie decided to publish it in the Range Life Series and sent the manuscript to Hertzog, who promised to get it underway before Dobie would leave for England to teach at Cambridge in the fall of 1943 (CH to JFD, 11 June 1943 HRC).

Dobie did not take the kind of hands-off attitude toward Benedict's book that he had toward McCauley's. In a June 25 letter to H. Bailey Carroll, director of the Texas State Historical Association, Hertzog says, "I now have Ms. from Dobie for a book by Carl P. Benedict and it is a sight. Dobie has edited every other line" (UTEP). By this time Hertzog and Dobie had worked together enough that the production moved ahead relatively smoothly. In a June 19 letter Dobie gave hasty instructions: "Carl, please use your own judgment in handling whole thing, type, binding, pictures, everything. I am writing on Ben Lilly and don't want to think about anything else. . ." (UTEP).

The book was to be illustrated with photographs printed on enameled paper inserts. Hertzog did want, however, a portrait drawing of the author at his prime, and to get it he turned first to Barney Lewis, who had illustrated *My Rambles,* and then to Elmer Boone. The Lewis drawing made Benedict look "too tough." Boone got it right the second time, however, and his modified drawing is the one stamped on the front cover of *Tenderfoot Kid* (notations on repro proofs in the Lowman collection). [Illus. 16A]

By September 10, two weeks before Dobie's departure for England, Hertzog was wondering if Dobie wanted a dust jacket and an advertising circular for the book (CAH). Dobie sent copy for the "dodger" as he called it and requested 2500 of them. They were printed on various scraps of paper stock. He left the decision concerning the dust jacket to Hertzog (14 September 1943 CAH), who decided to save money simply by putting it in a glassine wrapper. Again, the binding was done at the Becktold Company in Saint Louis and, of the 550 copies printed, the Texas Folklore Society was billed for 525 and twenty-five were sent gratis to Benedict (JFD to CPB, 18 September 1943 CAH), who was well pleased (CPB to Marcelle Hamer, 16 November 1943 CAH). So was Dobie, who wrote on the eve of his departure: "The Benedict book is handsome and has distinction" (JFD to CH, 23 September 1943 HRC).

On May 19, 1945, Mody C. Boatright, who had replaced Dobie as secretary-editor of the Society, addressed a letter asking the production cost of his own *Gib Morgan: Minstrel of the Oil Fields* (UTEP). Hertzog did not like the stationery on which the letter was written and came back with an inquiry to Marcelle Hamer, the Society treasurer who pretty much ran its day-to-day operation. "Who orders the stationery?" he wanted to know. "I would like to contribute the new lot with new officers' names. The attached is not only a poor combination of types, but also quite remote from an appearance of folklore. This type is usually used for bank checks or bookkeeping

J. Frank Dobie
Editor-in-Chief

Frank Goodwyn
President

Donald Day
Editor

Mody Boatright
Editor and Secretary

Marcelle Lively Hamer
Treasurer

TEXAS FOLKLORE SOCIETY

UNIVERSITY STATION
AUSTIN, TEXAS

Texas Folklore Society letterhead that Hertzog contributed to the Society in 1945 (Courtesy Al Lowman)

forms. Let me know how much stationery is needed and I [will] supply it with more appropriate type" (undated, CAH). And he did!

Concerning Gib Morgan, he wanted Boatright's opinion on type size and illustration, and then one last question: "Does the book have to be cheap, or do you want something better?" (25 May 1945 UTEP). Boatright's response came on May 29: "I have consulted the treasurer, and it looks as though the maximum we can spend is $1200. I suppose that means it has to be cheap" (UTEP).

Hertzog replied that a decent-looking book could be done for that amount, but he would have to delay production until fall, because he was at work on a deluxe project for Tom Lea, *Peleliu Landing* (8 June 1945 UTEP). Boatright accepted this arrangement, provided the books were ready by December 15. Alas Hertzog did not even start the project until the end of September. In a letter dated the 29th, he told Boatright, "We will have to rush to get it finished before Christmas." "I am starting typesetting immediately," he concluded (UTEP). Two weeks later Boatright asked his wife, Betty, to produce new illustrations (MCB to CH, 12 October 1945 UTEP).

Galleys were mailed to Boatright on October 27, with cuts of illustrations to follow shortly. Hertzog wanted suggestions on where to fit the pictures (UTEP). On the 30th he sent samples of binding cloth and expressed his own preference for a "loud orange color" (UTEP), which Boatright agreed to with a suggestion that it be stamped in dark brown ink (UTEP). At first Hertzog agreed (CH to Art Soucek of Universal Bookbindery at San Antonio, 12 November 1945 UTEP), but later opted for black.

Ten days later Hertzog shipped 1039 assembled books to the bindery with a plea to deliver 1000 in Austin by December 15. The extra thirty-nine were for Hertzog. Each book was to be wrapped in a glassine jacket (CH to Universal Bookbindery, 29 November 1945 UTEP). The new publication arrived from the bindery less than a week before Christmas 1945 (MCB to CH, 15 December 1945 UTEP). Already underway was the next Hertzog project for the Texas Folklore Society.

In the first three months of 1945 John A. Lomax in Dallas was writing Marcelle Hamer for information in the Folklore Society files to shore up his recollection of the organization's founding. He was trying his best to get help from L. W. Payne as well. Lomax wanted urgently to find a copy of the four-page folder that he and Payne had issued after the organizational meeting in Dallas. It contained a list of charter members. The search went on for much of the year (12 January, 2 February, 16 March CAH). Apparently Payne was of no help and neither was Stith Thompson. Then Payne died on June 16. But in September, about two weeks after Stith Thompson struck out, Mrs. Hamer located a copy. So In November, just as the Gib Morgan book was winding down, Boatright forwarded the Payne-Lomax material to Hertzog for printing (12 November 1945 UTEP). But sickness, war-time manpower shortage, the Christmas rush and year-end specials all conspired to prevent Hertzog from getting on with it (CH to MCB, 12 December 1945 UTEP). On March 11, 1946 Boatright wrote to ask: "What is the status of the Payne pamphlet?" (UTEP). A week later Hertzog replied:

Dear Mody:

I am glad I can write and not have to face you. In December I told you we could do the pamphlet on Payne in January. There is no use to alibi. The pressure is on and I take care of the chiselers and make my friends wait.

I can't find anywhere a mention of how many you want me to print, but assuming one thousand, the price will be $160. This includes reproductions of the first printed circular, the Payne picture, and signature. It will be a 24-page booklet with a good cover.

If this doesn't fit the budget, let me know and I will reduce the cost of the paper I planned to use. If you want more copies, you can let me know when I send you proofs which will be next week. Believe it or not.

Regards,
Carl (UTEP)

Boatright responded on March 18 with a request for 600 copies (UTEP). He was sent his page proofs on March 22, and with it came a note from Hertzog: "There is (and always has been) inconsistency in the use of Folk-Lore. Payne used Folklore, but Lomax uses Folk-Lore. Don't you think it high time for the Society to decide?" (UTEP).

Hertzog managed to finish the booklet with no further delay, and it was sent to members early in May, prior to the Society's annual meeting (TFS Newsletter, 6 May 1946 CAH). Over the years it remained one of Hertzog's favorites. In Becky Garrett's copy he inscribed, "I was always proud of this pamphlet—good typography, good printing, good paper!" It is also one of his scarcest.

Hertzog's final gesture for the Texas Folklore Society came in 1952 when he designed and printed the spring program for the joint meeting of the Texas and New Mexico Folklore Societies and the fall program for the joint meeting of the American and Texas Folklore Societies. Both meetings were held in El Paso, and Haldeen Braddy of the English faculty at Texas Western College was president of the T.F.S. Hertzog himself gave a paper at that fall meeting on "Charlie Russell—Cowboy Artist." He had become intrigued with the subject two years earlier when he created a deluxe portfolio of C. M. Russell prints for American Airlines executive C. R. Smith.

President Braddy had extended a special invitation to J. Evetts Haley to attend that fall meeting, but Haley's response to Hertzog—on letterhead of the Institute of Americanism at Texas Tech—was that "They usually have a bunch of dilettantes or pinks, and I cannot generate any enthusiasm for the meeting. Do you think I should accept?" (30 September 1952 UTEP). Hertzog countered, "The Folklore bunch may be dilettantes, but not pinks. . . . They would consider it a great honor if you would perform" (5 October 1952 UTEP). Haley was a no-show.

Hertzog and Braddy were always simpatico. Thus Hertzog responded to Braddy's printing need as a matter of friendship. Both programs utilized the same basic format—a front cover with a stylized drawing of a river coursing through a mountain pass. The drawing is then set within a cartouche. This device was adapted from the title page of *A Calendar of Twelve Travelers Through the Pass of the North,* Lea and Hertzog's 1946 classic.

Thus ended the Texas Folklore Society's association with the Southwest's premier book designer-printer. Two decades later the Society, under Wilson Hudson's aegis, would briefly boost another remarkably talented man, Bill Wittliff, whose Encino Press made its own significant contribution to printing arts in the Southwest. What the Society may have learned from these dalliances is that care and refinement and quality take extra time, and time means money. But, really, not that much more time, nor that much more money. What is vitally necessary is that the designer have taste—taste plus knowledge and appreciation of tradition. Slapdash printing may be OK with most folks. Perhaps most folks have little interest in such soul-satisfying endeavors as parks, libraries and museums either. But trashy, indifferent printing is expensive in its own way when the reader is too turned-off by appearances to examine the content. Who wants to pay to send a message that never gets read?

Today no books in the T.F.S. library are more sought after than the Hertzog items. For an organization like ours, that has always walked along a financial ledge, we are fortunate indeed to have such treasure in our backpack.

Endnotes

Correspondence is from Texas Folklore Society archives in the Center for American History at the Barker Center, University of Texas-Austin (CAH); from the Hertzog archives in the University of Texas-El Paso Library (UTEP); from the J. Frank Dobie archives in the Harry Ransom Humanities Research Center at the University of Texas-Austin (HRC); and the privately held Dudley R. Dobie collection at San Marcos (DRD).

PART TWO

★

FOLKLORE

Paisano

Vanquisher of rattlers,
Outdistancing stupid mutts
Out-maneuvering lizards,
Quick of eye and beak,
Essense of western tenacity and wit,
Like us wingless paisanos, the folk,
Who deal with what's on earth
And do not soar to useless heights.

Ernest B. Speck

5

Pistol Packin' Mamas: Gun Code for Western Women

Joyce Roach

THE CODE OF THE WEST WAS AN UNWRITTEN EXPRESSION OF THE philosophy of westering folk, notably people of the cattle kingdom. Included in The Code were such ideas as to always make strangers welcome but never ask their names, share what you've got, and be courteous with the women folk and children. There were at least a dozen more notions connected with decency, honesty, and fair play on the range. One legendary sub-heading of The Code addressed the unwritten rules governing the use of firearms, of revolvers, pistols, shot guns, rifles. Eugene Manlove Rhodes put the gun code into words in a piece of fiction, "Beyond the Desert": "It was not the custom to war without fresh offense, openly given. You must not smile and shoot. You must not shoot an unarmed man, and you must not shoot an unwarned man . . . " (459).

Women, too, observed a gun code in the West, and, while it had little in common with the ideas of fair play expressed by Rhodes, women's standards were fair, according to their own understanding of fair play. From diaries, reminiscences, books, letters and newspapers, it is possible to piece together the code for feminine gun play and to illustrate with examples.

Briefly put, the women's gun rules advised that strange men will do to shoot, or one can scare them to death. It is all right to shoot first, then ask questions later. If you shoot a man in the back, he rarely returns fire. Ambushing is effective. If a man needs killing, the woman should go ahead and do it, especially if there is no one else around to ask what to do.

I notice little romanticizing in the gun code of western women.

Just at the turn of the century, Mrs. Frank Adams, a Texas woman who rode, drank, and shot expertly, was thought to have plugged a man in the back because he needed it (Boatright files). An unnamed South Texas woman who ramrodded her own ranch and broke her own horses blew the top off a cowboy's head with a forty-five when he got fresh and pinched her ankle—in fun. He needed killing (Patterson).

The mother of Bob Crabb threatened to let her fingers do the walking when two strangers stole some oxen from the family ranch in the Texas Panhandle and then offered to sell them back to her for thirty-five dollars. Mrs. Crabb told them she didn't have that much money. They came back the next day with the oxen and said they would take five. When she wouldn't pay, they started to leave. Mrs. Crabb reached for her forty-five and said, "Go ahead, but I will kill both of you before you get away." The men didn't call her bluff, and it was a good thing because Bob testified that his mother could "kill a bird on a wing—she hardly ever missed" (Harrell 1–2).

A woman known in New Mexico as Lady Castile fired her gun and just missed her herder's ear when he got smart with her and refused to leave when she told him to. "I didn't try to hit you that time, but I just wanted to show that I mean what I say." The man left (Hurd).

Mrs. Cassie Redwine of the Texas Panhandle practiced the code on outlaws. While she did not necessarily shoot men in the back, she did ambush a few. Robbers were terrorizing the upper Red and Canadian rivers. When five hundred head of her own stock disappeared, Cassie decided to hunt down the culprits, who were under the direction of a man by the name of Black Pedro. It took three days for Cassie and her men to find some of the desperadoes who were in a secret camp, capture them, and change into their clothes. Black Pedro was not among them, but when he rode in later, among friends he thought, he was picked off by Cassie. She and her men had taken positions on either side of the camp. The rest of the men were either killed or captured. The next morning when the men prepared to hang or shoot the prisoners, Cassie would have no part of such awful business and refused to join them ("Frontier Sketches").

Another woman, unidentified except that she was dangerous, once made use of disguise and passed as a cowboy while she traveled over the cattle trails from one herd to another looking for her false lover. Part of her costume was a revolver. The woman located the object of her search and took care of him. She never said what she did to him, but she was known to remark, "I'll bet he won't trifle with another girl's affections" (Westermeier 324).

One gun wasn't enough for some ladies. A Mrs. Wheeler of Mobeetie, Texas, figured that two guns were better than one when she set out to get back her daughter who had been stolen away. Armed with six-shooter and Winchester rifle, the good mother prowled the streets of the town looking not for the daughter but for the one who had taken the girl. Bystanders watched from behind a fence. The marshall was among those behind the fence until more law arrived in the form of Cap Arrington, the sheriff. They both threw down on Mrs. Wheeler and managed to disarm her. Before they could get her to jail, however, she tripped them and drew a pistol from her bosom. After more scuffling, the law finally got her to jail (Reynolds).

The Fenleys of Uvalde were a close family, and like the rest of the family, Edie Fenley was good with guns, an expert with a rifle. She was much admired by many of the men in those parts. The woman got word that a Mexican had hit her brother, Sol Holland, in the head, killed him, and pushed his body in a vat of sheep dip. Mrs. Fenley picked up her rifle and went looking for a Mexican. Any Mexican would do. She leveled her rifle at the first one she found, but just before she pulled the trigger, someone who knew the circumstances told her that she was aiming at the wrong Mexican (Fenley 156).

Guns sometimes gave women the courage to wade into the middle of a group in order to see that justice was served. When a hand for the Bassett Ranch in Colorado was shot in the back by three strangers from Texas, Mrs. Bassett, Winchester in hand, approached the three, disarmed them, marched them back to the dying man and demanded an explanation. The one who had done the shooting claimed that Rollas, the Bassett's man, had shot and killed his brother in Abilene, Kansas. He intended to settle the score. Mrs. Bassett explained that shooting a man in the back was not the way scores were settled in Colorado. Lining up the three against the bunkhouse wall, the lady then invited Rollas to shoot one, two, or all three if it suited him. Rollas, by this time, however, was too weak to hold the gun (Willis 91–92).

Guns provided women with courage they might not have had otherwise. Ellen Casey of Lincoln County, New Mexico became excited when Apaches took both cattle and horses from their ranch. Declaring that she was not afraid, Ellen grabbed a shotgun, hastily loaded it, went after the horses and returned them. Her husband, watching her preparations, tried to advise against her going. When she returned he pointed out that she had loaded her shotgun with both charges of buckshot in one barrel, had put all the powder in the other barrel, and had only one cap, which was in the barrel of buckshot (Klasner 34–35).

Often a woman had to use her wits and invoke the rule of scaring men to death. Mrs. Mary Nugent was accosted by Apaches near her Tombstone, Arizona, ranch. Knowing she could not get to her gun quickly enough, she decided on another course of action. Letting it be known that she saw them and was not afraid, Mary invited the Indians to a fine breakfast. They feasted and afterwards she said she needed some help. Mary put the Apaches to work hauling various items to a storeroom with a heavy door. When the Apaches were off guard, Mary slammed the door and bolted it. Then she ran for her rifle and proceeded to shoot at the door where they might try to come out. There is no evidence that they tried. In time, the Indians were freed, but nobody ever asked why they had come to the Nugent home in the first place or whether they would be too scared to come back again ("Women Who Have Shown Rare Pluck").

No female was better known for weapons—pistols, rifle, shotgun, whip and a vocabulary in both English and Spanish that would have scalded the hide off a dog—than Sally Skull. Her life was the stuff of drama, and in the use of firearms, few were her equal. Sally rode in daylight and dark across the Mexican border to trade horses, went through at least three husbands, reputedly played poker with John Wesley Hardin, and drove trade goods in a wagon during the Civil War, among other things. Many of her activities were performed with guns blazing, sometimes two at a time (Roach 44–49).

Sally was described as a merciless killer when she got angry, and some testified that it didn't take much to make her mad. A story was that once when a man made unfavorable remarks about her she called him out and shot bullets at his boots until he danced. On another occasion someone testified that Sally and some unidentified man faced each other and that the lady's six-shooter spoke first. What the cause for gunplay was, nobody ever said, but the witness speculated that the victim was somebody who was better off dead (Nolen).

Ranch women sometimes dealt justice with weapons other than guns. Mrs. Victor Daniels ran a ranch jointly with her husband in the upper Gila Valley of Arizona. Ordinarily, the wife was on the range with her husband, but a sick baby had kept her home one day. Looking up from her work, Mrs. Daniels noticed two strange men driving off part of their herd. Springing into the saddle, she raced after them, built a loop and caught one by the neck, jerking him out of the saddle. As he fell, she drew her pistol and invited the other man to drive the cattle back to the ranch. The task completed, she told the man to clear out. When the other man was found later in the chaparral with his neck broken, there was no official inquiry as to how such a thing happened ("Women Who Have Shown Rare Pluck").

Alice Stillwell Henderson, who guarded the perimeters of the Big Bend country with her husband and brothers, was a crack shot. She often lived in a tent on the open range and was left alone in charge of both cattle and bandits who came through her part of the world. She defended her kingdom with a rifle. During one incident Alice disarmed five bandits who rode into her camp just after she had made an all-night ride alone to get help from a neighbor in order to get back some stolen cattle. She entertained them at gunpoint all day long until her men returned with their stolen herd (Shipman 101–103).

Women on the frontier often used guns well, and wisely. Central to the anecdotes and tales about pistol packing mamas is the idea that most were only trying to protect their families as well as themselves and their belongings. Those storytellers who passed on these frontier adventures seem to have embellished the facts. Or perhaps they didn't. It becomes difficult to tell. What sometimes seemed preposterous really did happen; what

Shotgun Totin' Mama aiming at some recalcitrant male, no doubt (Courtesy Southwest Cattle Raisers Association, Fort Worth)

appeared outrageous often happened too. Yet, there is the element of overstatement lurking just around the edges of the stories. It seems worth noting, however, that in most of the anecdotes the information pertaining to women and guns is rendered without much embroidering.

Popular literature of the early 1900s would feature female gunslingers, outlaws, and cattle thieves. Such real-life anti-heroines as Calamity Jane, Belle Starr, Cattle Annie, Little Britches, and Rose of Cimmaron would appear on the pages of dime novels and newspapers. These publications were not the sort that women of that time were expected to read or appreciate, and the books in which such females appeared were not morally uplifting according the standards of the time. There were, however, at least two other fictional heroines who were not at all wicked. They were both women of the cattle range, or cowgirls, as such women would later be identified by an international audience. Stella Fosdick and Arietta Murdock, heroines of *Wild West Weekly* and *Rough Rider Weekly,* respectively, were departures from the questionable images of the Belle-Starr type. Stella and Arietta were always on the side of law and order. The two rescued the hero with regularity, hurled dynamite, leaped chasms, shot revolvers, rode for the posse, produced Indian amulets and charms, stole guns or horses from the outlaws, and sometimes shot and killed the bad men of their stories. Theirs was a practical approach to the problems.

Perhaps only a folklorist is satisfied with both barrels of literary shot and has no need to separate fiction from fact-distorted images or from plain truth. Truth for the folklorist often encompasses fact, fiction, and folklore. Few critics, historical revisionists among them, would argue with the no-nonsense approach of one last cow-country heroine from the past and her sensible approach to firearms.

A certain Mrs. Stevens who lived in Lonesome Valley, Arizona, kept a gun handy at all times. When her husband, Lewis, had to go to town some thirty miles distant, he left his wife at home to guard the ranch and the children. Mrs. Stevens was going about her business when she looked out the window. She saw what looked like a rag on a bush outside, but since she did not remember hanging anything out there, she decided it might be an Indian. Grabbing her gun, she drew a bead on the rag and plugged an Apache right between the eyes. After the Indian had fallen, the frightened woman discovered that the ranch was surrounded. She reloaded, kept firing, and held off the Indians until, by chance, some cowboys who were in the vicinity heard the attack and came to the rescue. When things settled down, the cowboys prepared to ride on into town. They asked Mrs. Stevens if she wanted to send a message to her husband. On a piece of paper she wrote:

"Dear Lewis,

The Apaches came. I'm mighty nigh out of buckshot. Please send more.

Your loving wife" (Farnsworth 92–93).

Works Cited

Boatright, Mody C. From his files at the University of Texas, 1972. Clipping was from an undated, unidentified newspaper.

Farnsworth, Harriett. *Remnants of the Old West.* San Antonio: Naylor Press, 1965.

Fenley, Florence. *Oldtimers: Their Own Stories.* Uvalde, Texas: Hornby Press, 1939.

"Frontier Sketches." *The Denver Field and Farm.* April 29, 1911.

Harrell, Adelle. "Bob Crabb, Ranchman on Shoe-Bar Ranch." July 3, 1939. Unpublished manuscript, Panhandle-Plains Museum, Canyon, Texas.

Hurd, C.W. "Women Who Helped Make the West Wild." *Bent County Democrat.* Las Animas County, July 15, 1938. Western History Collection, Denver Public Library.

Klasner, Lily. *My Girlhood Among Outlaws.* Eve Ball, ed. Tucson, Arizona: University of Arizona Press, 1972.

Nolen, O.W. "Banquete's Gun-toting Woman Horse Trader. " *Corpus Christi Caller.* March 4, 1937.

Patterson, Paul. Letter to author. Crane, Texas. March 11, 1972.

Reynolds, F. Newton. "Pioneering in the West," as related by Newt Bowers. Unpublished manuscript. Panhandle-Plains Museum, Canyon, Texas.

Rhodes, Eugene Manlove. "Beyond the Desert." *The Best Novels and Stories of Eugene Manlove Rhodes.* Frank Dearing, ed. Boston: Houghton Mifflin, 1949.

Roach, Joyce Gibson. *The Cowgirls.* Denton: University of North Texas Press, 1990.

Shipman, O.L. *Taming the Big Bend.* Austin: Von Boeckmann Jones, 1926.

Townsend, E.E. Alpine, Texas. Unpublished reminiscences from the files of Mody C. Boatright .

Westermeier, C.P. *Trailing the Cowboy.* Caldwell, Idaho: Caxton Printers, 1950. Quoting "A Romantic Young Woman in the Role of a Drover," *Cherokee County Republican* (Columbus, Kansas), January 26, 1877. 324.

Willis, Ann Bassett. "Queen Ann of Brown's Park," *The Colorado Magazine,* April, 1952. 91–92.

"Women Who Have Shown Rare Pluck." *Denver Times,* Sept. 8, 1901.

6

"First Thing We Do, Let's Kill All the Lawyers"

★

Phyllis Bridges

SHAKESPEARE'S LINE IN *HENRY VI*, PART II, "THE FIRST THING WE do, let's kill all the lawyers" (IV.ii.76), is the remark of a folk character, a common man called Dick the Butcher, a follower of rebel Jack Cade. Dick's suggested annihilation of lawyers is meant to be taken as folk humor. This line, first spoken on stage around 1590 and first published in 1594, evidences a basic animosity toward lawyers among the folk of the Renaissance. In the four hundred years since the composition of this line, attitudes toward lawyers among the folk have changed very little.

Spanish novelist Francisco Quevedo, contemporary of Shakespeare and Cervantes, suggested, "A lawyer is like a cartwheel—he must be greased before he'll move." He also counseled, "A lawyer is one who picks your pocket and shows you a law for it." Sixteenth-century French essayist Montaigne observed, "Lawyers and physicians are an ill provision for any country." An anonymous proverbial definition states, "A lawyer is a learned gentleman who rescues your estate from your enemies and keeps it himself." English poet John Keats wrote, "I think we may class the lawyer in the natural history of monsters." American author Ambrose Bierce defined a lawyer as "one skilled in the circumvention of the law" and a liar as "a lawyer with a roving commission." Woodrow Wilson, 28th President of the United States, said, "I used to be a lawyer, but now I am a reformed character." Sir John Hamilton warned his contemporaries, "An attorney is like a porcupine; it's impossible to touch him without pricking one's finger." A nineteenth-century wit observed, "A client between two lawyers is like a fish between two cats." When James Oglethorpe laid out the city of

Savannah, Georgia, he stipulated that absolutely no lawyers would be allowed in the city.

A complete catalogue of the calumny visited upon lawyers cannot be incorporated in this short paper, but these samples from the past may suffice to show the unbroken chain of scorn heaped on the legal profession for hundreds of years. This tradition has come down to us, and we are surely going to add to it and pass it along.

Twentieth-century America, land of desktop publishing and support groups, evidently shares the sense of exasperation with lawyers that Shakespeare's character felt so keenly. Is it any wonder that our country, with five percent of the world's population but sixty-seven percent of the world's lawyers, is home to such special interest organizations as CALM (Citizens Against Lawyer Monopolies) and HALT (Help Arrest Legal Tyranny), the latter a Washington-based society with local chapters throughout the country (including the Texas Chapter which meets monthly in Dallas). In December of 1990, the *Dallas Morning News* published a column drawing attention to a new periodical called *AntiShyster,* a publication devoted to the expression of animosity toward lawyers. The columnist noted that he had received a hundred calls or more within two days from readers wanting to know how to subscribe (*DMN,* 12-21-90, 31A). These special agenda organizations and publications operate specifically to expose and attack lawyers. It is their goal to be taken seriously.

Another avenue which reflects contemporary attitudes toward lawyers is folk humor. We are killing the lawyers with laughter through stories and anecdotes which lampoon the legal profession and reduce its members to ridicule. The humor found in contemporary jokelore as well as in actual court cases about the legal profession ranges from good-natured tolerance to scathing, mean-spirited rebuke. Some of the stories which circulate are based upon real experiences from skirmishes with lawyers and courts; others are exaggerations built upon real experiences; and still others are pure inventions. The stories reflect personal and social values. In most cases the lawyer or his client is made the butt of the joke. The anecdotes are subject to many variations with repetition. Some are one-liners; others are highly developed; many are in the form of riddles; some have the form of proverbs; some are scatological. All remind us of Congreve's perceptive assertion, "Humor shows us what we are."

The following are a few of the items from the collection. First the riddles:

How can you tell when a lawyer is lying? His lips are moving.

Why won't a Texas rattlesnake strike a lawyer? Professional courtesy.

What do you call two hundred lawyers at the bottom of the sea? A good start.

What do you need when you have three lawyers up to their necks in cement? More cement.

What is black and brown and looks good on a lawyer? A doberman pinscher.

What is the difference between a lawyer and a vulture? A lawyer can take off his wingtips.

What do lawyers use for birth control? Their personalities.

What do you call a lawyer with an IQ less than fifty? Your honor.

What do you get when you cross a lawyer with the Godfather? An offer you can't understand. (Reminiscent of a remark made by Will Rogers: "The minute you read something you can't understand, you can almost be sure it was drawn up by a lawyer.")

What is the difference between a dead skunk in the road and a dead lawyer in the road? There are skid marks in front of the skunk.

What is the difference between an alligator and a lawyer? You can make a pet out of the alligator.

What is the difference between a chopped onion and a chopped lawyer? People cry when they chop an onion.

What do lawyers and bullfrogs have in common? Both have a big head that consists mostly of mouth.

Why are lawyers buried twelve feet deep instead of six? Because down deep they really aren't so bad.

If a lawyer and an IRS agent were both drowning, and you could only save one of them, would you go to lunch or take a nap?

If Saddam Hussein and a lawyer were standing in the road you were driving along, which one would you run down? Saddam Hussein. Business before pleasure.

Did you hear about the bus that went over the cliff with twenty-four lawyers on board? It was a terrible tragedy; one seat was empty.

Did you hear about the blizzard in Amarillo? The weather was so bad that schools had to close, pipes were frozen, streets had to be sanded. It was so cold in the Panhandle that a lawyer was actually spotted with his hand in his own pocket.

One evening an honest lawyer, a dishonest lawyer, and the tooth fairy were sitting around a table. There was a dollar on the table. Suddenly the lights went out. After a while, the lights came back on. The dollar was gone. Who got it? The dishonest lawyer. You don't believe in the other two, do you?

In these simple riddle stories as well as in more highly developed jokes and anecdotes, the lawyer has little defense against the wit of humorists. The following jokes—with variations—are in circulation now.

Over in Forney, Texas, which is an antique lover's paradise, a man was searching through the stores when he came across a sculpture of a rat executed in brass. He thought the piece would be interesting for office decor and conversation so he asked the merchant about it. The store owner said, "I'll let you have it for $100, but you have to understand I have a no-return policy. I sold that brass rat once before and the man brought it back. If you take it, you keep it." "Fine," said the customer. He paid his money and started to leave the store with his purchase. Just as he left, he noticed several rats scurrying through the store toward the front. He got in his car and headed out. As he looked in his rear view mirror, he saw an army of rats following him. In a panic, he stopped his car and threw the brass rat into a creek. All of the rats that had been following him jumped headlong into the creek and drowned. Mystified, he turned back toward the antique dealer's store. When he got inside, the shop keeper quickly cut him off. "Look, fellow," he snapped. "I told you I have a policy of no returns on merchandise. I will not give you your money back." "That's fine," said the customer. "I didn't come to get my money back. I came to see if you have any brass lawyers."

At the beginning of hostilities between Iraq and Kuwait, Saddam Hussein grabbed three thousand American lawyers working in the Middle East as hostages to use as bargaining chips in the negotiations. In his high flown rhetoric, he warned George Bush that if the United States tried to get into the fighting, he, the Tiger of the Euphrates, would begin to release the lawyers one a day until Bush capitulated.

A lawyer in Houston died penniless. The Houston Bar Association was concerned not to let a lawyer be buried by the county as a pauper, so members decided to raise money to lay to rest their unfortunate, poverty-stricken colleague. The plan was to ask for small contributions from many so that the burden would not be too great on any one. One member of the Bar approached a local judge, pointed out that money was needed to pay for the burial of a lawyer, and asked for a contribution of $10. The judge reached for his wallet, counted out $500, and started to hand the cash to the solicitor, who quickly said, "Judge, that's mighty generous of you." "Generous, hell!" the judge said. "At $10 a head, I want you to bury fifty lawyers for me."

A prospective client in need of a lawyer called on an attorney in his office. "Is it really true," asked the prospective client, "that you will answer any two questions for fifty dollars?" "Absolutely," replied the lawyer. "Now what's your second question?"

Two lawyers appeared in court on opposite and very hostile sides of a case. As they entered the court room on the first day of the proceedings, one turned to the other and said, "You're a no-good, conniving bastard." "Oh, yeah," said his opponent, "you're a lying son of a bitch." The judge banged his gavel and said, "Now that the attorneys have identified each other, let's proceed with the case."

A judge in a courtroom in central Texas was surprised to receive a handwritten note from a defendant who was appearing before him in court. He opened it and read, "If I am found guilty, your honor, would you please give me credit on my sentence for all the time my long-winded lawyer has taken up?"

A jury was sequestered for many days on a relatively simple case. They kept reporting to the judge that they could not reach a verdict. Finally the judge, exasperated and disgusted, called in the jury and in a stern voice declared, "I discharge this jury." One of the jurors jumped up out of his chair and yelled, "Hey, wait a minute, judge. You can't fire me. I work for that man over there," he said, pointing to the defense attorney.

A man was injured in a car wreck, but after months of therapy he was back to full strength. His doctor released him from care. Still he continued to walk around on crutches. Finally his wife said, "I don't understand. The doctor said you are fine. Why do you keep using those crutches?" "My lawyer said I still need them," he said.

The National Science Foundation has advised all of the major research universities in the country to make a change in laboratory experiments. From now on, instead of rats, researchers are to use lawyers as the hosts in scientific experiments. There are three reasons for the change: First, there are more lawyers than there are laboratory rats. Second, there is some evidence that laboratory staff members were bonding with the rats, a fact which made it difficult for them to sacrifice the rats at the end of the experiment. There is, however, no evidence at all of any bonding ever between a researcher or any human being and a lawyer, so the stress of making the sacrifice will be relieved. Third and most important of all, there are some things that a laboratory rat will not do.

A lawyer, a doctor, and an engineer had been good friends since their college days; and each year they spent time together fishing or hunting. One year during their hunting trip, they stumbled upon a big pile of bones along the trail. The engineer looked at the pile of bones and then whistled to his dog, "Hey, Slide Rule, come over here and show these guys what you can do with this pile of bones." Slide Rule ran over, began to pick up the bones and rearrange them. In a few moments he had a fabulous model of the Taj Majal created from the pile of bones. "Pretty impressive," acknowledged the doctor; but I have a good dog too. "Come here, Medicaid, and show them how a doctor's dog works." Medicaid methodically sized up the pile of bones, quickly made his decisions, and within a few moments stepped back, having rearranged the bones into a perfect skeletal form. "I'll have to say that is amazing," said the engineer. The lawyer said nothing. He turned to his dog, whistled, and said, "Go to it, Loophole." Instantly Loophole sprang into action. He screwed the doctor's dog, then the engineer's dog, and then he ran off with all the bones.

A lawyer with an extremely important and potentially highly lucrative case was distraught because all of the facts were against him. He could conceive of no strategy that would make him victorious. Still he was obsessed with winning. Finally he decided to make a deal with the devil, so he conjured up Satan. "Oh, Satan," he pleaded, "you've just got to help me win this case. I just have to win this case." Satan listened and then he agreed, but he said, "Look, fellow, this is going to cost you. I don't work free. If I help you win this case, it's going to have a price. Your wife, your children, and your mother will all suffer a plague. But I can see that you win the case." "Oh, that's great," said the lawyer, "but what's the catch?"

Once the devil was walking through hell, and he saw one of the big-shot lawyers who was a resident. Satan walked over to him and said, "You know, the trouble with you lawyers is you think you're the best people in hell. But you're not; you're just the most numerous."

One day a young lawyer died. He went to heaven and was waiting outside the Pearly Gates. In a while Saint Peter came over and said, "Welcome to heaven, Counselor." The young man replied, "Oh, Saint Peter, there must be some mistake. I am only thirty-seven years old. I am too young to die. I think I deserved more time on earth. Surely there is a mixup." Saint Peter said, "Only thirty-seven, huh? Well, let me go check." So off went Saint Peter, and the young lawyer felt elated that he might get a reprieve. In a few moments Saint Peter came back and said, "Well, I just took a look at your records on earth and according to your billable hours, you are ninety-four years old. So, welcome to heaven."

There was a young couple in heaven who had been living together. Finally they got married in heaven. After about three years, they decided they did not want to be married any more so they approached Saint Peter to ask for a divorce. Saint Peter looked at them askance and said, "Look, we like to have never got a priest up here to marry you. I know we'll never get a lawyer up here to handle a divorce."

The Pope died and went to heaven. He was standing in line at the Pearly Gates waiting for Saint Peter to let him in. He waited patiently, slowly working his way up to the head of the line. Just as he reached the first position in line, Saint Peter approached. Saint Peter looked beyond the pope and yelled for a man way at the back to come forward. The man came rushing forward; Saint Peter threw open the gate, and said, "Come in, come in, we're so glad you're here." Saint Peter took the man inside. The Pope could hear the angel choir singing, champagne corks popping, glasses clinking, great laughter and celebration. After a while Saint Peter came back to the Pearly Gates. The Pope addressed him, "Saint Peter, I am the Pope, the Holy Father, the spiritual leader of all Catholics on earth. I have been waiting here for a long time to enter heaven. But while I, the Holy See, stand here waiting, you usher some unknown person in with hallelujahs and leave me standing here. What is going on?" "Well, Pope, there is something you need to understand. We get a lot of popes up here. Heaven is full of them. But we've never had a lawyer up here before."

Three lawyers and their wives were out on vacation aboard a luxury yacht. A great storm blew up, the boat sank, and all aboard were drowned. The lawyers and their wives ascended to heaven and looked around. After a few minutes one of the lawyers went over to the Pearly Gates and started beating on them and calling for a response. "Hey, Saint Peter, we're out here," he yelled; "we want in. Come and let us in." Saint Peter came out and said, "Listen, this is heaven. You don't just beat on the gate and say you want in. Nobody gets in until I say so, and I can only say so after I review each case. I will take you one couple at a time." "Very well," said the first lawyer. "My wife and I are here, Saint Peter, and we'd like to get into heaven. We are asking for admission." "Not so fast, my friend," said Saint

Peter. "You are not a suitable candidate for heaven. While you were practicing law on earth, your only goal was to get rich. You would do anything for a dollar. You have worshipped possessions and money. In fact, you even married a woman named Penny. You can just go to hell." Quick as a wink, the first lawyer and his wife were gone. The second lawyer stepped up and said, "Well, what about us, Saint Peter, I wasn't so bad about money as he was." "Well, " said Saint Peter, "it's true that you were not obsessed by money like your friend. But still I am not convinced that you are worthy of heaven. Your problem has been alcohol. You've been a drunk all your life. You haven't drawn a sober breath in years. In fact, you even married a woman named Sherry. You can just go to hell." Immediately, the second lawyer and his wife were gone. The third lawyer looked over at his wife and huffed, "Come on, Fanny, let's get out of here."

All of these stories about lawyers help us to laugh at them and at ourselves and at the stressful situations which require us to deal with lawyers. And as Nelvin Vos has observed in his essay "The Freedom That Makes You Laugh": "If anything attempts to control us and imprison our vitality, we use laughter as a weapon to kill the oppressor." Thus with our laughter we kill all the lawyers.

An elderly matron was informed by her doctor that her health was failing and that her days would not be long. Mindful of her doctor's counsel, she thought it would be prudent to get things set up for her final days so she called in her preacher. She said, "Preacher, I am an old woman and I know I don't have many days left in this world. I want to get things arranged for my end. When my time comes and I am on my death bed, I want you to get my lawyer and put him on my right side and get my stockbroker and put him on my left side. I want them to be here at the end." The preacher said, "Certainly, whatever you like I'll be glad to arrange. But your request is a little unusual. Most of the time people want their families or old friends at hand at the end. Do you mind if I ask why you have chosen your lawyer and stockbroker?" She replied, "Preacher, you know I am a religious woman. And I want to go just like my Lord did—with a thief on either side."

Endnote

I want to acknowledge the contributions of the individuals who have helped me to gather my lore on lawyers over the past few years: Pat Ahearn, attorney in Travis County; Dr. Susan Brown of Dallas, Texas, and Santa Fe, New Mexico; Theresa Flowers, certified legal assistant in Denton County; Dr. Fred Fox of the University of Arkansas School of Law in Fayetteville; Judd Holt, attorney in Denton County; Dr. Carolyn Rozier of Dallas County; Dr. Brooke Sheldon of Travis County; Dr. Joyce Thompson of Denton County; and Sarah Weddington, attorney in Travis County.

7

Forked Stick Folkcraft

George Ewing

"FINGERS WERE MADE BEFORE FORKS" MAY EXPLAIN, AS PROPER, the table manners of the Colonel's dining room, but neither Moses nor Darwin wrote anything to support the truth of the statement. Admittedly, fingers predate the tined table tool, the hay-pitcher, the tongues that Native Americans observed in Europeans, the whiney instrument that *a cappella* singing directors tap on the podium and hold near their ears, and the behavior of roads with nonsequential destinations, but long before fingered primates, forks were already appearing in creeks, rivers, snakes' tongues (cf. Genesis 3), and, earlier than the dinosaurs, in trees, and pre-Georgian bushes. The many uses of the descendants of these pre-finger forks of the Carboniferous Period caught my attention early in my South Texas childhood during the 1920s and '30s, and I still find myself now and then taking a saw or pocketknife and remedying some situation with a forked branch. (*Forked* was pronounced with two syllables except when used as a verb in the simple past tense.)

My first memory of a practical utilization of a forked limb (other than for providing steps for climbing and seats for tree-sitting) involved our milk cow. We said she was a Jersey, but if she was, her mother must have been scared by a longhorn during pregnancy, for she had a set of cranial appendages, each a foot-and-a-half long, with which she could lift the top wire of any barbed-wire fence and step through it to the greener grass with no injury other than a deeply scratched and easily infected faucet on her five-gallon udder. Weary of regularly apologizing to our neighbors for our bovine trespasser, of losing one-fourth of a week's milk, and keeping a little tube cut from a rooster's

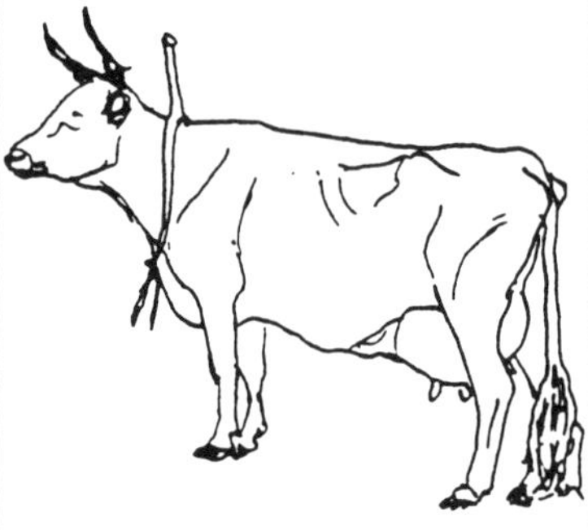

My yoke is *easy*—to make!

tail feather in the milk shed to drain the undrinkable fluid from the untouchable teat, my father, steeped from childhood in the folkcraft of the westward moving Scotch-Irish, simply cut a sapling about eighteen inches below a fork, then trimmed the two branches to about a yard each, and placed the Y-shaped stick on the neck of the cow. Pulling and tying the branches close enough to keep it from falling off, he had produced a "yoke"—not the team-joining type, but one that would keep a cow from going through a fence, and cost next to nothing.

Forked sticks appeared regularly from then on. Our clothes line sagged, so we cut a six-foot pole with a little fork at the top to prop it up. It was easy to move if we needed more room to hang a sheet. A rounded, smoothed three-inch fork on a branch the size of a broom stick was used to souse the clothes up and down in the boiling soapy water of the three-legged washpot and to lift them out when they were ready for rinsing. Six inches or so of forked branch was left on the end of the four-foot stick for rug-dusting. An injured foot or leg (not uncommon among the barefoot children of building contractors with nail-filled scrap lumber scattered around the yard) produced a correctly sized crutch from a forked limb, and gave the hobbler a

A movable clothesline prop

glowing sense of similarity to Long John Silver in the illustration in our edition of *Treasure Island.* A piece of cardboard stuck in the split branches of a forked twig made a fan—not often, for funeral directors kept church-going homes pretty well supplied. Fly swatters required folding the bottom corners of a five-by-seven-inch piece of screen wire over the two-inch branches of an eighteen-inch switch and fastening it with a strand of the wire pulled off the edge. We *had* reached the stage of store-bought kitchen tools and did not use the *lelè* I later saw brought from the West Indies—a foot-long stick hardly bigger than a pencil with three little branches forking out at right angles on one end. It was rotated at high speed by being rolled between the hands and used to stir gumbos and cactus soups.

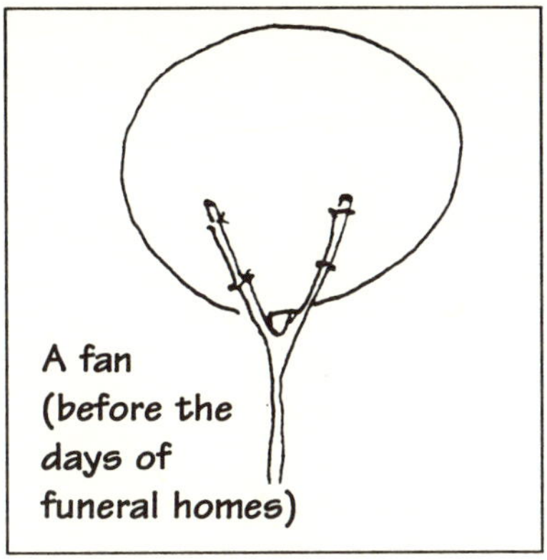

In those days when plastic was non-existent and metal was scarce, the advantage of the forked branch is apparent to anyone who has tried to make some gadget by nailing little sticks together; the joint is far stronger and the pieces are in the same plane. Mortising and gluing might achieve these benefits, but waterproof adhesives were almost unknown on the frontier. Then, too, the smooth round handle of things like the stick fly-swatter *felt* better than the wire ones I use today, and cost nothing.

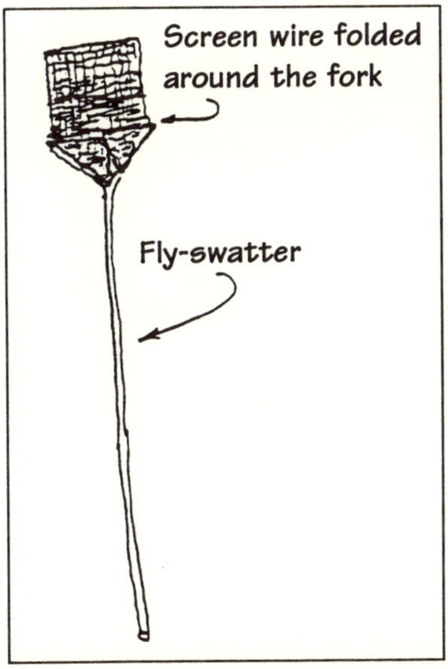

The agricultural uses on the older and less mechanized farms were many. Forked sticks held up the overloaded limbs of fruit trees and increased the tension on guy wires that held posts straight. Two sharpened stakes that forked at the top would support a light eight- or ten-foot pole that in turn held up the berry vines. A forked twig formed the hook for "the old oaken bucket" (I'm speaking literally) that hung in my grandmother's stone-walled well, and if the bucket was dropped it could be snagged with a little fork on the end of a fifteen-foot pole cut from a willow sapling. A cloth or leather pouch or tin can fastened to the fork on the end of a long slender pole made a fruit picker. Some houses had four-inch, V-shaped forks fastened to the back porch post near the shelf holding the water bucket and wash pan to hang the towel or dipper on; others near the door were for hats, raincoats, or anything too dirty to bring into the kitchen. Similar hooks for the wash tubs could be on the backside of the house, on a tree, or the toolshed—whichever was nearest the scrubbing bench and the blackened washpot. In the milking stall they held buckets and often a rag for wiping the udder.

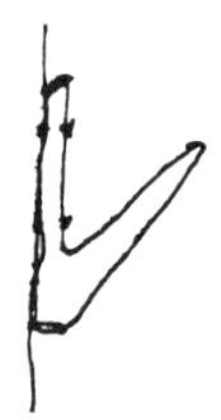

Fasten a form to a wall and you've got a hanger —for nearly anything!

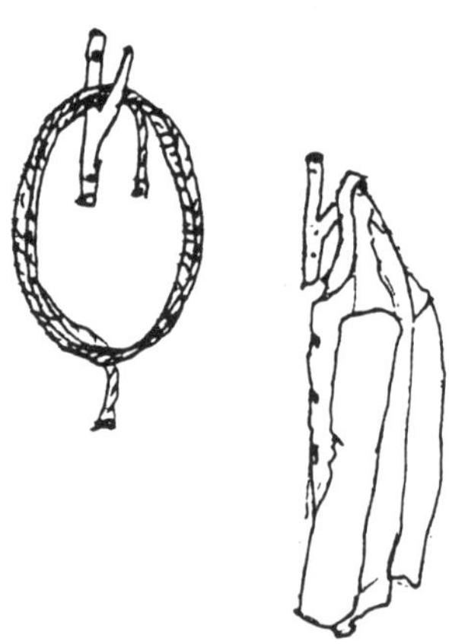

Still larger V-forks (eight to twelve inches) formed harness hooks inside the barn (Abernethy 155), but besides harness, they often held a lot of things, like buckets, rolls of wire, or a sack of anything rats or chickens were denied access to. A tight fork of a tree six or seven feet from the ground was also a sort of catch-all storage place for things, like machetes, that needed to be beyond the reach of children, pigs, and dogs. A similar fork closer to the ground could become a makeshift vise sometimes. If the closing of a door was important enough to demand a hinge hasp, most of the time it was secured with a four-inch twig (mesquite is best) with just enough of a forked branch on one end to keep it from dropping through the lock ring. Locks replaced these only when the danger of theft outweighed the inconvenience of keys. (The one I cut twenty-four years ago for the store-room of my then-new home is still in daily use.) In some chicken houses the inmates still slept on slender poles held up on each end by the forks on three-, four-, and five-foot stakes, driven in the ground with about two feet between each pair. A similar rack out in the sunshine supported anything (like a wet quilt) that needed drying but was too heavy for the clothesline, even after this modern convenience was added to the yard. Some modern conveniences even utilized forked stick hangers; *Built in Texas* has a picture of electric insulators on them (37).

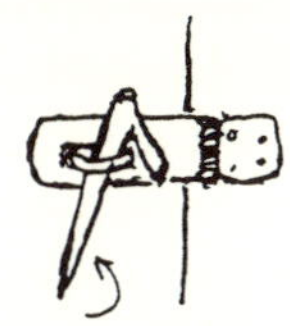

Hinge hasp fastener

Forked log plows had disappeared from the farms I remember, but are still in use in various Third World countries, and several varieties were used on the American frontier. A book published in 1949 shows a picture of one type still in use in New Mexico (Dickey 101). Flour and feed sack cloth had pretty well eliminated the need from homeweaving, so I never saw any of the forked stick "rests" that were used on some looms (Graham-Campbell 120). Another early use was the pack-saddle. A limb of a tree, forked with the proper angles, was cut to the right length and some boards attached to it with wooden pins. "A good fork was not to be found every day, and . . . Joseph Craig, an old pioneer preacher, once stopped short in his exhortation to a large congregation in the woods, and while his eyes were still turned devoutly to heaven, suddenly pointed his finger to a branch of the tree that shaded him, and exclaimed: 'Brethren, behold up yonder a first-rate crotch for a pack-saddle'" (Williams 30).

We knew about the use of the slender forked wand for water-witching, but did not have much use for it in the irrigated Lower Rio Grande Valley. (One of my father's friends, however, by tying a tiny vial of oil at the joint, demonstrated to us that the wand indicated a pool of petroleum deep beneath his water-logged pasture.) A more practical tool was the seven-foot stick, about two inches in diameter, with a foot-long fork, that was used to duck an animal that managed to do a belly-buster into a dipping vat without getting his head wet. Cutting a branch just below a fork provided a hook for carrying buckets of hot asphalt on the days when we repaired tar-paper roofs. My father recalled fork-topped posts that supported the poles of brush arbors or "tabernacles" for revivals, much like cattle shades used in parts of Africa today (Bynum 130). A number of old men I knew had watched for a fork with just the desired angle and cut themselves walking sticks. Boys made shinny sticks the same way for the game that, even though tin cans and sticks are still less expensive than Nintendo, has disappeared in my part of the country.

It was, of course, the remarkable strength of the joint that made the forked limb or post a sort of general-purpose fulcrum whenever a lever was needed, and it was this strength that produced its maritime uses: for anchors, for tholes or oar-pivots, and the mast-supporting projections on the keelsons of Viking boats (Graham-Campbell 50f). The curve of the grain around the fork of many hardwood trees may have inspired the making of the laminated wooden beams that fork high above the heads of many modern churchgoers.

When we headed for the great outdoors in those days of the Great Depression, we had little equipment, so we depended on our knives and nature's forks. A favorite toy was the stick water-wheel whose axle rotated in the forks of two twigs stuck in the mud. Green forked branches made better wiener roasters than the currently used wire coathangers that have little control over the squirming sausage. We knew about the half-dozen forked stick trail markers shown in the Boy and Girl Scout Handbooks, but never seemed to find an occasion for them except to pass the tests imposed by those organizations. A lot of other items shown in these manuals were old hat to those of us who had camped with our families long before we joined the Scouts. Making a lean-to shelter of sticks and cattails or a tent from a tarpaulin required the same two-forked-stakes-and-a-pole structure already described for chicken roosts and drying racks. A branch an inch or less thick—square-cut just below the fork—made a tent peg when the two other ends were sharpened, one longer than the other. Fork-topped green stakes driven in the ground on each side of a campfire held either a spit for roasting or a green stick over which a fork could be hung, with one side notched to hold a pot handle or bail. Green forked twigs could be converted into grills in several ways and either held by hand or propped up over the coals with another forked stake. A two-foot stick with an inch-long branch six or eight inches from the end with a notch in it could be slipped under the bail of a bucket of boiling water for lifting and pouring without burning the hands.

Many of our outings involved fishing. In the spring of 1928, the big barrow ditch by the East Main Canal near Edinburg was alive with perch and brim (we called them hump-backed perch), but the long willow pole I was fishing with was getting too heavy for my five-year-old arms, so my father cut and sharpened a forked willow branch about eighteen inches long and pushed it deep in the moist bank to form a rest for my pole—a common enough practice, but a marked beginning for me, for when we came back again weeks later, my pole holder had footed and sprouted, becoming the first of the dozens of trees I have planted in the sixty-three years since then. When we did not have a fish stringer, a willow switch the thickness of a pencil was cut about thirty inches above a little branch about two inches long. Slipped into a gill and out the mouth of each fish, this could be used to keep a dozen perch alive in the water until time to clean and fry them. A pole with wire or cloth netting—or even a syrup bucket punched full of holes—attached to a wide-angle fork on one end made a minnow dipper—cheap!

Since I have never hunted anything bigger than a jackrabbit, my knowledge of the narrow fork of a tree serving as a vise to hold the head of a deer or elk suspended above the ground while the less edible parts of the body were removed is limited to the pictures I have seen. My trapping was mostly with mouse and rat traps and catch-alive box traps for 'possums, but I did see a few steel traps attached to forked-stick pegs or drags that would catch on weeds and bushes if the animal tried to run away. Recently a gentle grandmother in her sixties aided my research by recalling her enjoyment as a child gigging frogs with a sharpened forked stick. She was overheard by a fortyish female English teacher who added her experience in the same sport, which must have been sex-oriented, for the boys I knew never got involved in it. Poisonous snake hunting, however, as a matter of course demanded a forked stick, or even two, so the wiggling body could be pinned to the ground with one until the second could be placed on the back of the neck just behind the jaws. Then the first could be released and that hand used to grasp the snake safely behind the head. Nowadays I notice various types of grabbers attached to rods and pipes used to capture and handle rattlesnakes, which I suppose is fully as sporting as hunting coyotes and polar bears with helicopters.

I do not know what to call the most common use of the forked stick in my childhood without sounding racist. African rock slingers? Whatever—I'm referring to the gadget that attached a little leather pouch to six inches or so of forked mesquite with bands cut from a natural rubber inner tube to propel marble-sized pebbles (or even marbles or ball-bearings if you could afford them) with incredible speed and accuracy at tin cans, cats, rats, rabbits, wayward livestock, birds, streetlights, signboards, vacant house windows, mailboxes, turtle heads sticking above the water, and yes, even gig-evading frogs. Our dialect reserved *slingshots* for the Davidic giant killer, but modern advertising is using that word for a mechanism similar to what I am talking about. Some homemade models are still around; the best are still made from mesquite, but the rubber generally must be of the type of tube we see disappearing up the noses of characters lying in hospital beds in soap operas.

Forked sticks may not be as great a part of life as they once were, but some of us are still using them, and not just in Texas. As late as 1975, Garrison Keillor tells us, some citizens of Lake Wobegon, seeking to organize a prestigious country club, offered a membership to Clarence, one of their fellow citizens. "If I had a thousand dollars and I wanted people to know I had it, I wouldn't join a club, I would walk around town with the money on a forked stick," Clarence replied. "I would wave it right in peoples' faces" (142).

Notes

Abernethy, Francis Edward, ed. *Built in Texas.* Waco: E-Heart Press, 1979.
Bynum, David E. *The Daemon in the Wood.* Cambridge: Harvard University Press, 1978.
Dickey, Roland. *New Mexico Village Arts.* Albuquerque: UNM Press, 1949.
Graham-Campbell, James. *The Viking World.* New Haven: Ticknor and Fields, 1980.
Keillor, Garrison. *Lake Wobegon Days.* New York: Viking Press, 1985.
Williams, John Augustus. *The Life of Elder John Smith.* Cincinnati: R.W. Carroll, 1890.
Sketches in this chapter by George Ewing.

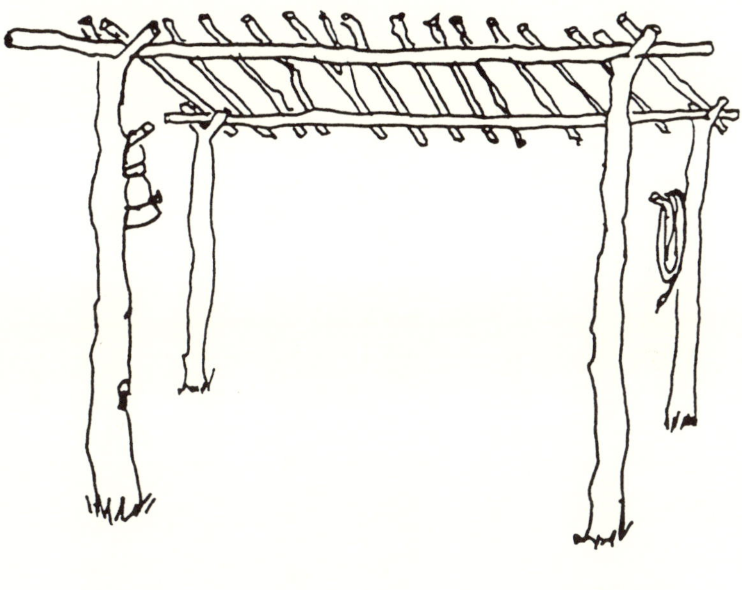

Cattle shades—or brush arbors for camp meetings

Steam-powered drilling rig (Courtesy of Thomas Sidney Hooks)

8

No-Eared Joe: Oil Field Folk Hero

Tom E. Breedlove

TO THIS AMATEUR'S EAR, LEGENDS OF LOCAL HEROES HAVE BECOME fewer and farther between in recent years. This scarcity of orally transmitted folk narrative can possibly be attributed to the migration of storytellers and their audiences to the wasteland of television or to the so-called sophistication of both the audience and the keepers of these legends.

This paper will attempt to resurrect some legends and portray a character—"No-Eared" Joe Ratcliff—whose name was connected with all sorts of escapades during my youth in the oil fields of South Texas. Unfortunately my memory was better then than now, so I will rely mostly on a few men I could find who knew and worked with him.

In the mid-1930s, drilling rigs were active in western Duval and Jim Hogg counties, developing such oil fields as the Seven Siters, Government Wells, Bruni, Randado, and many others. The Depression was in full swing, but in the oil field good wages could be had if a man was willing to work. And so they came—drillers, roughnecks, toolies, worms—from all over the country.

Freer, in Duval County, was a typical boom town: no pavement, no housing, precious little law, but lots of booze. Workers in the nearby Government Wells oil field lived in cheap hotels, in tents, and in the backs of their cars. The prime source of energy was kerosene and bootleg whiskey. (Prohibition had ended and only beer was then legal in Duval County.)

A corrugated tin building, called "Cowboys," served as the roughnecks' hotel. "Dub" Meek says that "You could get anything there but sleep." Rented rooms were so precious that crews working the same rig shared them. This was called "hot sheeting," because as soon as one man got out of a bed, another one got in before it could cool off. According to Getro Darden, one man would always leave the room early to relieve someone on the rig to come claim the room before the rest of the crew left for work. If a room were left empty, a homeless crew would move in, and a fight was sure to ensue.

Fist fights were the boom town's forerunner to 5K runs and aerobic dancing, common in today's metropolitan areas. They served the same purpose—release of tensions, cheap entertainment, and establishment of one's physical prowess. These were common, impromptu affairs, usually of interest only to participants. L. R. Hardcastle tells of seeing three fights going at once along Freer's Main Street and everybody going about their business, ignoring the combatants.

Usually, fights were not vicious, but were ways of letting off steam. Mostly the principals would fight till exhaustion, then share a bottle of liquid omnipotence. A good fighter was admired on one hand, yet constantly challenged on the other, much in the fashion of old-west gun fighters.

Into this environment, around 1934, appeared one Joe Ratcliff (Meek 4). About thirty-five years old, approximately six feet tall, and weighing roughly 240 pounds (Hellums), he was the kind of man who could "go bear hunting with a switch."

Mr. Ratcliff had a physical deformity. He had no ears! This deformity resulted in the obvious nickname, "No-Eared" Joe. The sides of his head were slick as a bowling ball. The more imaginative commentators said that Joe's earlessness was the result of a second place finish in a bar room brawl. Others, knowing the hazards of his profession, said the ears were lost in an oil field fire. Those who knew him personally assure me that the condition resulted from a birth defect.

This explanation holds with the further observation that Joe was hard of hearing. "Dub" Meek said that Joe carried a scratch pad and pencil with him whenever he went to town. He would hand it to various people with whom he was trying to communicate and ask them to write down just what they were saying so there would be no mistakes.

He must have forgotten these tools at Pearsall in 1942. It was at this time and place that "Blackie" Hellums made his acquaintance. Joe misunderstood something that Mr. Hellums' boss said. Joe invited the boss outside to settle things in a manly way. Only Mr. Hellums' command of the art of persuasion kept the invitation from being consummated.

Joe had a reputation of being a brawler. He was never known to back down from a challenge. However, he was not known as a bully, as many others of similar bent were at that time (Hellums).

"Dub" Meek tells of a time he was working with Joe and "Red" Tilley on a rig in the Bruni area. On this particular day drilling was slow and chores of routine maintenance were quickly finished. "Red," who was not without a reputation of his own, felt a need for physical activity. He challenged Joe to a fist fight, just to kill the time. Joe gladly accepted and promptly beat "Red" like a drum.

They rested up on the drill floor, "Red" counting his bruises, Joe with a smile of contentment. Seeing Joe's smile made "Red" forget the previous encounter. He suggested they start all over to establish just who really was the best. Joe, never one to ignore a challenge, accepted and straightway and again whipped "Red" like cream. Back on the floor, "Red" discovered his biggest bruise was to his ego. Looking Joe in the eye he said, "I bet you can't do that again."

Always game for another round, be it drinking or fighting, Joe answered, "I don't want to, but I guess I'll have to show you." Had it been a bullfight, Joe would have gone home with both ears and the tail.

Guiness Book of Records does not recognize the record number of fist fights during a tour [Editor: A "tour" is a work shift and is pronounced "tower."]. If it did, the record would surely belong to "No-Eared" Joe Ratcliff and "Red" Tilley.

If one is old enough to remember school playgrounds before days of physical education classes, it is easy to imagine how Joe became adept at fighting. His physical deformity must have been a constant source of taunts from calloused schoolmates. To a small boy there is only one way to put a stop to these taunts and that is to beat the living daylights out of the taunter. Always on the defensive, his poor hearing probably led to misunderstandings of some idle words and caused him to interpret them as "slanders to his manhood." It is easy to imagine that Joe had mastered the art of self defense and offense long before he hit the oil fields.

Joe has been described as a good worker. He fired boilers on steam rigs for A. O. Hellums at La Gloria Field near Premont around 1946. He stayed at the well site and cooked his meals on the boiler fire, thus saving money. This protestant work ethic lasted until he had enough money to hang on a good one. He would then take his leave and head for the nearest sign reading "Beer & Wine." Some days later and somewhat the worse for wear, he would show up again and apply for his old job. Mr. Hellums usually condescended, for as he said, "He never left you in a bind like a lot of those fellows."

Joe was not always successful in regaining employment. J. W. Meek started roughnecking when he was fourteen, on a crew with Joe. At that time they all called Mr. Meek "Kid" and went out of their way to see that he stayed out of trouble, both on the rig and in town.

Mr. Meek had a chance to repay this kindness four years later in Hebbronville. He was sitting in a cafe when Joe spotted him, came in, and sat beside him. "Kid," he said, "I'm in a hell of a shape. I haven't eaten, I'm broke, got no job and no prospects of one. Can you help me?"

Mr. Meek first fed him, then told him of a rig that was looking for hands. Joe replied that it wouldn't do him any good because he had no work clothes and no way to get to the rig to apply for the job.

Mr. Meek put Joe in his car and drove to the rig, got him the job, and arranged transportation from town to the rig. They drove back to town and went to the local mercantile store, where Joe was outfitted with shirts, overalls, and work boots, all at Mr. Meek's expense.

With tears in his eyes, Joe thanked his benefactor and promised to repay in full upon receipt of his first paycheck. Twelve days passed before Joe was seen again; it had taken that long to receive his pay. The first person he looked up, even before the bartender, was "The Kid." He repaid Meek in full, with the emotional expression, "Kid, you saved my life." Joe was not one to let a debt to a friend go unpaid.

On at least one occasion Joe's loyalty to a friend resulted in big trouble. In 1940, Joe was running with one T. P. Smith at Benavides. For reasons unknown, if indeed there needed to be a reason, Smith got into a fight. Unfortunately Smith misjudged his own prowess, as well as that of his opponent. Smith was getting an old-fashioned country whipping.

Smith was down. His opponent was on top of him and just getting started good when Joe decided that Smith was not going to be worth much if the altercation continued. Joe reached down and pulled the opponent off Smith, intending to stop the fight. Smith, seeing his antagonist in a vulnerable position, drew a knife and proceeded to terminate the argument, as well as his rival.

No one was more surprised than Joe. He had meant only to cause hostilities to cease and declare a winner, not to be an accessory to murder. The local constabulary did not see it that way. Joe was charged with murder along with Smith and taken to the county jail in San Diego.

After some difficulty Joe convinced authorities that he was indeed a more or less innocent bystander and gained release. Smith, however, went to prison (Hardcastle, Meek, Hellums).

This was not Joe's only brush with the law. Dorothy Abbot McCoy, in her book *Oil, Mud & Guts,* tells about Joe and about Freer's lack of jail facilities. In the early days, local law chained disturbers of the peace to the nearest immovable object. There they remained until sleep reduced their belligerence. Good citizens of Freer were offended by drunks chained in front of their establishments when they opened for business every morning. Because they were very vocal in their disgust, money was soon appropriated for construction of a jail. The appropriation was insufficient for inclusion of modern sanitary facilities.

Joe was an early guest of this municipal establishment. Awaking to the well-fermented stench of previous visitors, he proceeded to literally kick out the wall. Found nearby, basking in the sun and fresh air, he was asked, "Joe, why did you do that?" The answer was simple and to the point: "That thing is nasty," he said (18–19).

The earliest any informant can place Joe in the south Texas oil fields is 1934, when he appeared in Bruni, in extreme southeast Webb County. No one knows where he came from. He was last seen about 1946 in Premont, southern Jim Wells County. No one knows what happened to him. Yet in this period of just over ten years, he became a legend in the area.

Descriptions of him could fit many oil field workers in this place and time. Loyal to friends and job, a fighter, drinker, good worker, big and strong, a man who endured both good times and bad: these were not unusual traits. And, except for Joe's fighting propensities, these qualities are common in today's oil fields, as well as in other physical professions. It was Joe's physical deformity that made him stand out and set him apart as the stuff of legend, although I am sure he would have traded his fame and notoriety for a normal physical appearance.

But "No-Eared Joe"—what a name! John Henry Falk's Peavine Jefferies and Jerry Clower's Leroy Ledbetter pale beside it. It immediately attracts attention. Time was when his name and his exploits were common in barbershops, domino parlors, coffee shops, or wherever practitioners of folk narrative held forth. Mention of his name added spice and an aura of authenticity to the tale.

Unfortunately "No-Eared Joe" is virtually unknown to the younger generation. New characters have arisen to replace the old heroic originals. The days of steam-powered rigs are gone, along with the men who operated them. Only on rare occasions, when in company of reminiscing old timers, is Joe's name mentioned or his tales told.

This last story is from my memory of a cold night spent at a well site listening to Getro Darden tell of the early boom days in Freer.

A lot of people lived in tents in what was called "tent city," out on the edge of Freer. On one night a marital disagreement erupted in one of the tents. The husband, filled with the finest product of a bootlegger's art, shot his wife and proceeded to douse her and the tent with kerosene. A match concluded the argument. As the husband observed the blaze, he suddenly repented and decided he could not live without his consort. With much weeping and wailing he turned the gun on himself. The shot was poorly aimed and death was not instantaneous.

By this time a goodly crowd had gathered. Among them was "No-Eared" Joe, his batteries fully charged with liquid protest to the Volstead Act. Upon ascertaining the facts, he became righteously indignant. Grabbing a leaf out of a Model-T

Ford axle spring, he straddled the wounded and moaning spouse. Swinging this spring leaf with vigor and abandon, he warded off all potential Good Samaritans, explaining, "This sonofabitch wanted to die, and I'm here to see that his last request is granted ."

Notes and References

Darden, Getro. Alice, Texas. Drilling superintendent for J. W. Gorman and one the oil field's greatest story tellers, now deceased. Personal communication. Late 1950s.

Hardcastle, L. R. Freer, Texas. Presently a rancher but spent twenty-seven years working the oil fields around Freer. Personal communication. 14 August 1990.

Hellums, A. O. "Blackie." Freer, Texas. Retired driller. Personal communication. 16 August 1990.

McCoy, Dorothy Abbot. *Oil, Mud & Guts.* Brownsville, Texas: Springman-King Lithograph Co., 1977.

Meek, J.W. "Dub." Freer, Texas. Personal communication. 15 August 1990.

Steam powered drill and derrick crew: tool pusher (boss) in clean shirt, driller (#2) far right, motor man (#3) far left, tool dresser (#4) second from left, three roughnecks (Courtesy Clyde Gray)

Who would be a duck,
to swim, to swim throughout the world;
a duck to travel without passport,
and to cross and recross frontiers,
like someone who is only passing time.

Blas de Otero

Crossing the Rio Bravo in *un pato* (Courtesy Fernando Garza Quirós)

9

The Boat Called "*El Pato*"

Fernando Garza Quirós

THE FOLLOWING ARTICLE, WITH BROAD INTENTIONS BUT LIMITED contents, attempts to define and to describe an artifact of the Texas-Mexican border that the people call *el pato.* In this case, the meaning of the term is not the palmiped bird that walks with difficulty, whose meat is almost as appreciated as chicken's meat. *El pato* does not refer to the comical representation of such bird, which fails to reach the heraldic realms of the cock, the quetzal, or the eagle, and remains at the level of a cartoon character named Donald. Moreover, this work does not have or pretend to have metaphoric or analogical ends. No, our intention is to deal with the characteristics of an *embarcación*—half boat, half raft—that is used to smuggle wetbacks and contraband back and forth across the Rio Grande.

The main use of *el pato* is for transporting Mexican wetbacks, *los mojados,* from their native soil to the American side of the Rio Grande. But there is another use, returning the Mexican (or Latin American) national to his own soil when he gets ill in American territory. In the Third World (presently there is not a *Second* World anywhere from Mexico to Patagonia; all countries included belong to the *Third* World), one can still find some son of Hippocrates south of The River who will cure him on credit, or who will treat him according to his economic means. In the *norteamericano* elsewhere, among the defenders of democracy, the fees are absolutely fixed, and there is no credit at all. Even worse, the fees are figured in American dollars. That is the reason why wetbacks take *el pato* back across the river to look for a doctor or for funeral services in their own country. Besides dying decently, cheaply, and in their own beds, they can die patriotically in their own country.

The contraband that is smuggled across the Rio Bravo in *los patos* includes marijuana and other drugs. As a Matamoros *patero* (builder of *patos*) expressed it: "Making *los patos* is a way of life that injures authority." The biggest injury to the authority, of course, is traffic in narcotics.

We have no data on the inventor of *el pato* or on when it received such a name. When the first *pato* was floated on the Rio Grande there was no formal launching nor dedicatory bottle of champagne.

Dr. Jorge A. Bustamante, President of El Colegio de la Frontera, says that in Ciudad Juarez and El Paso "they call any floating item *un pato,* even pneumatics that can be used to cross part or the whole river with wetbacks" (letter to author, Feb. 12, 1991).

The research for this paper was based on observing the construction of one *pato* and on interviews with *pateros* and other people from the area between Laredo and Matamoros. The photos were taken in December, 1990, in El Capote, an *ejido* of Matamoros, Tamaulipas.

The *pato* is made of limbs and branches from a tree that grows along the banks of the Rio Grande. The tree is chosen because of its availability and straightness. Almost always the *pateros* use a tree called a *taray,* or yew-leaf willow (Salix taxipholia K.). Another name for *taray* is *huilote* (from *huila,* which means *kite* in Spanish). The taray is a *salicacea* that can reach fifty feet in height and eighteen inches in diameter but usually occurs in much smaller and more manageable growths (Vines 103–4).

As an interesting side note, when the experimental *pato* was ready to be launched, the rural police appeared and asked to see official authorization from the Secretary of Marine, permitting the construction of the boat. The rurales became less officious when they understood the academic motive for the *pato* project. They warned the builders, however, that if the *pato* project were repeated, the *pateros* must get the "Nihil Obstat" from Norman Schwarzkopf and other pertinent authorities to keep the American border patrol helicopters from using more drastic measures of control.

In regional history, the only mention of a vessel similar to *el pato* comes from Luis Berlandier and Chauvel, two Europeans hired by the Mexican government in 1826 to work under "La Comisión de Límites." They traveled through Nuevo Leon and Coahuila (At that time Texas was part of Coahuila.). They talked of a raft covered with cowhides as the only means available for travelers "in these deserts" to cross water. This is a description of a grandparent *pato*.

Because the *pato* is a folk-crafted object, built for a particular occasion, there are variations in the materials used and in the measurements of the craft. Basically, however, the form of the boat remains the same. The *pato* illustrated in this article was made from willows and scrap lumber and was quite large, measuring about fourteen feet long. The time required for the construction depends on the availability of the materials. It would take considerable time just to cut and trim the willows, if only one person were doing the cutting. In this present case, three

The skeleton of *un pato*, made from willow limbs (Courtesy Fernando Garza Quirós)

persons worked for three hours just building the framework from trees that had already been cut and dressed.

The first thing the *pateros* did with the limbs was to frame out the bottom of the rectangular hull. In the case illustrated, the hull rectangle measured six-feet ten-inches wide by nine-feet four-inches long. The framework was nailed together in this instance, but frequently the frame is wired or tied into place.

Next a triangle was added to the rectangle to form the bow. The bow extended the length of the *pato* by three feet. After the framework was complete, the *pateros* made a deck by placing limbs longitudinally across the ribs. The last step was to build the framework sides of the *pato.* In this case the height was eighteen inches.

When the framework of the *pato* was finished, it was placed on top of a tarpaulin spread out on the ground. The tarp was pulled up over the sides and stern and the boat was ready to float. In a large *pato* the edges of the tarp are tied to the framework; in smaller boats the tarp is just draped over the sides. The informants said the tarpaulin can be in contact with water for periods of almost three hours without leaking. Such a boat can cross the river several times before it needs bailing.

Finally the *pato* was launched into the river. The boat can be propelled with oars, with human arms, with one or several swimmers, with a line from the opposite side of the bank, or with lines from both banks. The means chosen to propel the *pato* depends on its size. The larger *patos,* such as the one in the illustration, are driven with oars.

A large *pato* can transport five to seven people. The passengers usually lie down on the decking to improve the stability of the *pato.*

After *el pato* has transported its people or goods, it can be hidden in the trees along the bank or completely disassembled and stacked in readiness for its next construction and crossing.

Or, because of the little or no money involved in its construction, the boat might be abandoned. Bill Toney of Austin, formerly a Border Patrol officer, describes "*los patitos,*" little ducks, small versions of *los patos. Los patitos* were three- and four-foot, hastily constructed, willow-branch frameworks covered with canvas that the immigrants used to carry their

Launching *un pato* (Courtesy Fernando Garza Quirós)

belongings. They pushed the *patitos* ahead of them as they swam alongside. When they arrived on the north bank, they pulled off the tarp, wrapped their goods in it, and took off for greener pastures. The framework was left behind.

In Matamoros and its neighborhood, *los patos* enjoy many uses. Informants from Rio Rico said that this type of vessel was frequently used in the region. They talked of all the *patos* hidden in the bushes along the banks of the Rio. The locals knew the owner of each boat. It is logical to think that in other areas of the Rio Grande the situation is the same. As one informant from San Rafael de las Peladas (a ranch located in the southern part of the Rio Grande, between Reynosa and Matamoros) expressed, "Before the bridges (over the Rio Grande) were built, the only way to cross the river was in a wooden box, made water tight with a sailcloth"—*un pato*.

The use of *el pato* has had a great increase since the 1890s, when the rural Mexican workers started going to the United States seeking better jobs, salaries, and working conditions than the ones prevailing in Mexico at that time. Later on, during the Revolutionary days, or at least during the Bellic period of 1910–1920, *los patos* were in even greater use as Mexicans crossed and recrossed the Rio, depending on who had won the last battle. Reports from people from Laredo, Reynosa, and Matamoros give accounts of floating mezcal and other alcoholic beverages across the Rio in *los patos* during Prohibition and The Roaring Twenties. Since World War II and the increasing demands for cheap labor in the States, *los patos* have become a way of life for those *mojados* who spend their lives moving back and forth between Mexico and the U.S.A.

Similar to the trucking industry, *los patos* always look for loads going both ways. That means on the return trip the *pato* is used to bring American goods, even iron stoves, from the States to Mexico. The carrying of iron stoves illustrates the capacity of *los patos* for transporting heavy weights.

The cost of contraband transportation across the Rio has increased considerably over the past years. When the Matamoros *pateros* made reference to this rise in prices, they said that the

Beaching *un pato* (Courtesy Fernando Garza Quirós)

cost of human transportation was one peso in 1943, and later (without citing any precise year) the cost increased to a peso and a half. Actually with the current financial instability—inflation, recession, danger of atomic and bacteriological warfare, and other strange terms used in the economic jargon that not even the economists understand—the cost of transportation from the Mexican banks of the Rio Grande to the America side is $400 per person. This is approximately 1,200,000 in Mexican pesos in 1992.

Great men of Mexican history have been forced from time to time to use *los patos* to cross the Rio Bravo for the sake of self preservation. So have the outlaws. But mostly, the *pateros* have built their boats and crossed El Rio de Misericordia for the poor and the desperate and the disenfranchised. Anytime two neighboring countries have different levels of wealth, or population density, the citizens of the poor country will flow to the wealthier. The same can be said for freedom; people flow toward countries of greater freedom than their own. They flowed across the Rio Grande in *los patos*. So many came to Los Estado Unidos via *los patos* that the immigrants are without number. Perhaps some day we shall see *un pato* in bronze or marble on a courthouse square, dedicated to those who endured the crossing of El Rio Bravo in such a boat.

Bibliography

Berlandier, Luis, et al. *La Comision de Limites, Diario de Viaje*, Cuadernos del archivo No. 39, Monterrey, 1989.

Bustamante, Jorge A. "El espalda mojada, un informe de un observador participante," Rev. de la Universidad de Mexico, Vol. XXVII, No. 6, Feb. de 1973.

Paredes, Americo. "Estados Unidos, Mexico y el Machismo," *Journal of Inter-American Studies*, Vol. IX, No. 1, January 1967, University of Miami, Coral Gables, Florida.

Vines, Robert A. "Yew-Leaf Willow: Salix taxifolia H.B.K.," *Trees, Shrubs, and Woody Vines of the Southwest*. Austin: University of Texas Press, 1960.

Weber, David J. "La Frontera Norte de Mexico, 1821–1846." *El Sudoeste Norteamericano en la Epoca Mexicana*." Mexico: Fondo de Cultura Economica, 1988.

But on this summer day you've cut a green bay tree,
Sheared the leaves away, stubbed the branches,
Stuck it upright in your yard, yard that it is,
And slipped bottles over the stubs,
many blue bottles.

Blueblazing in three o'clock sun
Above the raw rusted gulley,
It blares in elemental glory,
Your bluebottle tree, a hard-won
Stay against confusion. . . .

Jones Seay, "The Bluebottle Tree"

Jack Owens' bottle tree in Bentonia, Mississippi (Courtesy David Evans)

10

From African Spirit Catcher to American Folk Art Emblem: The Trans-Atlantic Odyssey of the Bottle Tree

★

Richard Graham

ALONG THE BYWAYS OF THE AMERICAN SOUTH ONE MAY YET encounter a bottle tree or two, those anomalous icons from simpler times when a tree festooned with colorful vessels gave peace of mind to restless souls. Passing motorists have seen them in East Texas, a hitchhiker reports one in tidewater Virginia, and a photographer recently captured one in middle Tennessee. A number of older folks in the Mississippi Delta and elsewhere can still recall the bottle trees of neighbors long departed from this world. They seemingly grow anywhere, and do, illuminating the Southern landscape with kaleidoscopic flashes of brilliance. To own a bottle tree, one need only have the inclination, a collection of old bottles, and a suitable tree or post on which to suspend them.

Like many other antiquarian aspects of Americana, the bottle tree phenomenon has Old World origins long forgotten. In this instance the tradition arrived with Bantu slaves from Zaire and Angola, coming to the United States, South America, and the West Indies. Dancing in the soft breeze, the bottle tree captures both sunlight and evil spirits, some folks say. Standing guard over rural homes, the bottle tree cleanses the land with hopeful splashes of cobalt blue, brown, and green, placating worried minds within its radiance. Yet the belief in the bottle tree's function as a talisman against evil spirits, thieves, and other interlopers is rapidly dissipating. Nowadays they are likely to be constructed as an aesthetic expression, akin to such other Southern folk art perennials as mail-box sculptures and car-tire planters.

The late Addie Burt, an African-American woman from Oxford, Mississippi, said "I got the idea from a lady over in

Pontotoc, Mississippi, and I thought it was pretty so I came back and started one. I just tried to beautify, to put something pretty out by the highway." Just down that highway, in Sarepta, Mississippi, Hubert Glenn, a Caucasian cultivator of bottle trees told me: "I saw one in a magazine, twenty or twenty-five years ago. I wanted to try something different, so I put one up." Glenn also discovered that one of his bottle trees was a good lightning rod when it was struck a few years back: "Glass went everywhere." A more common function of the bottle tree in Mississippi and Louisiana is to promote growth in fruit trees, which is precisely why Jack Owens, a famous blues singer, hangs them in his trees. An anonymous soap-opera fan in Johnson City, Texas, created hers because she had seen them elsewhere and thought they were pretty. In a novel attempt at recycling, Elise Quigley of Eureka Springs, Arkansas, turned her late husband's antique bottle collection into a stunning bottle tree.

The creations of the individual bottle-tree cultivators are as varied as their motivations are, changing form from one example to the next. Geographical and racial trends are apparent, although as in most folk art expressions, there are exceptions to every rule. African-Americans tend to produce sparse bottle trees, at times sporting only a half dozen vessels. Conversely, Caucasion makers, possibly influenced by Christmas tree traditions, prefer tightly clustered arrangements with fifty or more bottles adorning a single tree. Although nearly any tree can be used, makers do have their preferences, favoring cedar, crepe myrtle, and green bay trees. Of these, cedar is the most popular, largely because

Bottle tree forest in East Texas (Courtesy F. E. Abernethy)

Blue bottle trees bring the best luck, in Johnson City, Texas (Courtesy F. E. Abernethy)

of its resistance to decay and its upward pointing branches that facilitate the displaying of bottles. Another stylistic difference between African-American examples and European-American variants is the former's preference for live trees. Caucasion bottle trees are usually either hewn from a dead cedar shorn of its branches, or, alternatively, a wooden post set into the ground. In these examples the bottles are hung on nails driven into the wood.

The choice of vessel accoutrements also varies from one species of the bottle tree to another, the makers using nearly every shape or color of bottle, whatever is available to them. However, blue bottles, particularly cobalt blue antiques, are the most prized. According to old Southern folk beliefs, the color blue wards off evil and brings good luck, hence the blue bottle tree or any number of homes with blue trim around the doors and windows. It keeps the evil spirits away, so some say. For contemporary makers of blue bottle trees, milk of magnesia bottles do just fine. In Alabama, Mississippi, and Tennessee, some folks have incorporated plastic clorox bottles and tin cans in their totemic compositions, although purists scorn such innovations. The aforementioned Christmas tree connection has produced some interesting hybrids. James D. Martin, bottle tree scholar par excellence, reports that an elderly African-American woman of his acquaintance had an indoor bottle tree poised in a Christmas-tree stand of commercial manufacture. A retired rancher in San Jose, California, has topped his bottle tree with a Santa Claus figure. Hubert Glenn crowns his creation with an old Volkswagen headlight unit and a tin star. Still, it is the colored

Santa Claus bottle tree in San Jose, California (Courtesy Ron Carraher)

bottles that are of paramount importance in the bottle-tree paradigm, remaining its most salient feature. Clear bottles may be hung up as they are or else colored by pouring paint inside them.

Other elements and ideas incorporated into bottle trees suggest the efficacy of its magical properties, at least according to the more mystically minded makers. On their trees the throats of the bottles are likely to be greased with fat to facilitate the capture of evil spirits fatally attracted to the colored glass. Once sucked inside, it is believed that the spirits cannot escape, the morning sun sealing their fate. When a strong wind whips through the bottle tree causing it to emit a low, aeolian whistle, folk belief explains that it is the death moan of imprisoned spirits. During the 1878 yellow fever epidemic in Memphis, Tennessee, families victimized by the disease hung blue medicine bottles on tree limbs outside their homes to ward off evil spirits associated with the plague.

Another important function of the U.S. bottle tree, closely linking it to its African and West Indian origins, is that it is believed to have power to ward off thieves and other menacing intruders. In these instances, it is thought that conjured bottles hung on the branches of fruit trees will plague pilferers with a variety of physical ailments including hernias and sexually transmitted diseases. Another common belief is that the thief's stomach will explode if he climbs or devours fruit from a tree thus protected. Protective talismans concerned with both home and garden are common in the Kongo/Angolan area, traveler's reports dating them back to at least 1776. The bottle tree becomes a part of a larger complex of magical power containers known collectively as *minkisi*, or "Medicines of

God." Robert Farris Thompson believes that the U.S. bottle tree is derived from this African charm pool (personal communication 8/22/92). An examination of ethnographic evidence gathered by missionaries and other travelers lends credence to Thompson's assertions (Proyart 192–93; Bentley 261; Weeks 239). One common talisman used to expel interlopers in nineteenth-century Kongo was *nkisi nkandu,* consisting of a basket, gourd, bag, or similar container of magically imbued substances ritually elevated to a conspicuous height over a doorway or hung in a fruit tree. It was meant to insure honesty. With the availability of European bottles in Africa came innovations in the production of these protective devices. Albert Schweitzer, the Nobel Prize-winning physician and missionary, noticed these changes in his account of a Bantu-speaking farmer living along the Ogowe River in Gabon: "Opposite the mission station a negro has laid out a small cocoa plantation, and the fetish which is expected to protect it in a corked bottle" (Schweitzer 35).

Additionally, bottles, jugs, and other such vessels were important grave decorations in the kingdom of Kongo, especially if they were the last-used objects of the deceased. It is also apparent that in some cases such vessels were interpreted as *minkisi* "medicines," and were at times ritually elevated on trees and posts over certain graves to honor the dead and preserve their talents in symbolic gestures or spirit containment. Less elaborate variants of these graveyard decorations survived the middle passage, and I have seen them in both Tennessee and Mississippi. Other writers have reported them elsewhere in the U.S. (Bolton 241; Lawton 197; Michael 132). These grave-decorating traditions, possibly reinforced by Arabian and European folktales concerning the containment of spirits in bottles, gave rise to similar attributes assigned to the bottle trees. It is also noteworthy that elevated traps and corked calabashes are common spirit catchers in Zaire, and this may have had a mediating influence on U.S. customs as well.

The first New World notices of this complex of Kongo/Angolan talismans occur in Suriname, where a Moravian missionary reports them around 1778 (Schumann 6). In his notice he includes the name *Kandu,* a Ki-Kongo term still current there for such protective assemblages of bottles and gourds. Examples on the island of Hispanolia date back at least to 1791, and by the late nineteenth century reliable reports of bottle-tree talismans from other West Indian islands include Jamaica, St. Vincent, Grenada, and the Bahamas (Atwood 265; Kingsley 439; Carmichael 254; Bell 3; Shattuck 415). By the mid-twentieth century notices of bottle trees escalate in the islands, suggesting the great importance which African peoples assigned to this custom (Thompson, *Black Art* 126).

Problems arise in a study of U.S. distribution of bottle trees, there being no literary notices of the phenomena before the mid-twentieth century. This makes reconstruction of the bottle tree's social history in this country a difficult task at best. It is possible that bottle trees were present in antebellum America, escaping the limited attention most writers bestowed on slave culture then. A second scenario is equally possible; the tradition might have been introduced to the U.S. by West Indian migrants in the late nineteenth century. As a number of other African-American cultural expressions experienced an equally circuitous journey before arriving in the States, this theory does seem tenable.

The photographer-author Eudora Welty provides us with our first pictoral evidence of U.S. bottle trees in a photo she took in Simpson County, Mississippi, during the Depression era. She later used the bottle tree as an important motif in her 1943 short story, "Livvie." Oral tradition, however, traces the presence of the bottle tree in the U.S. back to at least the late nineteenth century, as the following reminiscence of the late North Carolinian root doctor Jim Jordon (1871–1962) illustrates:

> He learned the fine points between right and wrong when a neighbor's watermelons ripened early and he and his brother Paul were abruptly thwarted: "Don't you pick that melon." He saw blue bottles containing an assortment of things hanging from a white lady's peach trees. Older folks said the bottles contained such things as chicken toes, hair, feathers and red flannel; warned: "Better leave dem peaches alone; she is throwing (conjuring) fer dem dat pick 'm (Johnson 31).

Contemporaneous with the Caucasion appropriation of the bottle tree talisman to prevent theft were similar circumstances in Grenada. In a lengthy passage in his 1889 book on Obeah, an African religion practiced in the West Indies, Hesketh J. Bell explained how a farmer, plagued by thieves, hired an Obeah priest to conjure his fields by hanging bottles in the trees (1–5). Despite the farmer's lack of faith in the mystical properties of the Obeah priest's remedies, superstitious thieves were, as elsewhere, dissuaded, insuring a fruitful, multicultural future for the bottle tree in the New World. Combined with their aesthetic appeal, such pragmatism helps explain the bottle tree's wide dispersal today.

In the U.S., European-Americans are just as likely to construct bottle trees as African-Americans are, and I have seen more examples in Ozark Mountain communities than in the Mississippi Delta. As the bottle tree diffuses to such far-flung places as New York, Alaska, Colorado, and Nova Scotia, magical motives are in great decline, and form and meaning change with each new social context. Bottle trees have provided artistic inspiration for the poet James Seay, writers Eudora Welty and Samuel Selvon, filmmakers Ken Harrison and Julie Dash, and sculptors David Hammons and Thornton Dial. So if time has dimmed the magical impulses emanating from these spirit-charged sentinels, the bottle tree's odyssey seems far from over, and as an enduring emblem of the South, these glittering totems will be with us for some time, charming us in new ways.

Acknowledgements

My thanks to F. E. Abernethy, David Evans, Bill Ferris, Glen Fitten, Wyatt MacGaffey, James D. Martin, and Robert Farris Thompson for their valuable assistance.

Bibliography

Abernethy, Francis Edward, ed. "Folk Art in General, Yard Art in Particular." *Folk Art in Texas*. Publications of the Texas Folklore Society XLV. Dallas: Southern Methodist University Press, 1985.

Atwood, Thomas. *The History of the Island of Dominica.* London: J. Johnson 1791.
Bell, Hesketh J. *Obeah; Witchcraft in the West Indies.* Westport, Connecticut: Negro Universities Press reprint, 1889/1970.
Bentley, Rev. W. Holman. *Pioneering on the Congo.* London: The Religious Tract Society, 1900.
Bolton, H. Carrington. "Decoration of Graves of Negroes in South Carolina." *Journal of American Folklore* Vol. IV. July–September 1891.
Carmichael, Mrs. *Domestic Manners and Social Condition of the White, Coloured, and Negro Population of the West Indies.* New York: Negro Universities Press, 1833/1969 reprint.
Johnson, F. Roy. *The Fabled Doctor Jim Jordon.* Murfreesboro, N.C.: Johnson Publishing Company, 1963.
Kingsley, Charles. *At Last: A Christmas in the West Indies.* New York: Harper & Brothers Publishers, 1871.
Lawton, Samuel Miller. *The Religious Life of South Carolina Coastal and Sea Island Negroes.* Doctoral Dissertation in Philosophy. Nashville: George Peabody College for Teachers. June 1939.
Martin, James D. "Bottle Trees." *The Encyclopedia of Southern Culture.* William Ferris and Charles Reagon Wilson, editors. Chapel Hill: University of North Carolina Press, 1989.
Michael, Dorothy Jean. "Grave Decoration." *Backwoods to Border.* Mody C. Boatright and Donald Day, eds. Publications of the Texas Folklore Society XVIII. Dallas: Southern Methodist University Press, 1943.
Orr, Ellen. "The Bottle Tree." *Mississippi Folklore Register.* Vol. III, no. 4, 1969.
Proyart, L'Abbé. *Histoire de Loango, KaKongo, et autres royaumes d'Afrique.* Paris: Berton and Crapart, 1776.
Schumann, C. L. "Sacramaccanisch Deutsches Wörter-Buch." *Die Sprache der Saramakkaneger in Surinam.* Hugo Schuchardt, ed. Amsterdan: Johannes Müller, 1778/1914 reprint.
Schweitzer, Albert. *On the Edge of the Primeval Forest.* New York: MacMillan Company,1952.
Shattuck, George Burbank. *The Bahama Islands.* New York: The MacMillan Co., 1905.
Thompson, Robert Farris. *The Four Moments of the Sun: Kongo Art in Two Worlds.* Washington, D.C.: National Gallery of Art, 1981.
———. "The Song That Named the Land." *Black Art: Ancestral Legacy.* Exhibition Catalog. Dallas: Dallas Museum of Art, 1990.
Weeks, John H. *Among the Primitive BaKongo.* New York: Negro Universities Press, 1914/1969 reprint.

11

A Hog Race

★

Bill Brett

THE HOG RACE TOLD ABOUT IN THIS STORY WAS NOT FOR SPORT, AS most races are nowadays. This one was primarily for money. Bowen Taylor of Daisetta, the man chasing the hog, intended to catch this young boar, ear-mark and castrate him, and then turn him loose. The next winter the fattened hog would be penned and brought out of the woods, butchered, and sold. It would probably dress 150 pounds, with the head and feet on, and bring ten cents a pound. That'd be fifteen dollars. (That's equal to five twelve-hour days in the oil field at three dollars a day or fifteen days as a farm hand or cowhand at a dollar a day.) And if they couldn't peddle all the meat, they'd salt and smoke it and eat it the next summer.

The hog Bowen Taylor got after turned out to be old and rank.

When Mr. Taylor realized that he couldn't catch that old boar, the next thing to do was to kill him to get him off the range, even though it'd mean wasted meat. The reason he wanted him off the range was because that old boar could be the death of dogs during a hog roundup. The reason the meat wouldn't be used was because boar meat is so strong and musty it's inedible. I've seen an old boar's carcass lay until it was nearly dried out before the buzzards and 'possums would eat it. Cooking even a young boar the odor is so stifling you have to do it outside, stand upwind, and turn it with a long fork.

You didn't need many boars in the woods for breeding purposes. Sows and barrows (Barrows are castrated boars, and that was pronounced *bars* in my country.), usually stayed in the same bunch and had a range of only five or six miles. Boars, though, went from bunch to bunch (I think *drift* is the correct

Big Thicket hog hunters with game across the saddle (Courtesy Glenn Beasley)

word for a herd of hogs but *bunch* fits better.) and would travel up to eighteen or twenty miles if needed to be with a bunch.

A young, two-year-old boar could service as many sows as an older one and was a whole lot easier to handle. If the dogs bayed a bunch he was with, he'd usually stay with them until they was penned. If he did happen to run off, the dogs would stop him, and he'd fight a little and come back.

Not a big three-year-old though. One of them would always leave the bunch before they'd pen, and he was big enough and fast enough that even if the dogs stopped him he'd leave again when he got ready. Some dogs used in a roundup would catch, which wasn't bad if the boar they caught was a young two-year-old. A young boar's tushes was just long enough to cut a dog up kinda bad, but a three-year-old's tushes was maybe two or two-and-a-half inches long and could kill a dog like a cane knife. That was the reason these older hogs was either caught or killed.

These hog dogs were the same kind of dog that Stephen F. Austin wrote about in 1832 and said was worth the price of a good horse or a yoke of oxen and was needed too much to be used up needlessly. There's no way you can work cattle or hogs in this timber country without them. So you do everything you can to keep a good dog and an old boar apart—like killing the boar.

This following yarn about a three-year-old unmarked spotted boar is one told me by Bowen Taylor of Daisetta. Later on I had the same story from his brother R. E. This is how Bowen told it:

I had a good big bunch of hogs one time that stayed close in around that Tin House slough. You know where it is, just above where McMurty had that still, and me and R. E. was down there one time hunting them. Just before we got to the old house, the dogs went to baying up ahead. I had Lindy and my old Rock dog, and R. E. had a little dun dog come from Buddy Caruthers he called Rowdy. Before we could get there they left runnin' a wild-assed shoat and went out of hearing toward Fishtrap, just 'uh yow-yow-yow ever' breath. I knew Rock and Lindy would quit and come back in a little, so we just pulled up and waited where we was.

There was a big old down tree just off from us a little piece, and we's setting there listening for the dogs, and directly I heard a hog pop his teeth out toward it. "Listen, R. E.," I says. "There's a damn hog right there," and I rode up to where I could see a little better.

I could see that old hog backed up under some briars and vines between the tree and the first big limb, and I told R. E., "Come see, it must be one of them old bar's of mine, he shore is a big'un. Looks like he's got four inches of ivory sticking out of his mouth." He rode up and looked and says, "Come on back 'fore you make him run. When we get the dogs back we'll catch him and carry him out."

"Oh, hell, no," I told him. "He ain't going to stay that long; he'll be long gone before them dogs get back." I studied a little and says, "R. E., you go down there and come back the other side of that log. I'm going to bay that hog while you catch him."

"You're going to what?" he says. "You try that and that damn hog is going to rip you down both sides."

"Go on," I told him. "We ain't got another chance of gettin' him."

I waited 'til I seen him come to the other side of the clay root. Then I got down on my all-fours and went to barkin' and going in toward the old hog, tryin' to keep him from noticing R. E. That old sow was poppin' them teeth and threatening toward me, and directly I pulled back and got my breath and told R. E., "Hell, come on, R. E., this old dog don't like to fight too close," and went back to baying, trying not to get so close he'd run at me and still keep him from seeing R. E.

I was up, I guess, in ten or twelve foot of him, gettin' hoarser ever' bark and just knowing he'd be on top of me any second, when I seen his behind go up in the air, and I says to myself, "Uh-huh, ole bully, you waited too long, and R. E.'s gottcha."

Big Thicket hunter bringing in meat (Courtesy Garland Taylor)

I jumped up and ran in and got him by the ears, and we laid him down and I seen I was crazy as R. E. thought I was. It wasn't a bar'; it was about a three-year-old unmarked boar. If I'd knowed that I'd never pulled that stunt. We had him, though, and I knelt on him while R. E. got a piggin' string out of his leggin's pocket and tied him.

After we stood up R. E. went to laughing and says, "Bowen, if you had a little better mouth, and was a little younger, I believe I could work you a while with a good dog and make a pretty fair hog-dog out of you. You think you could learn to catch?"

Bowen went on to tell another story about a razorback hog.

The longest I ever knowed of a razorback hog running was one Papa tied into back east of Daisetta one morning. Me and him and Uncle Hubert and my brother Jack had been camped in there three or four days and was coming out down the old Mainline Tram. Me and Jack on the wagon and them horseback, and maybe two miles before we got to the oil field at Daisetta, the dogs went to a bunch of hogs just off from the tram a little piece.

Me and Jack pulled up and waited while Papa and Uncle Hubert went to see whose they was. Directly they called the dogs off and come back, and Papa told us they was his. Uncle Hubert had seen a good big hog slipping off from the bunch when they'd rode up.

Papa set and studied a minute and finally told us, "That hog's done that the last two times I've bayed that bunch. Both times it was getting late, and I was afraid I'd lose my dogs, or it would get dark on me and I'd have to go off and leave them, and I've let him get by with it. I believe, though, I'll just look at that bully this time. You boys leave me Mutt and Maggie, and catch them other dogs and go on, and if I don't catch up before then, wait for me at Stengler Slough.

Time we got the other dogs tied under the wagon, old Mutt and Maggie was opening, and it wasn't but a few minutes 'til they was running straight east. They hit Jerome Slough and then went due north, justa yow-yow-yow 'til they went out of hearing.

We drove on up to Stengler Slough and got down and waited and listened, and finally about 12:30 they come in hearing, coming back the same way they'd went, right down Jerome Slough in the worst country in them woods.

They'd just got in good hearing to where we could tell they'd cross maybe a quarter east of us when Papa popped out on the tram and hollered to us to turn loose old Jeff and Hattie.

"Uh-huh," Jack says, "If he can head him off in that strip of open woods by the tram and them two can hold him 'til Mutt and Maggie get there, it'll be 'Katie bar the door.' They'll stretch him like a fresh coon-hide."

They didn't make it, though. Papa said later that old Jeff hung him by the ham and turned him around just as he hit the edge of the thicket on the other side but didn't stop him. The last we heard before they went out of hearing, they was going into what we call the Bad Bend on Batiste Creek. Old Hattie was carrying the lead and putting the pressure on.

Papa always said that old bitch was good as he ever went in the woods with. I know one thing, if she ever barked behind a hog you could go home, get coffee, love up your wife and come back, and old Hattie'd either be looking at him or still running. She didn't have no quit.

That was, I guess, about 12:30 or 1:00. They'd started about ten, and we started waiting and listening again. Once or twice they got to where we could hear them, but they'd make a whip back and go out of hearing again.

The woods was awful bad and boggy that winter. We'd had lots of rain, and a horse 'ud bog half-knee deep ever' step. I mentioned to Jack once't maybe Papa'd quit and come in because it was so hard on his horse.

"Oh, hell no," he says, "Papa said he was going to look at that hog, and he'll kill hisself and old Henry both to do it."

Uncle Hubert hadn't tried to stay in the race, just stay'd along where he thought he'd have a chance of cutting them off if they come back. About 3:30 or 4:00 we saw him ride out on the tram, back toward the creek. Me and Jack was both tired of just sitting, so Jack got his Winchester off the wagon and says let's walk down that way. Well, we hadn't got a hundred yards before we heard a dog coming, and in a minute we could tell they was all four coming, with old Hattie still carrying the lead.

Directly they got close enough we could tell they was going to hit the tram on ahead of us, and Jack made a break that way. 'Bout then I seen Uncle Hubert coming toward us, and I grabbed Jack and told him, "Hold up, hold up, Uncle Hubert's coming to cut him off, and if he don't kill him he might turn him this way to us!"

Shore 'nough, that's just what happened. That hog come up in fifty yards of Uncle Hubert and musta seen him and turned. When Hattie got there and turned where the hog did, Uncle Hubert whooped to her to "Go on, Hattie, go on!" And Lawd God, she did turn on the steam behind that old shoat and come on.

Me and Jack was drawed up in a knot the next two or three minutes, but directly I heard a palmeter break, and I told Jack, "Get ready, he's coming square out on top of us."

Jack says, "If he does I'm going to stop the race." Time he said that, I seen that hog come out of the palmeter, 'bout 'uh three-year-old unmarked spotted boar, still traveling pretty strong even after the run he'd made.

I don't know whether that old hog didn't see us or just wasn't skeered of anybody afoot, but anyway he never made a bobble, just come right on, and when he hit the tram about thirty foot from us Jack's ole .38-40 went "Ka-blam!" and the race was over.

You know, there's something I never seen but two or three times; time that hog was dead five minutes he was so stiff you could stand him up on his all-fours. From being run so hard, I guess.

Well, anyway, old Hattie was there in a minute or two and the other three dogs right behind, and Uncle Hubert rode up and looked at his watch and it was 4:30 exact. That hog had run since ten that morning. Six-and-a half hours. Run hard.

Papa rode out of the woods in just a few minutes, and it wasn't hard to tell what kind of country he'd been through. Muddy, god, him and his horse both, plumb to the top of his head. Hat gone, scratched all over, shirt ripped, and he'd snapped a stirrup and broke the leather and was riding with one stirrup and carrying the other'n in his hand, buckaree and all.

We just looked at the pore old feller a minute. Finally Jack asked him, "Papa, why couldn't them dogs ever stop that hog? He ain't big enough to be all that bad."

"They did stop him," he says. "Stopped him ever time he hit a little open country where they had room to fight in, but before I could get there he'd make a break and get back in them bad vines and briars, and all the dogs could do in there was follow him 'til he hit another opening."

Uncle Hubert spoke up and says, "Albert, the shape you're in, danged if it don't look like you're the one that lost the race."

"Hubert," Papa told him, "To tell the truth, the way me and this old horse feel right now, we'd 'bout as soon it'd been us got shot instead of the hog!"

Wild boar in the Big Thicket (Courtesy F. E. Abernethy)

12

An East Texas Lynching: The Humphries/ Wilkinson-Greenhaw Feud

Mark Busby

THE CEDAR CREEK DAM AND RESERVOIR IN HENDERSON COUNTY not only contains catfish, bass, and water moccasins, but it also holds the secret of the feud that led to the Humphries lynching at the turn of this century. In 1966 as part of an assignment for Jim Byrd's Texas Folklore class at East Texas State University I set out to interview two older members of my family about an event both of them followed carefully. I interviewed my great-great aunt, who was eighty-five at the time of the interview, and my grandfather, who was eighty-three. Within a year and half after I interviewed them for the project, both were dead. Aunt Maggie Hill, or "Aunt Shang" to us kinfolks, was a young girl of eighteen at the time, and her knowledge of the deed came from women talk at Fate Scott's store in the now defunct town of Aley, Texas, which used to thrive just east of Tolosa on the Henderson County border. My grandfather, Louis Steven Scott, was a lad of sixteen and also a daily member of the crowd at his brother's store. After recording the story as they remembered it in 1966, I forgot it until earlier last October when my mother died and I went through some of her things and found a copy of my original paper. It piqued my interest and I decided to find out how my relatives' recollections in 1966—almost seventy years after the fact—corresponded to the history.

First, here is the story as I originally heard it.

On a cold winter night in 1898, Joe Wilkinson, his son Walter, the Greenhaw brothers—John and Arthur, John Gaddis, John Sparks, Sam Hall, Bob Stevens, and a fellow named Mahan—rode out to the Humphries' farm on the blackland prairie on the pretext of looking for a murderer. Jim Patterson was accused of killing John Rhodes, a friend of this group of vigilantes. Someone said he had heard that the Humphries were harboring Patterson, and they wanted him.

When the Humphries failed to produce Patterson, the band of hangmen forced the men to mount up and follow them down to the Cedar Creek bottom—a dense country thick with hog plum, sweet gum, pin oak, catalpa, slippery elm, dogwood, sassafras, ash, chitwood, chinquapin, and other varieties of trees and brush. The executioners tied the Humphries boys' hands behind their backs and then tossed their loops—three in a row—over the long branch of a gnarled old hickory tree where tradition had it that Howdy Martin had made a speech to rally a group of Henderson County boys to ride off for the honor of the Confederacy in 1861. According to the group's account, one of the lynchmen tightened his loop around the neck of the patriarch of the Humphries' clan, old Jim Humphries, in an attempt to get him to tell them where Patterson was hiding. But old Jim fought and cursed them with a strength that belied his years. As the story goes, in the struggle to get the old man to talk, the vigilantes "accidentally" hanged him.

As old Jim's boots dangled in front of them, the vigilantes looked at each other and realized in an instant what they had to do. In order to escape the Humphries' wrath, the men decided that they would have to lynch them all.

As the three bodies swung from the old tree, Joe Wilkinson called his group together and said, "We'll all take this oath: If one of us tells this tale, the rest of us will hang him from this same tree."

My grandfather had told the story numerous times by the time I interviewed him: "Old Mahan had thought over the events of the night and had decided what his best course should be. So, instead of takin' the oath, he galloped his horse off 'bout ten steps, then turned him 'round sharply, tipped his hat to the rest of the men and said, 'As you see me now, you'll see me no more!' and rode off never to be heard from again."

The story of the Humphries lynching was the most talked about event in Aley for quite a while. The reason for the lynchings depended on which side you took in the feud. My grandfather and aunt stood clearly on the Humphries side. My

"The Three Bodies Hanging on the Stooping Hickory, From a Sketch Approved by Eye Witnesses" in the *Dallas Morning News*, May 29, 1899

Aunt Maggie told me what her side believed the real reasons for the lynching were: "Rumor had it that the Humphries were accused of stealing some hogs that had really been stolen by the members of the lynching party. These men were afraid that if the trial ever came up before Judge Dickerson, the Humphries would be cleared, and they rigged this lynching to get rid of that threat."

Maggie's Uncle Eli Hugh Garrett found the swinging bodies the next morning in the hanging tree, which supposedly became "haunted" by the Humphries' ghosts. If anyone went out to that tree at night, he could still hear the Humphries gagging for breath. That tree is now at the bottom of the Cedar Creek Reservoir.

To Pampa Scott, the most memorable outcome of the lynching was the investigation by the legendary Texas Rangers. To the lad of sixteen, the Texas Rangers were about the most important people in the state. But my grandfather's story altered some of the legendary elements. To investigate the lynching, more than one Ranger rode into town. And they didn't gallop in on fine stallions. As Pampa recalled,

> The Rangers came to town in the finest buggy I'd ever seen. It was pulled by two black stallions that would make the front of the buggy jump up in the air when they started off. They had a big lap rug to keep them warm pulled up over their legs, and it had the face of a lion on the front of it. There were two rangers, but only one of them did the talkin'. The other one sat there with a razor strop tied to his arm. While the other one asked the questions, the man with the razor strop sharpened a dirk. He ran it along that razor strop so loud that it came off with a "ting." If any man hesitated in his answerin', the first ranger, the one with the dirk would whip it up with a "ting," and say, "Answer the questions as asked you, sir," in a firm, loud voice. He always got an answer.

The Rangers questioned all the men in town first and then began to single out the ones they thought were guilty. My grandfather had a youth's faith in the Texas Rangers, and he told me in all sincerity that he was sure that the Rangers were so smart that they could tell just by the man's tone of voice if he were guilty or not.

One of the first men to be singled out by the Rangers was John Sparks. Pampa remembered hearing the story in his brother Fate's store. "It seems as though one of the widder Humphries seen one of the hangmen, and the Rangers was trying to get her to identify Sparks as the man. They carried Sparks to the porch of the Humphries house and made him lie on a table. Then, they covered him up with a sheet and called the widder out to look at him. They pulled the sheet off Sparks' head and said to the widder, 'Look at him close, ma'am; look at him close.' She couldn't identify Sparks as the man, but it scared him so that he went home and died of shock."

Under the Rangers' questioning, the two Greenhaw brothers of the original hangmen turned state's evidence and identified the rest of the men. At the trial, Aunt Shang remembered that the judge looked at the men and said, "You were all mighty good men, but you lost it in one night." They were sentenced to ninety-nine years in prison.

The only male survivor in the Humphries family was the youngest boy, Willie, who along with "Boy" Greenhaw, was a fishing buddy of Pampa Scott. As Pampa remembered it: "Boy Greenhaw's old man had turned state's evidence and didn't go to jail. About two months after the trial, him and Old Lady Greenhaw stepped out of church one Sunday morning—I think they was primitive Baptists—and Willie Humphries shot him through the belly. Old Lady Greenhaw stepped in front of him and said to Willie in a real steady voice, 'Don't shoot no more.' Willie jumped a fence and began runnin' off wavin' his gun over his head and yellin' to beat sixty. Somebody finally caught him and told him not to worry because almost everybody was glad he done it. Old Man Greenhaw lingered on about six months but then died."

With the completion of the Cedar Creek Reservoir, the last relic of the Humphries lynching—the hanging tree—slipped into the past. Names on the headstones in the Henderson County cemetery are the only physical reminders of the most important event in that small east Texas town in the waning years of the nineteenth century.

That was the story as I first heard it. Then I decided to research the history of the feud and the lynchings, but it took me a while to find the story. Because my grandfather was so detailed about the cold weather, I was sure it happened in winter and began looking in the Athens and Corsicana papers on microfilm at the Barker Texas History Center in Austin, examining newspapers from October 1897 to March 1898, then October 1898 to March 1899, with no success. Finally I contacted the Henderson County Historical Society and learned to my surprise that the lynching took place in May 1899, not winter 1898 as my grandfather recalled. With that information I found the stories beginning with the May 26, 1899, issue of *The Dallas Morning News* detailing the lynchings that took place around 4:00 A.M. on Wednesday May 24, 1899, under a moonlit sky in the area that was then called the Trans-Cedar region of Texas.

I learned not only that it was a major event in Henderson County, but *The Dallas Morning News* treated it as "the blackest spot in Texas history" (May 29, 1899) and covered the lynching, the investigation, the preliminary hearings, and the trials with front page stories for days. The story was enhanced by drawings of the crime scene, the hanging bodies in the hickory tree, the various investigators, the men charged with the crime, and the grieving widows. My grandfather was wrong about the date and time of year, and John Greenhaw was shot after leaving a hearing not after church. Also, the lynchers were sentenced to life instead of ninety-nine years. But almost all of the rest of my grandfather's and aunt's details—the original hog theft as reason for the dispute, the death oath by the conspirators, the disappearance of Mahan, the hangings in a hickory tree—told from memory sixty-seven years later—are accurate.

I discovered some details that Pampa did not remember. I learned that Jim Patterson, the man the lynchers said they were after, eventually turned himself in and swore that he had not seen the Humphries for at least a year before the lynchings. And I was surprised by a particularly gruesome detail Pampa forgot: the hangmen initially botched the job, because the limb they had selected was too low, and the Humphries' feet touched the ground. The mob then had to tie their legs up so they would die.

By checking the news accounts I also learned the correct spellings of names. My great-great-great uncle who discovered the bodies was named Elihu, a single name, but the family called him Eli Hugh. Uncle Elihu was a justice of the peace in Aley, and on the day after the lynching he began holding daily hearings with written transcripts of testimony about the event—hearings that lasted for thirty straight days. It was this original testimony that partially broke the conspirators' will and led people to tell what they knew even though there was intense fear that those who talked might themselves be seized by the same mob. The two Rangers who investigated were

Ranger Captain W. J. "Bill" McDonald, who investigated the lynching

Capt. W. J. "Bill" McDonald and Ranger A. W. Olds of Company C. And I discovered that some of Pampa's story—the story of Sparks being scared to death and Mahan's words as he took his leave—appear nowhere else. More importantly, I think I learned why this event preoccupied Texans for a few months at the turn of the century and then dropped into the abyss of unrecorded history for years.

First, why did the story capture the public's attention? In 1893 the famous historian Frederick Jackson Turner had seized the public's interest by pointing out in his seminal essay "The Significance of the Frontier in American History" that the American frontier was officially over, since the 1890 census had demonstrated that the country was settled from sea to shining sea. The result was that Americans feared that the kind of values that had defined America would disappear with the end of the frontier. Those values—industriousness, self-sufficiency, agrarianism—were about to enter the popular imagination. But the basic conflict as the story of the lynchings was told, upheld these values. As the story was told in the press, it was a basic American story of hard-working, industrious but poor farmers who were set upon by a mob of profane, drunken men roused by the wealthiest members of the community. John Greenhaw is described as "one of the wealthiest farmers" in the county and Joe Wilkinson—the one-armed, one-eyed leader of the lynchers—is called a man with "wide experience and no small property." In the story presented to the public, justice for common men and women prevails, and good eventually wins over evil in this morality play in Henderson County.

So with this initial interest and intense newspaper coverage, it is surprising that none of the books about feuds in Texas mention the Humphries lynching. C. L. Douglas in *Famous Texas Feuds* does not discuss it, nor does the great Texas feud collector, the late C. L. "Doc" Sonnichsen, include it in either *I'll Die Before I'll Run* or *Ten Texas Feuds.* The official history of Henderson County, written by J. J. Faulk and published in 1929, *History of Henderson County Texas; Recording Names of Early Pioneers, Their Struggles and Handicaps, Condition and Appearance of the County, Advancement and Progress to the Present,* does not mention it. Nor does Walter Prescott Webb discuss it in his famous history of the Texas Rangers, although Webb profiles Captain McDonald and attribues the now famous "one riot, one ranger" quote to him (458).

Why did this event capture the public's mind and then drop into obscurity? I think there are some local reasons for the event to have dropped from public records for years. The first reason is that again and again in the newspaper accounts the good citizens of the Trans-Cedar region are described as being dismayed at the negative publicity that their small community received as a result of the lynchings. They did not want to be identified with the lawlessness, disorder, and violence associated with the old frontier. They were quiet people, people who shunned public displays. The lynchings brought them much more than fifteen minutes of infamy, and they wanted to be left to their work, their homes, and their families. The official Henderson County history by J. J. Faulk fails to document the event for another reason. Mr. Faulk was the attorney who defended the lynchers and lost. So it is natural, I suppose, that he tried to forget the defeats.

The story did not completely disappear from the historical record, of course. Although it did not enter into the mythical region like the more famous Sutton-Taylor feud or the El Paso Salt war, it did receive mention by a relatively famous writer in 1909 when Albert Bigelow Paine, who wrote the first definitive biography of Mark Twain, published *Captain Bill McDonald, Texas Ranger: A Story of Frontier Reform.* Chapter XXXI, "The Trans-Cedar Mystery: The Lynching of the Humphries and What Happened to the Lynchers" presents McDonald's story and Paine's interpretation of what happened. Originally published by J. J. Little and Ives in 1909, a facsimile was reprinted by State House Press in 1986. According to Paine, Captain McDonald discovered the real reasons for the lynchings by convincing the frightened people of the area that he would insure their safety:

> Little by little evidence collected. Men willing to testify gained confidence from Captain Bill's assurance of protection and told what they knew. Men unwilling to testify found themselves unable to hide their facts where they could not be reached by the keen persuasive probing of the man with those ferret eyes, that quiet voice, and those alert extended ears. The testimony brought out the fact that the Humphries had known of an illicit still run by two men—one Polk Weeks and a man named (W. A.) Johns. Also that they had known of John Greenhaw stealing cattle and hogs, and that John Greenhaw had once drawn a gun on the elder Humphries, who had taken it away from him, unloaded and returned it, instead of killing him with it and rendering the community a service (Paine 256).

The story did not catch the public's interest, since it was only one of many in this long book about an interesting but less flamboyant Ranger than some of his compatriots like "Rip" Ford and L. H. McNelly.

For almost seventy years, Paine's account of the lynching was the only historical account recorded. Then in 1976 the story told by the leader of the lynchers, J. L. Wilkinson, was published by Carlton Press, edited by his daughter Bertha Drager. Old Joe Wilkinson's story tells of hog thieves and conspirators. According to him, the Humphries and James Patterson had stolen hogs from him. The Humphries were arrested, but they were able to delay their trial and eventually were able to get friends to lie for them to get them off scot free. But the evidence against Patterson, Wilkinson said, was strong, so Patterson escaped to Indian territory only to return and kill John Rhodes, a local constable appointed to the post with Wilkinson's support and the man responsible for arresting Patterson for stealing Wilkinson's hogs. According to Wilkinson, he and his friends were convinced that the Humphries had engaged Patterson to kill them one by one.

That was the reason, he said, that he organized the group to go out and round up the Humphries that night. Here is Wilkinson's version of the actual lynching:

> With the ropes around their necks, we then put them upon horses, fastened the ropes, thrown over a bending tree; then gave them further chance to surrender Patterson. Not the slightest unnerved was a single one of them.
>
> Amid cursing and vituperations more vindictive than before, the horses were driven from under them; we rode away in the darkness, leaving them to their fate, conscious of whatever fortune or misfortune might follow us we had made Trans-Cedar a safer and a better country in which to live, with every honest man in all that country, who craved the right to enjoy the fruits of his toil unmolested, ready to applaud their taking off (32).

Of Ranger McDonald, Wilkinson says with heavy irony, "[H]e was brave enough to charge hell with a bucket of water" and "notorious because of the number of men he had been able to put under the sod by the six-shooter routs [sic]; a fit subject for hanging, but who had been given office upon the theory that he knew the 'ins and outs,' from experience, by which criminals escaped the penalties of the law; and would, therefore, be a fit tool for the state to use" (35–36). Wilkinson further asserts that he and his innocent friends were railroaded: "The court of inquiry was continued for three weeks without getting a scintilla of evidence upon which a conviction could be based, though they had nearly everybody before them, living within a radius of ten miles" (33).

But most of his scorn he directs toward the "Judas" among his band, John Greenhaw, who confessed so that he could get the $1,500 he paid in legal fees out of the reward money: "No one except the confederates of the Humphries were making the promises; but with no more nerve than a rabbit, Greenhaw drank it all in as if it were sweet cider; then, taking his brother with him to the attorney general, he closed the compact" (34). The Greenhaw brothers were joined by Polk Weeks, called "Poke" by Wilkinson and described as "too sorry for the dogs to bark at" (34).

Adding to the public record, in 1989 Jim Monaghan of Dallas, who is married to one of old man Humphries' granddaughters, transcribed the newspaper accounts, the chapter from Paine's biography of McDonald, and selections from Wilkinson's book and published the results as *The Trans-Cedar Tragedy.* Even though the public record contains much more than it did just a few years ago, the questions about why the mob lynched the Humphries is still shrouded partially in mystery.

In an epilogue to his collected material, Monaghan conjectures about what he thinks are the reasons for the lynching. Like my grandfather, Captain McDonald, and the juries who convicted the lynchers, Monaghan finds the Humphries innocent and speculates about the psychology of Old Joe Wilkinson, suggesting that Wilkinson had both obvious and deep-seated reasons for leading the lynching:

> [T]he two obvious reasons for Wilkinson's fear of the Humphries were alluded to in the text. First, that they knew of Wilkinson's bootlegging activities and were a threat to reveal these facts . . . . Second, that they knew Wilkinson had sold the hogs (he claims the Humphries had stolen and butchered them) to someone in Corsicana while they were still obligated as collateral on a loan held by a bank in Athens that Wilkinson had not paid off (258).

Monaghan also suggests that Wilkinson "really didn't trust the law" and turned to mob action when "the justice system did not operate the way he thought it should." Finally, Monaghan speculates that "Joe Wilkinson's apparent hatred for James Humphries may also have exposed an element of envy buried deep in his psyche. . . . Perhaps the fact that James Humphries was a Confederate veteran of that war and represented the 'hero' Joe could never become worked on his mind as he made plans to eliminate this 'enemy' from this life" (258).

Although the town of Aley has disappeared beneath Cedar Creek Reservoir, the questions surrounding the event almost a century ago remain. The story has timeless elements of suspicion, jealousy, injustice, murder, betrayal, determination, and courage. These are classic aspects of the human experience that ensure that all of those touched by the story—such as my grandfather, my great-aunt, and now me—will continue to retell it.

List of Sources Consulted

Douglas, C. L. *Famous Texas Feuds.* Dallas: Turner Co., 1936; reprinted, Austin: State House Press, 1988.

Hill, Maggie. Personal Interview. Ennis, Texas, December 1966.

Monaghan, Jim, ed. *The Trans-Cedar Tragedy: Triple Lynching in Henderson County, Texas.* Dallas: Homemade Publishers, 1989.

Paine, Albert Bigelow. *Captain Bill McDonald, Texas Ranger: A Story of Frontier Reform.* New York: J. J. Little and Ives Co., 1909; reprinted, Austin: State House Press, 1986.

Scott, Louis Stephen. Personal Interview. Kaufman, Texas, December 1966.

Sonnichsen, C. L. *I'll Die Before I'll Run: The Story of the Great Feuds of Texas.* New York: The Devin-Adair Co., 1962.

———. *Ten Texas Feuds.* Albuquerque: Univ. of New Mexico Press, 1957, 1971.

Webb, Walter Prescott. *The Texas Rangers.* Austin: Univ. of Texas Press, 1935, 1965.

Wilkinson, J. L. *The Trans-Cedar Lynching and the Texas Penitentiary.* New York: Carlton Press, Inc., 1976.

The following issues of *The Dallas Morning News* contain stories on the lynching: May 26, 27, 28, 29, 30, 31, 1899; June 1, 4, 7, 8, 12, 27, 28, 29, 30, 1899; August 9, 10, 11, 12, 13, 1899; December 14, 15, 16, 17, 18, 19, 20, 21, 22, 23, 28, 29, 30, 31, 1899; January 2, 3, 4, 14, 1900; July 30, 1900; August 2, 3, 4, 9, 11, 17, 21, 22, 1900.

13

Hammered Dulcimers and Folk Songs: The Musical Heritage of the C. A. Lee Family

★

Jean Granberry Schnitz

THE HAMMERED DULCIMER IS A MUSICAL INSTRUMENT WHICH originated around the tenth century A.D. The dulcimer got its name from the Latin *dulce melos* or "sweet melody." The early history of the hammered dulcimer is closely related to another ancient stringed instrument, the psaltery. Both instruments originated in the Near East and probably evolved from a common ancestor, a type of zither dating back to the eighth century. The basic difference between the two instruments is in the method of producing sound. The strings of a psaltery are plucked, while the strings of the hammered dulcimer are struck with mallets or hammers. The psaltery is mentioned in the Bible in the books of Psalms (33:2; 92:3; 144:9), and the psaltery and dulcimer are mentioned in Daniel (3:5). The dulcimer was probably transplanted to Western Europe by returning Crusaders.

The hammered dulcimer found favor among the aristocracy in Europe until the seventeenth century, when it lost status because it had become "an instrument of the people." Thereafter, the hammered dulcimer went through alternating periods of popularity and disfavor. It became a popular instrument because of the ease with which common people could produce simple melodies which could be understood and enjoyed.

The first dulcimers in North America arrived among the household effects of British and other European colonists. They became popular in frontier America because they were easy to transport and most were relatively inexpensive (Groce 1–22).

When Miller Lee and Nancy Wheeler Lee moved from Tennessee to Missouri in 1840, they established a home at the Lee Spring in Barry County, Missouri, near where Cassville later became a town. Columbus Addison Lee (sometimes known as "C. A. Lee"), was born in Rhea County, Tennessee, on May 10, 1836. He was the ninth of Miller and Nancy Lee's thirteen children.

In 1859, before the beginning of the Civil War, C. A. Lee bought a hammered dulcimer which had been built in a small woodworking shop in Sedalia, Missouri. He did not like the legs that had been put on the dulcimer, so he designed new legs for it and had them carved to his specifications.

Southern Missouri was a bad place to be during the Civil War. Conditions were particularly turbulent since both Union and Confederate troops occupied Barry County for most of the years of the War. One of the main roads though the area ran through Cassville, making it a strategic location. "Brother against brother" was a reality in the Lee family because of intense and opposing feelings among the many sons of Miller Lee. That C. A. Lee's hammered dulcimer survived the Civil War is amazing!

Columbus Addison Lee and Permelia Caroline Yandell eloped on January 3, 1861, and lived in Barry County, Missouri, until they decided to move to Texas in 1878. By then their family consisted of nine children, including Dora Belle Lee, who was born on October 2, 1874. (Dora Belle Lee became my grandmother, Dora Lee Scudder.) When she was about four years old, in 1878, the family moved to Texas in a wagon train of thirteen wagons and a hack. After the evening meal each night on the train, Ida Lee played the hammered dulcimer while a young man named Newton Meador played the fiddle. The group favorite was a folk dance called "Steppin' Over the Line," with another favorite being "Fisher's Hornpipe." The weary travelers enjoyed music that reminded them of home.

The C. A. Lee family came to Comanche County, Texas, near Hogtown (now called Desdemona). Desdemona is in Eastland County, but the Lee property was located just across the county line in Comanche County (near where Highway 16 now runs toward Palo Pinto). It was near the Comanche/Eastland/Erath County lines. The family's principal business was ranching.

C. A. Lee's hammered dulcimer is rectangular, thirty-six inches from side to side and fifteen inches from top to bottom.

The Columbus Addison Lee family in Seymour around 1891. Columbus and Permilia, parents in front row center, Dora Belle Lee (Scudder) in back row at far left (Courtesy Jean Granberry Schnitz)

The sound box is four inches deep. It stands twenty-five inches tall in front and thirty inches tall at the back. The strings are arranged in a trapezoidal shape as shown in pictures of ancient hammered dulcimers dating back to Biblical times (Groce 5–19).

Seasoned cherry wood is used as the sound board under the strings and comprises the top part of the hammered dulcimer. The legs and cover are made of walnut. When it was new, two pieces of glass about one inch wide with the names of the notes painted on them were positioned under the strings so that the children could see what note was represented by each string. The pieces of glass did not survive the wagon trip to Texas, but the wooden braces which held the glass are still in place at the top and bottom of the middle bridge.

The original hammers with which the dulcimer was played were made of whalebone and gutta percha, a resilient rubbery material made from the latex of tropical trees. (The earliest golf balls were made of gutta percha.) The original hammers were lost many years ago, but Dora Lee Scudder made hammers of corset stays with cork covered with leather on the ends.

Each treble note has three strings, while each bass note has two strings. The strings are permanently attached on the left side, with the tuning pegs on the right. The pitch of the note to the right of the middle bridge is a fifth lower than the pitch of the same string to the left of the bridge (which can sometimes cause problems in tuning the instrument). The bass notes are struck on the far right side of the top, and the strings run through holes in the bridge so that it is difficult to strike them on the left side of the bridge. The strings are tuned so that an octave is in "courses" of four strings, with the second half of the octave played to the left of the bridge. The tuning allows playing in the keys of D, C, G, and sometimes A, although there are only two sharps.

Originally, a hinged lid covered the stringed top. The top of the lid or cover was slanted at the same angle as the top of the dulcimer and made a convenient writing table when closed. There was a level spot on the right hand corner of the lid so that a coal oil lamp or candle could be placed there. The family owned another hammered dulcimer that Dora Lee Scudder later referred to as the "red lap dulcimer," the present whereabouts of which is unknown.

C. A. Lee was a "music master," as music teachers were called in those days. He played several musical instruments, including the violin, which was frowned upon in those days because it was an instrument which was frequently played in places not esteemed by the church-going people of the time. When C. A. was a child he had not been allowed to play the violin for this reason, but after he was grown, the story is told that "he stood on a stump and swore" that all of his children would be taught music, including the playing of fiddles.

All of the nine Lee children learned to sing solfeggio (by the do-re-mis). There was much music and singing around the Lee household because the teaching and learning of music was given a high priority. Each child was taught to play several musical instruments, including mandolin, fiddle, ukulele, piano, and hammered dulcimer.

The Lee children sang many songs, some of which were popular songs of the era, while others were folk songs which had been passed down through many prior generations of folk singers. Dora Lee Scudder remembered that when she was a girl, people from miles around the Hogtown area of Texas came in their wagons on Saturday or Sunday afternoons to make music far into the night. Each family brought food. After the meal, the music began. People played pump organs, guitars, fiddles, banjos, hammered dulcimers, mandolins, and/or whatever homemade instruments they fashioned. Everyone sang.

When the children got tired, they went to sleep in the wagons. Later, the parents came out to the wagons, where they counted children, and went home. On more than one occasion, a family went home with the correct number of children, but some of them were not their own. Usually there was no panic over this situation, because the proper exchange would be made the following weekend when the neighbors gathered again, if not before. Dora Lee Scudder told of one time when a family got home only to discover a missing child. They wore out the horses getting back to retrieve him.

When the music was at the church, hymns were the order of the day. When the music was at the Lee home or somewhere other than church, the music that was sung and played by the Lee family included sentimental songs of the day such as "Listen to the Mockingbird," "Red Wing," and various Stephen Foster songs.

Irish hornpipes were popular, including "Durang's Hornpipe," (sometimes called the "Wobble Wheels Hornpipe" because it was supposed to sound like the wagon wheels were about to wobble off), "Peekaboo Hornpipe," "Mountain Hornpipe," and "Fisher's Hornpipe."

Fiddle tunes and breakdowns were played, including "Devil's Dream," "Turkey in the Straw," "Mississippi Sawyer," and "Choked Goose."

Among the marches were "Yankee Doodle" (which was *always* played in a medley ending with "Dixie"), "Bonaparte's Retreat," "Washington's March" (which was the marching music used by George Washington), "Java March," and "Cathedral Hill March" (which was the marching music for Teddy Roosevelt's troops in the Cuban campaign).

Waltzes included "Glide Waltz," "Over the Waves," "Wednesday Night Waltz," and waltzes with unknown names played in the keys of C and D. Other melodies like "Eighth of January," "Arkansas Traveler," and "Soldier's Joy" were popular. "Stunt" songs such as "Leather Britches," and "Dusty Miller" brought laughs to player and listener alike.

Dances such as "Rochester Schottische," "Jenny Lind Polka," and "Laughing Cotillion" were played, but it should be noted that the Lee family was quite religious and only permitted folk dancing which did not require couples to hold each other. There was much hand clapping, knee slapping, and foot patting.

Dora Scudder told that one night a stranger rode up on horseback and asked C. A. Lee for the night's lodging. After supper the family gathered for music. After an evening of music and singing, the stranger became very excited and spoke to Lee, but Lee became very angry and ordered the stranger from his property. Dora Scudder remembered hearing the sound of the stranger's hoofbeats as he rode away into the night. When Caroline Lee asked her husband what had made him so angry, the answer was that the stranger had asked if he would bring his family to perform at the World's Fair. At that time, people who performed on stage or were in show business were generally thought of as being "rough" and without morals. C. A. Lee had considered the stranger's invitation an insult rather than a compliment.

Many of the songs sung by the Lee family are more or less traditional. Some may be found in some of the Lomax collections but others are not well known. One of these is what Dora Scudder called "The Giant Song." This song tells the story of a young boy who told one lie and continued to tell lies until it was necessary to confess. Dora Scudder taught this song to me when I was about six or seven years old:

When I was a little boy as fast as I could go, (Whistle)
When I was a little boy as fast as I could go,
They sat me on a copy bench for a show.
To my ty, rinky ty, rinky ty-da-la-de-ay.

And while I was sitting there, a giant passed by. (Whistle)
And while I was sitting there, a giant passed by,

He looked down on me, and his head touched the sky.
To my ty, rinky ty, rinky ty-da-la-de-ay.

He challenged me to a wrestle, and a hop, jump and run.
(Whistle)
He challenged me to a wrestle, and a hop, jump and run.
I beat him at his own game and killed him when I's done.
To my ty, rinky ty, rinky ty-da-la-de-ay.

When the neighbors seen what a deed I done, (Whistle)
When the neighbors seen what a deed I done.
They gimme a little money, about three thousand ton.
To my ty, rinky ty, rinky ty-da-la-de-ay.

I built me a box about three acres square. (Whistle)
I built me a box about three acres square.
And I put my money there.
To my ty, rinky ty rinky ty-da-la-de-ay.

When I trabble, I trabble like an ox. (Whistle)
When I trabble, I trabble like an ox.
And in my britches pocket I carry my little box.
To my ty, rinky ty rinky ty-da-la-de-ay.

I had a little hen and her color was fair. (Whistle)
I had a little hen and her color was fair.
I set her on a mussel shell and she hatched me out a hare.
To my ty, rinky ty, rinky ty-da-la-de-ay.

This hare it turned to a horse about sixteen hands high.
(Whistle)
This hare it turned to a horse about sixteen hands high.
And if anybody beats this, I think he'll tell a lie.
To my ty, rinky ty, rinky ty-da-la-de-ay.

Another song I learned from my grandmother during the 1930s or early 1940s was taught to her by her father when she was a child. C. A. Lee told Dora that he had learned the words as a child and that some of the words were Indian words. He explained that "Tuscavalalalavoo" was the name of an Indian girl and "shacka loo rye ree" means "I love you." The chorus contains the same phonic sounds in other combinations with unknown meanings. The tune is the same ancient Irish tune which has numerous other words, including "Johnny's Gone for a Soldier."

Chorus
Shoo, shoo, shoo laka shack,
Shoo laka shacka lacka shoo rye loo,
Fa la mussa sa la va la la voo,
Tuscavalalalavoo, shacka loo rye ree.

Roses are red and the grass is green,
Joys are fled that I have seen,
Others in the place that I have been,
Tuscavalalalavoo, shacka loo rye ree.

Chorus
I'll set me down on yonder hill,
Cry till my tears could turn a mill,
Till this poor head lies cold and still,
Tuscavalalalavoo, shacka loo rye ree.

Chorus

In 1891 C. A. Lee sold his property in Comanche County and moved his family, cattle, and other property west to Seymour in Baylor County. When C. A. and Caroline Lee lived in Seymour, they were surrounded by their children and grandchildren. Dora Lee married William Ira Scudder in December,1891. Later, Dora and Ira Scudder and their seven children lived in Seymour as did Cora Lee and G. B. Morris and their twelve children. Other Lee family members who lived in Paducah, Amarillo, and Oklahoma visited often.

During the years in Seymour, many musical sessions were held when the traditional melodies were played and sung. Dora Lee Scudder's daughter, now Esther Scudder Orton, was one of the children who liked to sit on the floor in front of the dulcimer with her back against the leg of the instrument while enjoying feeling the vibrations as the dulcimer was played. Later, in 1959, she sketched the dulcimer. Her sketch shows details better than most photographs.

Dora Belle Lee Scudder and William Ira Scudder, the author's grandparents, playing the fiddle and hammered dulcimer (Courtesy Jean Granberry Schnitz)

C. A. Lee died in Paducah, Texas, on August 18, 1896, at the age of sixty. Permelia Caroline Lee died on July 21, 1926. Some time after C. A. Lee died, the hammered dulcimer passed to Ida Lee Weldon, the eldest daughter, who had moved with her husband and family to Oklahoma. When hammered dulcimers went out of style again around 1910, no one in Ida's family played the instrument, so it was stored in the barn. On a trip to visit Ida, Dora saw the dulcimer hanging in the barn. Later word reached Dora that Ida's children were playing with the dulcimer, swinging it on ropes in the barn, and dragging it around on the ground.

Dora wrote to Ida and asked if she might have the dulcimer. Ida replied that Dora could have it if she would pay the shipping charges from Oklahoma to Abilene, Texas, where Dora

Scudder was living at the time. The year was 1931. Times were hard and money was difficult to come by, but Dora and Ira were determined. In time they raised the grand sum of $13 to have the dulcimer shipped to Abilene, much to the chagrin of the older Scudder children who thought this was a frivolous waste of money.

When the dulcimer arrived, it was in terrible shape. Over the course of the next two years, Dora and Ira worked to restore the old instrument. Ira took the top off so they were able to see the inside. They found that the tuning pegs on the right side and the pins to which the strings are attached on the left side are set in metal. The fact that the pegs and pins are set in metal probably explains why it has been possible to keep the instrument in tune. Had they been set in wood, they no doubt would have worked loose many years ago.

Ira Scudder replaced the missing metal cap on the top of the main bridge with a piece of coat hanger. Dora and Ira replaced the strings that were missing with strings removed from the treble strings of several old pianos. Since the original hammers of whalebone and gutta percha were missing, Dora made new hammers from pieces of cork glued to the ends of corset stays. She covered the cork with pieces cut from leather gloves. The leather was hand sewn tightly over the cork.

The wooden cover had been removed from the top of the dulcimer. It was never reattached since it was more convenient to play without having to remove the top. The cover was stored in a barn outside the Scudder's home on Stowe Street in Abilene. That house burned in 1938, destroying almost all the Scudder family's possessions. The hammered dulcimer survived the fire because Dora and Ira Scudder had taken the dulcimer with them when they went to visit a daughter in Slaton, Texas.

Articles in Abilene newspapers reveal that Dora Scudder began playing the hammered dulcimer for various musical programs in 1933. Dora Scudder played the dulcimer for all kinds of gatherings from church groups to teas, luncheons, parades, and school groups. It went everywhere that Dora Lee Scudder went from the time she acquired it in 1931 until early 1967. She continued to play it until 1969, the year before she died at the age of ninety-five.

Henry Ford had established the Ford Foundation in 1936. As one of the Ford Foundation's first projects, teams were sent out across the United States to find people who were playing traditional music. The object was to record that music and its history for posterity. The music of the hammered dulcimer was especially favored by Henry Ford.

While the Scudder family was in Abilene, representatives from Henry Ford's Foundation heard about Dora Lee Scudder's dulcimer and came to visit her. Dora told them all she knew about it and the Ford Foundation people recorded the tunes she played that had been learned from C. A. Lee. The Ford people became very excited when Dora played "Washington's March." They told her that she was the first person they had encountered who knew all four parts of the tune in the correct order. She was proud of her participation in Henry Ford's project.

After the Scudder's house in Abilene burned in 1938, the Scudder family spent many years with the Granberry family in Victoria and Alice, Texas, and then in the late 1940s and 1950s with the Granberrys and with Esther Scudder Orton in Raymondville, Harlingen, and Beeville, Texas. Several nights a week, the Granberry family and the Scudder family had musical sessions where Dora played the hammered dulcimer, Ira played his fiddle, Lena Belle Scudder Granberry played the piano, and the Granberry children clapped their hands and sang to the music.

When the Scudders left Abilene in late 1938 or early 1939, they forgot about the dulcimer cover out in the shed. Esther Scudder went to retrieve it several months later, but the shed had been cleaned out and the cover was gone.

The first time I realized that Grandmama's dulcimer music was something special was in 1945 when my grandparents were living with us in Alice, Texas. Grandmama and Grandpapa were visited by a man whose name I do not remember, who had known them since before they had married. He was a fiddle player. Each day and night while he was there, Grandmama, Grandpapa and their friend made music on the dulcimer and fiddle, accompanied by my mother, Lena Belle Scudder Granberry, on the piano.

After they played for a Sunday School class from the First Presbyterian Church in Alice, somebody asked them to do a program for an assembly at the William Adams High School in Alice, where I was in the ninth grade. I was horrified when I heard that they had accepted the invitation and the assembly would be held at 11:30 during a school day! I loved to hear Grandmama's music on the dulcimer, and I enjoyed hearing the visitor and Grandpapa playing with Grandmama, but I was thirteen years old and the idea of my grandparents, mother, and another man playing for an assembly at the high school I attended was terribly embarrassing. I felt sure that the other teenagers would not like it. The music my family played was very different from the music of the 1940s.

The day of the program came. All the students of the high school assembled in the auditorium, with one member of the audience cringing low in her chair. By the time Grandmama stood up and told the crowd about the instruments and how they had played together with the visiting man before 1900 (Grandmama was nearly seventy at the time), the audience was somewhat restless. When the music began, however, the audience was immediately enthralled. Each tune was greeted with thunderous applause. I felt better after each piece.

The bell rang for the beginning of the lunch hour during the playing of a tune. No one moved. When the tune was over, Grandmama announced to the crowd that she understood that the bell for lunch had just rung and that all who wished to go to lunch were dismissed. The principal made an announcement to the same effect. No one moved. They all sat there. At first I was absolutely horrified, then I realized that this was a terrific tribute to the performers coming from a couple of hundred teenagers who were so enraptured by their music that they would give up part of their lunch hour to hear more.

At that time I decided that I, too, would learn to play the dulcimer and would learn everything I could from Grandmama. The program ended only when Grandmama announced that it had ended and they would play no more. A resounding standing ovation erupted from the crowd. I was the proudest person in the world that day.

After Ira Scudder died in Beeville, Texas in 1954, Grandmama lived in Slaton, Texas, where she played the dulcimer frequently for many and varied groups. Each year during the winter she traveled to visit her daughters in Alice and Beeville; my brother, Bill Granberry, and his family in Corpus Christi; and me and my family in Kingsville, Texas. She rode the bus (until she was ninety-four) and with her traveled the dulcimer, packed in a flat box in the luggage compartment.

Each year Dora Lee Scudder performed on the dulcimer for several groups in each of those Texas towns. When she visited me, her favorite activity was to "entertain the old folks." She was in her nineties but we went to the local nursing home to entertain. She was usually older than most of the people we were entertaining. I played the piano or the guitar and Grandmama played her hammered dulcimer.

In January of 1967, when Dora Scudder was ninety-two, I was helping her pack for the long bus ride to Lubbock. As I started to pack the dulcimer, she said. "No. The dulcimer is not going to make the trip this time. It's staying here with you. I want you to take it places and play it for people. Don't leave it sitting in your living room."

After 1967, Dora Scudder made three trips back to Kingsville. She set out to teach me all of the tunes that she knew how to play on the dulcimer. Each time we spent up to eight hours a day on this project for her entire three-week stay. The music was taught by rote; that is, she played the piece section by section. When I played each part over and over until she decided I knew it correctly, we would go on to the next movement of the song. Piece by piece, C. A. Lee's music was passed on.

The last time Grandmama Scudder came to Kingsville, in January of 1969 when she was ninety-four years old, she could barely see the strings to play and hear the notes to tell if tunes were right or wrong. She told me that she had taught me everything she knew except two, "Money Musk" and "Fisher's Hornpipe." Finally in frustration, she had me get my notebook, and she sang out the musical tones solfeggio. I wrote down what she sang. I have since transcribed the notes to music.

On the last evening she spent in Kingsville in 1969, my family was invited to a friend's house for a music session.

Everybody brought guitars and other instruments. On this evening, Grandmama agreed to go since I was taking the hammered dulcimer. She told me not to ask her to play since she "just couldn't do it any more." How sad I was!

After the instruments were tuned and the music began, I played one of the tunes Grandmama had taught me. When I finished, she said, "Jean, you played that too fast." Someone said, "Grandmama (all my friends called her that), "why don't you show us how?" She said, "I believe I will." Grandmama went to the dulcimer and played what we all knew was her last performance. I would have given anything for a recording, but no recorder was available. Grandmama Scudder played nonstop for more than an hour to the accompaniment of many guitars and a fiddle. She had never played more beautifully! There were few dry eyes in the room by the time she finished. She told me on the way home that she knew she had just played her "swan song."

Dora Scudder died August 26, 1970, at the age of ninety-five. Her music and that of C. A. Lee live on. The Lee musical heritage has been heard indoors and outdoors in nursing homes, museums, historical houses, parades, churches, auditoriums, school rooms, festivals, Mayfests, Bayfests, Texas Folklife Festivals, and in other likely and unlikely places. It has been heard by the Texas Historical Commission, Texas Historical Foundation, Texas Federation of Music Clubs, Texas Folklore Society, and other such groups.

I am in the process of writing the music on paper, along with what history I know about each tune. Recordings need to be made.

C. A. Lee's hammered dulcimer has traveled by wagon and surrey; by automobiles such as the Ford Model T, Ford Maverick, station wagon, Whippet, Hudson, Blazer, and Suburban; and by bus, train, pickup, trailer and truck. It has ridden in parades on flatbed trailers and floats. It has not yet traveled by airplane, but I will not be surprised if someday it does.

During the 1980s and 1990s the hammered dulcimer is repeating history by being "discovered," resulting in increasing popularity of the instrument and the music which had faded into obscurity about 1900. A musical style is developing that is

Jean Granberry Schnitz playing the family dulcimer at a Texas Folklore Society meeting (Courtesy F. E. Abernethy)

a departure from the traditional style, as played by C. A. Lee and Dora Lee Scudder. This "progressive" style involves the use of arpeggios and other musical embellishments, resulting in the hammered dulcimer's becoming more sophisticated and more successful as a solo instrument. Dora Lee Scudder never even considered playing solo. She insisted on piano or guitar accompaniment. When I first heard the new style of playing, I was amazed, but thrilled at the prospect of using an old instrument in a new way. I enjoy playing and hearing the new style, but I believe that it is important for traditional music to continue to be heard and enjoyed. I believe that C. A. Lee and Dora Lee Scudder would agree.

Works Cited

Groce, Nancy. "The Hammered Dulcimer in America." *Smithsonian Studies in History and Technology.* Number 44. City of Washington: Smithsonian Institution Press: 1983.

14

The Rabbit, The Lion, and The Man: Race Relations in Folklore Fieldwork

Patrick B. Mullen

HERE IN THE LATE TWENTIETH-CENTURY UNITED STATES OF America, we are still living in a racist society. Prejudice against black people, along with related economic and political causes, are at the root of the social problems of the inner cities; the situation is complicated by the intertwined forces of race, class, and culture. One result has been a backlash against civil rights and affirmative action. Race relations seem to have gotten worse after the hopeful dialog that began during the civil rights movement of the 1960s. The attention to black concerns in the sixties accelerated the academic study of African American culture with the establishment of Black Studies Departments in universities throughout the country.

Folklorists have been collecting and analyzing African American folklore since the nineteenth century, but our efforts have often been separate from social and political processes. Our fieldwork has been academic research in the ivory tower sense. We have not always recognized the fact that when a white folklorist interviews black informants it is within a political context. Fieldwork interview situations are influenced by and reflect larger patterns of race relations in America.

In 1967 in Sabine Pass, Texas, I interviewed and recorded two black men about traditions in their lives, and both what we said and how the three of us interacted have racial implications in society and in the profession of folklore studies. I was a twenty-six-year-old folklorist, still in graduate school, on one of my first field research trips, interviewing Captain Son Brill and his friend Jr. Carter on the bridge of Captain Brill's fishing boat. Captain Brill was sixty-four and had been a commercial pogie fisherman since he was twelve in Jacksonville, Florida. Jr. Carter was in his early thirties, originally from South Carolina, and worked in the plant which processed the pogie fish. We talked about occupational traditions and race relations in the fishing business. Jr. Carter also told several jokes and tales.

I have written about Son Brill's legends and beliefs elsewhere (*I Heard the Old Fishermen Say* 84–93), and I have used Jr. Carter's stories in folklore classes for years, but in all my previous work on them I had concentrated on the texts within their cultural context without considering the immediate context of the interview, specifically how the racial and cultural differences influenced what went on. This, then, is an exercise in "reflexive ethnography" (Clifford and Marcus), a looking back at an incident in my professional life, trying to see it within the historical context of 1967 from the perspective of the present moment which has been influenced by the intervening twenty-five years of fieldwork experience and writing folklore. My perspective now is that of the white liberal recognizing the influence of racism on his personal and professional life, and what follows is in somewhat of a confessional mode.

The boat Son Brill, Jr. Carter, and I were on was tied up less than twenty-five miles from where I was born, Beaumont, Texas, a segregated city in housing, schools, and all facets of social life at the time I was growing up. I remember the "colored" drinking fountains at the White House, the big downtown department store, the "colored" waiting room at the Greyhound bus station, and Negroes in the back of city buses. The only black person I knew as a child was Melissy, the woman who did the ironing for everyone in our family. One day when I was six or seven, Melissy was in the dining room ironing, and I was in the kitchen eating lunch. I was playing with the salt and pepper shakers and said, "This one is white, this one is a nigger." My mother scolded me, pointing to the other room where Melissy could hear me. I remember being embarrassed because I had been taught to say "colored" or "Negro" and to be kind to black people in the patronizing way that polite southern whites had at the time. Black people were all around us, but as far as I could tell, there was no cultural contact.

This all changed for me when I was in junior high. The schools were still segregated, but white kids were listening to black radio. Like many white southerners my age, I became fascinated by African American culture when in 1954, at the age of thirteen, I heard Ray Charles, Lavern Baker, and The Penguins for the first time. This inevitably led to Robert Johnson, Leadbelly, and Sonny Terry, and eventually to Duke Ellington, Charlie Parker, and John Coltrane. This interest in another culture was instrumental in my becoming a folklorist. I wrote a paper entitled "Folk Elements in Modern Jazz: The Soul Movement" for Francis Abernethy's undergraduate folklore course at Lamar Tech, and I read the same paper at my first scholarly conference, a meeting of the Texas Folklore Society in 1964. I was reading James Baldwin as an undergraduate and Eldridge Cleaver as a graduate student, and by 1967 had taken a graduate seminar in Afro-American folklore at the University of Texas, and I still did not know any black people except for my ex-wife's grandmother's maid and my father's yardman.

I slowly learned about what was later called "cultural hegemony," but at the time I was barely aware of such things as the exploitation of black musicians by white producers and record companies, and I had no idea that white scholars were also exploiting black folk, that, in fact, I was part of a process of academic exploitation. Even after I became more politically aware, I still had the tendency that white fans have of romanticizing African American culture, a more subtle form of racism than I had grown up with. In this, I was part of a much broader cultural process of the 1950s—the beatnik emulation of black hipsters that can be seen in Jack Kerouac's "wishing I were a Negro, feeling that the best the white world had offered was not enough ecstasy for me, not enough life, joy, kicks, darkness, music, not enough night" (148), and later in Norman Mailer's imagining a Negro who "subsisted for his Saturday night kicks, relinquishing the pleasures of the mind for the more obligatory pleasures of the body" (303); in Jerry Lee Lewis, Carl Perkins, and other white rockabillies' craving for black hedonism in "Drinkin' Wine Spo-Dee-O-Dee" and "Dixie Fried," and finally in the very birth of rock 'n' roll with Sam Phillips' success in finding a white man who could sing like a "nigger" (Mullen, "Hillbilly Hipsters" 79–92).

Out of this background came the young white folklorist interviewing black people for the first time. My academic knowledge of the culture had not prepared me for this kind of fieldwork. I didn't know how to talk about race with black people. In some ways, this may have been an advantage since Son Brill, Jr. Carter, and I had to work out together the way we would talk about black/white relationships.

We didn't talk directly about race at first; rather Jr. Carter told a series of obscene jokes—the country bumpkin who doesn't know about modern toilets, the man who complains about the size of his wife's vagina, the man who is worn out from sexual intercourse with an insatiable woman, a boy having intercourse with his grandmother, and the man looking for crabs in a town called My Ass, Florida. The first joke he told established the tone.

"Say that guy left from Georgia, going to New York. He had never used the bathroom on the train before, so he asked the conductor if he could go to take a crap, you know. The bathroom—the conductor told him, 'You can go right back in there and use that room right in there.' He went in there and the lights was off. So he pulled his pants down and sat down, and the bowl was real cold, you know. So he jumped up and reached up and tipped the light on, you know. So he say, 'Damn, my mama ain't never let me shit in her bread pan before.'" Brill chuckled. "So he saw the window heisted, backed up there and sticks his ass out the window, you know, and started shitting. So after awhile, they passed by the street, and there was men scooping up the sidewalk with a shovel; they saw that ass out the window, and they went to whipping him with that shovel, you know. So when he came back, the conductor say, 'How you find the shitting?' He say, 'I find it successful, but that electric asswiper you got gonna kill somebody yet.'" Brill and I laughed.

Jr. Carter told this story first because he assumed that Brill and I shared certain attitudes with him—a modern urban perspective and an awareness of the country bumpkin stereotype. Jokes of this nature are often told among white and black storytellers who are members of groups freshly removed from the country. My parents both grew up in rural environments, and Jr. Carter's and Son Brill's probably did too. We could share in our superior status as we laughed at the ignorance of the bumpkin. Race was not mentioned directly in the story, but the assumption might have been made that the man on the train was black. In which case, this could be part of the minstrel stereotype, and Jr. Carter was laughing with a white man about the antics of a black bumpkin, thus making the storyteller superior to the racial stereotype.

Another early story Jr. Carter told also had an implied racial stereotype in it.

"Said, uh, one time a man had a mule, you know, a pretty mule way back there in the olden days with a saddle on him, you know. He had the mule trained, you know, ever time you goose him in the side the mule would break wind, you know, phhht. A woman standing on the corner, says, 'Hey. Give me a ride to town.' He say, 'I don't mind getting you to town, but I got a deal.' She said, 'What is it?' 'Ever time my mule break wind,' said, 'we gotta stop and fuck.'" Brill chuckled at this point. "She says, 'Okay, okay.' So they went on down the road a little bit, and he hit the mule on the side, you know, and the mule say, 'Phhht.' 'Whoa! Fuck time!'" I laughed then. "He stopped and him and her fucked, you know. Goddamn, really giving it good to the woman, you know. They went on up a little further, about another mile or two, he goosed the mule in the damn side, and the mule hauled off and farted again. 'Phoooo.'" Brill chuckled again. "'Whoa, fuck time!' And he gave that woman a good fucking that time. Got on the mule and started on back to town. So she saw what he did. She goosed the mule in the side, and the mule broke wind. Say, 'Hey, your mule done broke wind.' 'Get up, mule, go on into town.' After awhile they got in there by a puddle of water, you know, where it was cool and a lot of trees. Hauled off and goosed the mule in the side. Said, 'Hey, mister, your mule done broke wind. Time for us to fuck.' He said, 'I wouldn't give a goddamn if that mule shit, I'm going to town.'" All three of us laughed.

Roger Abrahams says of this story, "This picture of women as sexual creatures is not simply one projected into expressive lore. To the contrary, the image of the sexually demanding woman arises from real situations which the men themselves see as taxing" (*Positively Black* 115). The story may be culture specific in the gender roles it portrays, but it is also cross cultural: both black and white men have the insatiable woman stereotype as part of their expressive lore. Jr. Carter, Son Brill, and I were interacting on the basis of shared stereotypes and of common experience with women. This was partly based on a sexist stereotype and partly on an admission on the part of men that they cannot keep up with a woman's normal sexual desire.

Some of the jokes Carter told were indirectly about race since they projected certain stereotypes about black men and women, but they also established a masculine bond between the three of us that temporarily transcended race. I didn't recognize what was happening at the time, since I had brought my own sexist attitudes to the situation. My education in feminism was not to begin for another couple of years, but from the perspective of the 1990s I now see the irony of momentarily displacing racism with sexism. We were all laughing together at this locker room humor even though segregation would not allow us to share the same locker room. We came together as men laughing at women as sex objects. This sexist process actually enabled us to establish a rapport which made it easier to talk about race later.

The subject of race came up as a result of talking about the pogie fishing industry which in Sabine Pass was all black, from the crews to the captains. I asked, "How did that come about, that it's all Negro?" Son Brill replied: "Well, [six second pause], most of that is [seven second pause] from uhh, I would say, getting along, one part, it's hard to mix uhh [Carter agrees "Um umm" at this point as if he knows what Brill is going to say and wants to encourage him to mention race directly] colored captain, white captain." I interjected, "Yeah," also to help him talk about something that is difficult for a black man and white man to talk about. Clearly, Brill was hesitant to talk about race directly; before he did there were long pauses, false starts, and formulaic phrases. A few minutes later in bringing up another aspect of racism, he did it again: "I would say, I'll tell you something else now [four second pause], believe it or not [five second pause before he mentions an example of racism]." As an elderly southern black man from a segregated society in 1967, Brill may have been talking directly about race with a white person for the first time, and this was certainly the first time I had done so, which helps to explain our hesitance.

Captain Brill also talked hesitantly about racism within the black community, and Carter was again in agreement with what he said. Brill told me, "I can take a crew of men and you could take one. I hire a crew of colored men and you hire a crew. They work for you better than they would work for me." Carter agreed, "They would." I asked, "Why is that?" And Brill replied, "Well, I don't know, but they will." Carter again agreed, "They will. They will." Brill's point here was about the racism of black against black, the acceptance of the oppressor's racist stereotype of the black man as incompetent for leadership positions. Carter was supportive, encouraging, and in emphatic agreement with Brill when Brill started to talk about race, establishing solidarity between two black men as they explained their attitudes toward race to a white stranger. They were attempting to educate a white person about the intricacies of race within the black community.

Even after several minutes of talking about race, there was still indirection in the discourse. Carter and I talked about "it," whites and blacks working together, without ever saying the words "integration" or "segregation." Instead of segregation, I said "all colored," and they used "mixed up, white and colored" for integration. We kept the discussion personal and occupational, not acknowledging the political implications. I said "Negro" first, then they said "colored," and we settled on "colored" as the agreed upon term. Folklorist and informants were both feeling their way around what they all realized was a sensitive subject in a racist society. We negotiated the language to be used. On those rare occasions when blacks and whites talked about race in the Old South, this was probably the nature of the discourse. Son Brill, Jr. Carter, and I were engaging in and extending a tradition.

Our discussion of race gradually shifted from deference on Brill's part to a stated recognition of agreement. Brill said, "If I was captain of this boat and was to hire a white chief, why, we wouldn't get along," suggesting that because of white racism, a white chief would not take orders from a black captain, but he never said directly that racism was the cause. When he did seem about to explain this behavior as racism, he hesitated and backed off: "That's everywhere. You see [four-second pause], it's just something, I don't know, it just won't work." I stated it more directly, "Is it that the white man doesn't want to work for the colored man?" Brill responded, "I would say that." Except that he didn't say it, he waited for the white man to say it. As a white person, I was in the position of power, and Brill and Carter deferred to that power; they accommodated themselves to the white interviewer and got their points across indirectly. Finally, Brill did state it, "He don't want to take orders, I would say." He then said something that brought us together in agreement: "*You know as well as I do* that a lot of mens don't want to do this" [emphasis added]. "You know as well as I do" suggested not only agreement but also an attempt on Brill's part to move the discussion to another more honest and direct level.

After all this discussion of race, Brill revealed the deeper reasons for pogie fishing boats having all black crews and captains. He explained the mechanisms an oppressed people must use to get some economic advantage: "Understand me now, a whole lot easier for a colored man to make a captain in a way than it was for a white man. White man would—the fishermen were all Negro, just about. If you was to come on this boat as a captain, and we's all colored on here, why we say, 'We ain't going to learn him nothing.'" Carter agreed, "Unn uhh." "You couldn't make it." Carter said, "No." "You'd probably be on here a couple of weeks, and man they'd put you off because you couldn't produce. Therefore the colored man had a better chance . . . . Otherwise, we never would have had no Negro captains." Carter's interjections indicated that he was aware of these mechanisms and agreed with the need for them. This open discussion of strategies of the oppressed with a representative of the oppressor came only after hesitations, indirections, and careful negotiations about appropriate language, and only after they were sure that I was sympathetic to their position.

After he told me of the in-group mechanisms to get work, I indicated my support by saying, "Sounds fair enough though," and laughed. Brill continued with other incidents of racism in his occupation, "That's right. I know the time right aboard these boats, [four second pause] colored man wasn't allowed on the bridge." Carter asked, "Wasn't?" And Brill said, "No sir. He didn't come up on the bridge." I said, "They carried their prejudices out to sea with them." Brill said, "That's right." I said, "That's bad. But now you're running them." Brill agreed, "Oh yeah. Yeah. The highest position a colored man could get 'board these boats was dry boat. You see that little boat sitting on the back of the 'Sandy Hook'? That little boat. That was about as high as he could get, in that little boat. That's the highest position he could hold, dry boat." Brill's image of "that little boat," repeated three times, became a visual metaphor for the racist attempts to deny blacks equal opportunity to advance in their chosen occupation. We were sitting on a boat that dwarfed the small dry boat, signifying both white power and Brill's success in overcoming it.

In order to indicate my support of Brill's point and to make it clear to him that I was not a racist, I told him and Carter about working for and taking orders from a black man whom I respected. By talking about my experience working with black men in New Jersey, I was attempting to establish my white liberal credentials and to distance myself from southern white racism, and this did seem to open up the discussion to more political concerns. Brill then mentioned his own white boss in a way that suggested it was a parallel situation. "I know what you mean. Just like our boss." However, it soon became clear that his boss was a racist, and that the case was entirely different for a black man with a white boss. "Now, uh, I was telling him the other day. He like to raise a lot of hell, you know, when he's talking to you . . . . And he talked to me just like he would, you know, to the boys or something. He—this kinda old stuff, off the wall. And I talk to him just like he is the boss." He was critical of his white boss, but again in an indirect way, characterizing his abusive speech as, "He like to raise a lot of hell," and "This kinda old stuff, off the wall."

As a younger man who grew up in the generation of the civil rights movement, Jr. Carter was able to express his feelings about race more directly than Son Brill. He made the conversation more explicit when he said, "Now you take just like up in Carolina, they had that thing about discrimination up there. What they thought up there, they wanted, the colored boys wanted to marry the white girls, but that wasn't it. What they wanted was the equal—if you do a job, and you get paid, and if I'm colored if I can do the job, pay up the same money." He seemed about to use the politically charged phrase "equal rights," but instead switched to an example to make his point. Carter then called for equality: "Shucks, if I see a place out there that I want to buy me, build me a house and I worked for it, and let me spend my money. If I want to go places, I can go if it's a public place. But they don't figure that way. A lot of people figure it different." He was clearly in favor of integration in housing and public facilities, but he was still careful not to directly criticize whites, referring to them as "some people," and he still wasn't sure if I was one of those people who "figure it different."

By 1967, the civil rights movement and the ideas of Martin Luther King had become widely accepted by southern blacks, and Carter had been involved in the civil rights movement in South Carolina. "No, I told them one day, they had a big meeting up there in Carolina. I told them, 'That's all we want. If I go in there and if I can operate, or if I can fly an airplane, if I got education enough in the world and if I pass that test, let me have it. If you know more than me, you take it.' A lot of people don't see it." "A lot of people" might have included his white listener, and this formulaic phrase was a closing disclaimer, allowing his listener to express a different point of view.

The earlier telling of dirty jokes made it easier to talk about race and sex. Jr. Carter brought the subject up directly when he referred to the white stereotype of black men wanting white women, but when Brill talked about race and sex, he was extremely vague: "It's just as many colored people, I would say men, as far as the women, will never change . . . . And you couldn't make them change, as far as that part. But it feels, some people just feel like that's all they want, that's all they want, but that ain't it. No, that ain't it." Carter was able to talk about sex more directly because he was younger; Brill represented an older generation which would not feel comfortable talking about sex with a white person.

As with the discussion of race, talking about sex and race became more revealing the more we talked. Carter said, "But you take colored people now, and you take like you say 'white,' you just one color. But you take colored people—" Brill interrupted,

"And any color they want." Carter continued, "Any color you want. You can go out there and get a woman that looks just like she's white; you can get a dark, dark woman, or you can get a black woman, or you can even get a high yellow, or a red woman. All the women is out there; all you got to do is pick out one." This seems to be an early expression of the Rainbow Coalition and of the concept of "women of color" although expressed in a sexist way since the women were viewed as sex objects. Still, a definite racial pride came out: the implication was that white is bland and lacks variety.

I shifted the discussion to traditional narrative poems, toasts (Abrahams, *Deep Down* 97–172), which we had talked about earlier. I said, "Well, getting back to some more of this traditional material, you say both of you have heard the toasts that I was talking about a while ago?" Carter asked, "What ones was that?" I said, "Well, any of them." Carter said, "Any of them, yeah I've heard them." "And they tell them around here? How often do you hear them?" Carter said, "Sometimes you get with a bunch of boys." And Brill added, "Anytime just sitting around." Carter said, "Bunch of boys ain't got nothing else to do, sit down shooting the bull." After they described the usual contexts of performance, I said, "I'd like to get together with them . . . . I'd like to catch them all sometime. I'd like to get some of those toasts." And Carter began to tell a story.

"You ever, you ever hear that one about that rabbit and that lion got talking about who ruled the heaven and who ruled the earth? Er ah, say the rabbit told the lion one time said, 'Brother Lion,' said, 'God rule the heaven and man rule the earth.' Brother Lion told him, 'that's shit!' He say, 'God rule the heaven and I rule earth.' So the rabbit told the lion, said, 'I'm gonna let you meet man.' So that Sunday morning, they went out. Rabbit went by and picked the lion up, told him, 'Come on, let's go meet man,' you know. So they left going on down the road. And after awhile they met a little boy rolling a hoop along. Lion broke at him, you know. Rabbit told him, 'No, no, Brother Lion,' say, 'That *will be* man.' 'God damn I thought that was man!' They went up the road a little bit further, and there's a old fella, you know, cutting up wood on the woodpile with an axe. He broke at him. The rabbit said, 'No, no, said, That *have been* man!'. They went on down the road a little further, say they met a man on a horse with a Winchester rifle and a forty-five on his side and big bull whip. So the rabbit say, 'Now damn if that ain't man there!.' So the old lion squared off and made a pass at him. Say that man went to shooting him in the face with that bull whip, and when he turnt 'round he went to shooting him in the ass with that damn Winchester. Say that damn rabbit asked that lion, said, 'Did you meet man?' He says, 'You goddamn right!' He said, 'I ain't never seen the lightnin' so fast in my face and thunder in my ass in all my damn life!" Brill and I laughed. "Said, 'If you think I'm lying, take a glimpse at my ass when I pass.'" We laughed some more. "He had fucked him up" (Aarne, AT 157 "Learning to Fear Men"; Dorson, Tale #18 "King Beast of the Forest Meets Man").

Jr. Carter took my interest in traditional stories as an invitation to tell one, in this case not a toast, but a related genre, the animal tale. Since there are a number of toasts about animals, "The Signifying Monkey" being the most widespread, the story of the rabbit and the lion was a logical choice to tell. I assume that Jr. Carter did not perform the rhymed metrical toasts, but this story was probably the closest to a toast in his repertoire. There was another reason for telling this tale: it fit into the context of the preceding discussion about race. Within the African American tradition, animal tales are often symbolic stories about race relations. Jr. Carter was demonstrating his abilities as a storyteller and at the same time continuing our discussion of race.

Unfortunately, I have not had the opportunity to interview Jr. Carter again to determine what his interpretation of the story is, but I have worked out a possible interpretation based on the text, the interview context, and knowledge of African American folk culture. Roger Abrahams has influenced my interpretation of the story since he was one of my professors at the University of Texas while I was conducting this field research. His book *Deep Down in the Jungle* and a seminar I had with him had a profound influence on my view of African American folklore. I gave him transcriptions of Jr. Carter's stories, and he used several of them in another book *Positively Black*. He says of the rabbit and lion story, "This is a parable of accommodation, not the sort of story one therefore finds among the young men; but, like the newer stories, it talks in terms of learning to live with fear and of defining one's relations with others in terms of power" (*Positively* 50). I must have incorrectly attributed the storyteller's age when I gave Roger the transcriptions since Jr. Carter was a young man when he told the story. Roger's point is still valid, I think; a young black man in Texas in 1967 could still be an accommodationist, but the situation was actually more complex when seen in the context of the rest of the interview, including the dynamics of interaction between storyteller and folklorist.

Roger says that the man on the horse is the "white man-boss," and I agree. In terms of the previous discussion with Brill and Carter, the man on the horse is also Brill's racist boss in the pogie fishery, and the "old heads" in South Carolina who do not understand Carter's call for equality; "The Man" is also me, the white folklorist in the position of power to collect, transcribe, and present to the public the words of the two black men, to represent them to the world. There is potential for oppression in this situation: the fieldworker can become the "schoolteacher" figure of Toni Morrison's *Beloved*, a social scientist who uses his research materials to reinforce racist stereotypes. I like to think that I have not abused the power of that position in my own fieldwork and publication. Brill and Carter may not have known the intricacies of the academic process, but they did know that I was a potential interpreter of their culture.

Here, then, is my interpretation of the story, recognizing that meanings are multiple and fluid, that my understanding will not be the same as the storyteller's, and that his may have changed as much as mine over the years. From a historical perspective, the lion during slavery times could be thought of as the young African prince, the slave newly arrived from Africa who does not yet realize the power of the white man and the consequences of confronting him. In that case, the man on the horse has all the characteristics of the white overseer on the plantation. In the late 1960s, the lion could be the young militant black who thinks he can win in a confrontation with white authorities—the police, highway patrol, or national guard. The rabbit then becomes the older, more experienced black man, the accommodationist, who uses trickery and indirection in dealing with whites, who always wears "the mask that grins and lies." His job is to teach the lion a lesson by tricking him into a direct confrontation with "The Man," and, of course, the outcome of the story proves the accommodationist point of view.

Is the storyteller, then, himself an accommodationist? Again, the context of the interview, including the story he told next, suggests a more complex role for Jr. Carter. He had already established his political stance as an integrationist, not just in word but in deed, having taken part in civil rights meetings in South Carolina. We cannot, then, take the attitude expressed in the story as a direct representation of the storyteller's politics. Throughout our discussion, Jr. Carter had directly expressed a more militant attitude than the older Son Brill, but he still recognized the need to disguise his true feelings and to express them indirectly at times, depending on the circumstances. He wore many masks and could be an accommodationist if the situation called for it. The rabbit and lion story more clearly expressed Captain Brill's point of view, and Jr. Carter could have been telling it for him, respectfully supporting the older man as he had done throughout the interview. The story, then, is about all three of us: the man on the horse is me, the rabbit is Son Brill, and the lion is Jr. Carter, defeated here but ready to fight, in different circumstances, another day.

As soon as Carter finished the rabbit and lion story, he launched into another one without a pause, insuring that he would maintain the floor. This story is thematically related to and comments on the previous one.

"Say that colored fella going on down to Georgia going to Baltimore, some way, you know, down that highway down there, said, ain't got no trees, you know, and you can't shit on the highway, you know. So he had to shit, boy! So, he shit, and he had a big old straw hat on. So he covered that shit up. He saw the highway patrolman coming. Throwed the hat on top of that shit, covered it up, you know. He were holding it. So the patrolman come up there and say, 'Hey!' Say, 'What you got underneath that hat?' Says, 'Boys, I've caught one of the fastest son of a bitches you ever seen in your goddamn life!' He said, 'Let me see.' He said, 'No, no, no.' Says, 'He's faster than your eye can see.' He said, 'Damn if I ain't got to see it!' He said, 'No sir!' Say, 'I can't let you get underneath a here,' say, 'he'll get away.' Say 'I just caught him in my hat.'" Brill chuckled here. "So the patrolman said, 'Goddamn if I ain't gonna see.' So he, he reached down there and grabbed his hat up, and stuck his hand underneath, and say he stuck it in that shit. Said, 'Goddamn, look at that!' He say, 'I told you he was a fast son of a bitch! Done shit all over your hand and gone, and you ain't seen him yet!'" Brill and I laughed. "Done shit all over his hand and gone" (Aarne, AT 1528 "Holding Down the Hat").

Jr. Carter didn't say that the highway patrolman was white, but it was understood that in Georgia in the 60s, he would have to be. By identifying the hero as a "colored fella," Carter established racial confrontation as the theme of the story. The story indicates the complex, multidimensional nature of the label accommodationist. The man who shit on the highway is like the rabbit in that he uses trickery and indirection, but he does not just stand off to the side and watch, he has been pulled into a confrontation because of segregation laws which forbid him to use any public toilet. The highway patrolman is the modern version of the man with the Winchester rifle and bull whip, the white authority who enforces the racist laws. His defeat extends the political implications of the rabbit and lion story; there is no fight, but through wit and deceit there exists the possibility of overcoming fear in the neverending struggle for power.

The "colored man" of the story is someone that both Jr. Carter and Son Brill can identity with. This is the Son Brill who used deceit to undermine white captains in order to become a captain himself. This is the Jr. Carter who wants equal access to public facilities: "If I want to go places, I can go if it's a public place." The accommodationist role includes the indirection and deceit of the trickster and the protest of the bad man; it is a pragmatic role for survival and change. If the last two stories are related and both reflect the immediate circumstances of the interview, then I have to recognize myself in the highway patrolman. Even though I was a supporter of the civil rights movement, I was still part of the white southern power structure that supported the police in their enforcement of racist laws.

Jr. Carter had talked and told stories until he had me laughing at my own race; he tricked me as surely as the colored man tricked the highway patrolman. But in this case, the manipulation was part of a strategy to get me to agree with his point of view: the three of us laughed together at the predicament of the white man. From our first tentative discussion of race, we moved to an understanding and an agreement expressed through storytelling, recognizing that beyond our little circle racism still prevailed.

When a black folklorist interviews a black storyteller, there is an assumption of agreement on certain issues from the beginning; they don't have to go through the same process of establishing rapport that Son Brill, Jr. Carter, and I did. For example, Paulette Cross was a black student at Indiana University when she tape recorded Ronald Tylor telling jokes in 1968, one year after my fieldwork on the Gulf Coast. The political climate was similar in the two years, but Ronald Tylor and Jr. Carter were very different black men, and the relationship of fieldworker and informant was vastly different. Tylor was a twenty-three-year-old graduate student from Milwaukee, and he and Cross appear to have known each other for some time. Their discussion of race was direct from the beginning.

C: Why do you usually tell [the jokes] and where?
T: I tell jokes about white people cause they're funny. I tell 'em with the fellas . . . .
C: Because white people are funny or because the jokes are funny?
T: Well, because number 1, white people are funny and number 2, because the jokes are funny . . . . If you can laugh at someone then you don't have to hate 'em so much.
C: Oh I see; I take it that you don't particularly care for them?
T: For whom?
C: White people.
T: Oh I don't mind them. They're negligible you know . . . .
C: Why have you gotten so wrapped up in this black nationalist movement? Oh I don't really mean wrapped up—
T: Oh, I'm definitely wrapped up in it. That's a good statement. Well, because I don't believe we're going to get anything

> through white America. I don't believe that we're going to get anything unless we can address the power structure in America as a group of people, you know (652–53).

The first joke Tylor told directly expressed his political views, and it is related to the last two stories that Jr. Carter told.

"There's this black cat from the north, ya know. He's a bad nigga, and went down to the south, driving his white Eldorado Cadillac, and he drove into this gas station in southern Indiana. Right in front of him was another black man in an old beat-up pick-up truck. And the filling station attendant walked out, and he said, 'Whatcha want boy?' And the black cat in the pick-up truck said, 'Uh, gimme a dolla wortha regula' And the station attendant said, 'Gimmie a dolla's worth of regula, what?' The black man said, 'Ah uh, please mista Charlie.' So mista Charlie gave him a dolla's worth of regula and charged him a dolla fifty and said, 'Naw git on outa heah, boy.' So the black cat in the pick-up left.

"So then the nigga from the north, he pulls up in this white Eldorado Cadillac, in his sharkskin suit, silk socks, Stetson hat, Stacy Adams shoes, just clean, you know. So the nigga reaches over and pushes a button and the window slides down a little bit, and the white cat say, 'Whaddyah want, boy?' And the nigga say, 'Fill it up.' And the white boy say, 'Fill it up, what?' He say, 'Fill it up, man, I ain't got all day. Come on, fill it up.' The white boy say, "Fill it up, what?' 'With gas, fool. Come on I ain't got all day.'

So the white boy went inside the filling station, and he got his rifle, and he came back out with his rifle, and he looked dead in the nigga's eye, and he pointed over at a bush about 200 yards away, and he said, 'Nigga, see that fly on that bush 200 yards away?' And the nigga say, 'Yea, I see it.' So the white boy took the rifle, aimed and fired, and he killed his fly without touching the bush, and he looked back at the nigga waitin for the nigga to respond with, 'If you please, mista Charlie.'

"But instead the nigga pushed this button and rolled the window all the way down and leaned over and pushed a button to the glove compartment, and pulled out a saucer. And he said, 'Hold that, boy,' to the white cat, and he reached over to his glove compartment and pulled out an apple, and he reached in his inside coat pocket, and he pulled out a razor, and he threw the apple in the air, and he grabbed the razor and sliced around the air with all kinda fast beautiful motions so quick and so fast that he peeled the apple, cored the apple, and sliced it so thin in that split second with that razor that when it hit the saucer it was applesauce.

"And the white boy said, 'What, uh, what was that, uh, regular or ethyl?'" (Cross 650–51; Abrahams, *Positively* 72).

This seems to be a retelling and updating of the rabbit and lion story; all the same types are represented in the same confrontational setting. The man on the horse becomes the racist filling station attendant, the accommodating rabbit becomes the timid black man in the pick-up truck, and the lion is now the aggressive "black cat from the north." The difference, of course, is in the ending: the lion defeats the man with the rifle, and the story reinforces the need for militant confrontation and rejects the accommodationist attitude. The militant black man fulfills the white stereotype of the urban black criminal, specifically the pimp with his white cadillac, expensive clothes, and razor blade as weapon, thus inverting the image from a white negative to a black positive.

Ronald Tylor as an urban, northern, educated black man had been influenced by black intellectual movements of the late 1960s; Jr. Carter as a small town, southern, uneducated black man was a product of the civil rights movement of the late 50s and early 60s, and their stories reflect the different political contexts. Paulette Cross as a black folklore student interviewing a black friend was able to deal with the politics of race more directly than I was, and Tylor was able to express his opinions about racism more forcefully than Carter. In their case, race and culture were the common ground that overcame gender difference; whereas, for Carter, Brill, and I, common gender made it easier to talk about racial difference.

Tylor's comments support the symbolic interpretation of the story. Cross asked Tylor, "I take it that you really approved of the actions of that black cat from the north?" And Tylor replied, "Yeah, I really do. For one thing, he's the typical stereotype that whites have about city niggas, you know. They think that all any nigga wants to do is to make a little money and then spend it all on a big car, like that Cadillac. Only in the joke, it shows that that city nigga ain't so dumb after all." Later Cross asked, "What does that black man in the pick-up truck mean to you or what makes him important?" "He typifies the 'black sambo' type, you know, the old accommodating 'colored' man. He's important because he shows that there are two types of blacks in this country today, the passive 'uncle Tom' type and on the other hand you have the type of black man who isn't going to take any shit from anybody. In a way, this last type sort of fits in with my views on violence."

"What type of violence?"

"You know, organized to help the black man in this country. To help him get that white monkey off his back" (Cross 655).

Tylor knew that he had a sympathetic listener in Cross; Carter wasn't sure about his white listener and had to proceed more carefully even in expressing his less militant views. My interview with Carter and Brill took place about a year before this one, but in some ways it could have been twenty or thirty years earlier. Son Brill, Jr. Carter and I were still saying "colored" and "Negro"; the term "black" never entered our discussion.

To Ronald Tylor, Carter and Brill might both be accommodationists: ". . . there are two types of blacks in this country, the so-called colored who would prefer being called colored since it doesn't seem so close to black and more closer to being white. And then there's the black man that's proud of being black and being called black; he doesn't try to assimilate his cultural value within the mainstream of the white society by trying to be something he ain't and by demeaning his own values by attempting to replace them with something that is close to whiteness" (Cross 655). Son Brill and Jr. Carter were to some extent accommodationists, but as I pointed out earlier, this was a more complex stance than Ronald Tylor acknowledged. They did accommodate themselves to me during the interview, but both also condemned racism and called for social equality. The accommodationist role can include protest as well as deceit; wit and guile are used to defeat the white oppressor, a figure who is clearly delineated in both the accommodationist and protest stories, whether he is the overseer, the highway patrolman, or the gas station attendant.

As different as they were, both interview/storytelling situations indicated dynamic change was taking place. As Son Brill, Jr. Carter, and I interacted, we were creating new kinds of relationships between the races, and Jr. Carter's storytelling was a performance which commented on and extended those relationships. His stories, as traditional expressions, were being used as part of a process of social change, drawing on the past to reshape the present and offer hope for the future. Paulette Cross's interview with Ronald Tylor spoke more directly to the need for political change, but since Cross and Tylor were from the same community and shared certain attitudes, their interaction did not itself involve change, although Tylor, like Jr. Carter, was drawing upon traditional stories to illustrate the need for new relationships between the races.

Reflexive ethnography involves more than stepping back to observe your own field research in the past; it also involves trying to determine the social and cultural influences on the researcher in the present, recognizing subjectivity then and now. I re-read this essay and think maybe I have been too hard on myself, but that is part of the cultural and psychological baggage white southern liberals can never quite put down. I recognize myself in Andrew Hacker's statement, ". . . liberals stand in dread of black disfavor, which must be mollified by admitting to oversight or error. Rather than deny the indictment, the liberal tendency is to admit to such bias, and pledge renewed vigilance against future errors" (56). This essay has been a catalog of oversights and errors in my fieldwork of twenty-five years ago, but I think it is a productive endeavor for understanding not only what happened then but also for recognizing the continuing importance of race in fieldwork now.

From the perspective of the early 1990s, a time when issues of race are still at the center of American consciousness and racism is still a political reality, we can look back at the late sixties and see that the idealism about change in race relations of that period has not come to fruition; many racist attitudes remain the same. Just as Son Brill, Jr. Carter, and I were tentatively beginning a racial dialog, the need for dialog still exists.

Just as Ronald Tylor pointed out the need for radical change in attitudes of both blacks and whites, that need still exists. The folklorist's interview can be a microcosm of larger social issues, bringing forth not only interesting and revealing texts, but also revealing political contexts which can be better understood from a historical perspective.

References Cited

Aarne, Antti. *The Types of the Folktale: A Classification and Bibliography.* Translated and enlarged by Stith Thompson. 2nd rev. ed. Helsinki: Suomalainen Tiedeakatemia Academia Scientiarum Fennica, 1964.

Abrahams, Roger D. *Deep Down in the Jungle: Negro Narrative Folklore from the Streets of Philadelphia.* Rev. ed. Chicago: Aldine, 1970a.

———. *Positively Black.* Englewood Cliffs, N.J.: Prentice-Hall, 1970b.

Clifford, James and George E. Marcus, eds. *Writing Culture: The Poetics and Politics of Ethnography.* Berkeley: Univ. of California Press, 1986.

Cross, Paulette. "Jokes and Black Consciousness: A Collection with Interviews." In *Mother Wit From the Laughing Barrel: Readings in the Interpretation of Afro-American Folklore,* Alan Dundes, ed. Englewood Cliffs N.J.: Prentice-Hall, 1973.

Dorson, Richard M. *American Negro Folktales.* Greenwich, Conn.: Fawcett Books, 1967.

Hacker, Andrew. *Two Nations: Black and White, Separate, Hostile, Unequal.* New York: Scribner's, 1992.

Kerouac, Jack. *On the Road.* New York: New American Library, 1957.

Mailer, Norman. "The White Negro." In *Advertisements for Myself.* Rpt. 1981. New York: Random House,1959.

Mullen, Patrick B. *I Heard the Old Fishermen Say: Folklore of the Texas Gulf Coast.* Austin: Univ. of Texas Press. Rpt. 1988. Logan: Utah State Univ. Press, 1978.

———. "Hillbilly Hipsters of the 1950s: The Romance of Rockabilly." *The Southern Quarterly* 22, no.3, 1984.

Instruments for a string band (Courtesy of F. E. Abernethy)

15

Longino Guerrero's Corrido on J. Frank Dobie

★

F. E. Abernethy

THE TEXAS FOLKLORE SOCIETY MET AT THE DRISKILL HOTEL IN Austin on April 16–17, 1965. This was a memorable meeting for me because I was president of the Society that year. My family and I were accorded the Jim Hogg Suite in honor of the occasion, and the children were much impressed. I remember the Saturday morning session very well because John O. West gave a paper on Jack Thorp and John Lomax that indicated that the latter had borrowed significantly from the former. John Lomax, Jr., was in the audience, and everybody got real quiet during the reading. Academic objectivity was maintained, however and fortunately, and no enmities were incurred.

The other thing I remember about that session was that Américo Paredes was accompanied by two of his corrido singing friends, Longino (Lonnie) Guerrero and Frank Rios. Américo gave brief introductory remarks on the corrido as a continuing and modern folk tradition and introduced the two musicians. They concluded the Saturday morning session singing two of Lonnie's latest corridos, "La Tragedia del Presidente Kennedy" and "El Corrido de J. Frank Dobie," also called "Homenaje a J. Frank Dobie." Kennedy had been assassinated in 1963 and Dobie had died in 1964, so these events were still fresh on members' minds.

During the 1960s Lonnie Guerrero wrote and recorded thirty-five songs. He continued his work in music, and in 1983, when he was sixty-seven years old, was inducted into the Tejano Music Hall of Fame as a singer and composer.

The Frank Dobie corrido was not commercially recorded in 1965 but was taped and deposited in the folklore archives at the

University. The tape has since disappeared, but I was able to locate Lonnie through Américo. Lonnie was seventy-four when I wrote him in 1991, and he was still picking and singing. He wrote on November 26, 1991, that he had read Dobie's stories of the Mexican border and wrote the corrido, with some help from Frank Rios, as a memorial to Dobie. Lonnie Guerrero very graciously allowed the Society to use his words and music, transcribed by Dan Beaty, in this publication.

El Corrido de J. Frank Dobie
by Longino Guerrero

Año del sesenta y cuatro, desde la altura del cielo,
Se recibio la noticia que conmovia al pueblo.
Herido de sentimiento, y sollozando he venido
Porque murio en Austin, Texas, un escritor conocido.

Refrain:
Una oracion en su nombre, pro el descanso de su alma;
Ha muerto Francisco Dobie, un hombre de mucha fama,
Un escritor renombrado por su lectura divina,
Y su cancion favorita fue siempre "La Golondrina."

Era costumbre de Dobie andar por los chaparrales,
Y conoció las espinas del mezquite y los nopales.
Entre los montes y valles su vida habia pasado
Fue partidario del campo como hijo de Coronado.

De muchos pueblos de Texas, el conoció los paisajes,
Y anduvo en muchas haciendas del valle del Rio Grande.
Allá en su rancho bonito, que le nombraba El Paisano,
Alli escribio muchos libros recordando al Mexicano estribillo.

Refrain:
En sus novelas y hazañas el conocio mucha historia,
Desde la flor de la tuna, hasta la flor de magnolia;
Los Hijos de Coronado tendre mos en la memoria
Gratos recuerdos de un sabio, que semerece la gloria.
En el panteon del estado situado en la capital
Alli descansan los rostos del escritor inmortal.

Lonnie Guerrero, Austin, maker of corridos (Courtesy Longino Guerrero)

The Corrido for J. Frank Dobie
by Longino Guerrero

In nineteen hundred and sixty-four, from Heaven on high
There came the news that deeply moved everyone.
Full of sorrow, sobbing have I come
Because in Austin, Texas, a well known author has died.

Refrain:
Say a prayer in his name, for the repose of his soul;
Francisco Dobie is dead, a man of great renown,
A writer who was famous for his divine learning,
And his favorite song was "La Golondrina."

It was Dobie's custom to go about in the chaparral,
He was acquainted with the thorns of mesquite and cactus.
Among mountains and valleys he spent his life;
He loved the open country like a son of Coronado.

He knew the features of many Texas towns,
And he visited many haciendas in the Rio Grande Valley.
Down on his pretty ranch, which he called "El Paisano,"
He wrote many books in remembrance of the Mexican.

Refrain:
In his novels and his deeds he saw much history,
From the flower of the prickly pear to the magnolia
blossom;
We children of Coronado will keep in our memory
Pleasant recollections of this wise man who well deserves
his place in Glory.
In the state cemetery, located in the Capital,
There lie the remains of the immortal writer.

16

Peripatetic Proselytizing

★

Julia Whitsitt

MANY FUNDAMENTALIST CHRISTIANS NO LONGER DELIBERATELY separate themselves from the corrupt and decadent world as "saving remnants." Instead, they try to enter the mainstream of society and establish themselves as members of the secular middle class. Such social and economic—not to mention spiritual—integration carries with it inevitable stresses as new and old value systems strive to reach an uneasy accommodation.

During the past nine years, my spouse and I have studied the phenomenon of religious enthusiasts in an aggressively materialistic, upwardly mobile context by collecting their own messages to the world at large. These messages can be found on their bumper stickers. We have copied, with notations of graphic and typographical design where significant, some 550 different examples of religious roadway rhetoric, most within a few miles of Lubbock, Texas. The stickers express in miniature the religious fundamentalists' effort to join a dominant secular culture without entirely surrendering to it.

For fundamentalists seeking membership in the middle class, the automobile—or pickup truck—constitutes an icon uniquely suited to mediating the tensions between theological concerns and socio-economic mobility. Exhorted by religious tenets to proselytize, yet uneasy about the economic and social class implications of doing so, eager to live out the materialistic American dream, yet bombarded continually with otherworldly theology, they resolve these contradictions in part by affixing religiously oriented bumper stickers to their cars or trucks.

Despite variations among specific types of stickers, several common paradoxes underlie the texts of the stickers we have observed. First, almost all stickers assert an in-group versus out-group mentality (e.g. "Experience Jesus," "Our God Reigns"). The message invites the reader to join the in-group and thus increase its clout in the secular world. Yet such an invitation, communicated by means of a sticker on an automobile, precludes face-to-face contact with the potential new member. This enables the sticker bearer to enjoy the spiritual rewards of preaching to the heathen without the potentially embarrassing need to stand on a street corner or engage in conversation with a hostile or satirical prospect.

Secondly, stickers on automobiles are what we might call anonymously assertive, as are automobiles themselves, which are creations of mass production yet regarded as uniquely expressive possessions by their owners (as demonstrated, for instance, by the common bumper sticker "I love my truck"). To affix a religious sticker to one's automobile is to assert one's faith in a way that both does and does not make one responsible for the assertion. The stickers are mass produced in great variety, like automobiles, but because they are mass produced, and not the product of individual testimony, they carry with them no anxiety about the rightness of the message. They are displayed most while the automobile is moving on the streets, thus shielding the driver from most comments on the message of the sticker. At the same time, however, some kind of direct statement is being made, using one of the most personally resonant artifacts of everyday life. In this sense "Honk if you love Jesus" represents the epitome of the religious bumper sticker, because it places the burden of action on the observer while the driver remains the anonymous communicator of his spiritual superiority. *He* never has to honk his horn to prove anything.

Finally, many stickers try to be clever or humorous, in the tradition of what Paul Fussell in *Class* characterizes as "legible clothing." Fussell notes that for lower and middle class people, legible clothing is a way of asserting such a quality as sophistication (A "Je [heart] Paris" t-shirt, for instance, proclaims at once European travel and linguistic accomplishment.), or wit (as in the "Even Paranoids Have Real Enemies" t-shirt, which implies the ability to laugh at complex psychological terminology), without having to demonstrate either in any truly significant way. Similarly, the bumper sticker, creating what we might call "the legible automobile," can communicate cleverness, loving kindness, concern for others, and spiritual commitment without requiring much direct action toward exercising those virtues once the sticker is affixed.

Within these broad patterns, however, lies great scope for variety and inventiveness. The rhetoric of religious bumper stickers makes use of many verbal and graphic techniques, and the personalities posited by the stickers range from the sweetly brainwashed to the thunderingly prophetic. While most are what might be called purely religious, a small but significant number yoke religion to conservative politics, either in general or in reference to specific issues such as abortion or women's rights (against both), local boosterism, or America-love-it-or-leave-it patriotism. Beyond "Pray for Peace" and "If you want peace, work for justice," we have observed no stickers that could be characterized as politically moderate or liberal, although such varieties might well exist beyond the confines of the Texas Panhandle. Some stickers even allude directly to other stickers ("Tithe if You Love Jesus/Anyone Can Honk"), as religious groups continually seek to outdo their competitors.

In this short survey we will not have time to ponder all the implications of all these characteristics. Instead, we will investigate some striking examples of several major thematic genres of stickers: first, those taking political stands; second, those asserting national or local chauvinism; third, those warning the heathen of the error of their ways; fourth, several variations on the theme of assertions of the joys of being a Christian; and finally, a few with which the research team asks your help, because they have so far defied our interpretive powers. While most of our attention will be on the messages as opposed to the media, we will pay particular attention to the ways in which stickers in various categories play on traditional sayings and on contemporary secular advertising.

The issues addressed by the political stickers range from the nebulous admonition to "Vote" with a cross forming the "t" in the word, to the specificity of "Kids Need to Pray" and "American Abortion: Hitler Would Have Loved It." Interestingly enough, for at least one sticker, peacefulness and loving kindness are not essential to the Christian message: the affixer of "Three that Set Us Free: Guns, God, Guts" seems unlikely to follow the Biblical admonition to "turn the other cheek." We presume this sticker to be a statement against laws regulating firearms, and, as such, invoking divine sanction, patriotism, and macho bluster all at the same time. The ironic echo of the doctrine of the trinity in the "three" is also worthy of notice.

The specific-issue or candidate-oriented stickers are less numerous, however, than those which chauvinistically assert some special relationship between the deity and either the United States as a whole or some smaller part of it. "God Made Notre Dame #1" and "If God isn't a Longhorn, Why is the Sunset Burnt Orange?" may stand as academic examples of this genre. "God Loves Abilene and So Do We," a similarly self-congratulatory instance of local chauvinism, resembles "On the Eighth Day God Created Texas" [the word "Texas" surrounded by stars] in asking the reader to simply accept the superiority of a place rather than to take any particular stand on an issue. The stickers asserting that the entire country is somehow an especially blessed nation rely more on vague uplift—analogous to the "it's morning in America" theme of 1984 electoral fame—than on the blustering bellicosity of the local varieties. Thus, for instance: "Thy Kingdom Come in America" [top line blue, bottom line red, white background], "JerUSAlem" [letters USA highlighted in red, other letters in blue, white background], "Thank God for AMERICA" [in outline map of USA], and, of course, "Good News America/God Loves You." A few of these imply some reciprocal responsibility from a country so blessed: "America/Don't Forget to Thank God" [with flag], "Jesus Christ/America's *Only* Choice" [possibly political as well], "Blessed is the Nation/Whose God is the Lord," and "America/Handle with Prayer." On this theme, a final example in a minor key is "God Bless America/and Please Hurry."

As these last few examples suggest, a major function of the bumper sticker is to warn the reader of the consequences of not agreeing wholeheartedly with whatever political/religious stance the affixer of the sticker holds. Many stickers in this third group seek to show the heathen the error of their ways, often through striking plays on traditional or current phrases and concepts. For instance: "Our Only Means of Survival/Is REVIVAL," "Without Jesus/You Haven't Got A Prayer," "READ THE BIBLE/It'll Scare the *Hell* Out of You," and "SALVATION/Don't Leave Home Without It." A subset of this group contrasts the perfection of the unseen world with the daily hassles of this world—automotive: "God's Filling Station/Never Runs Out of Gas"; financial: "LIFE Insurance? Jesus Christ"; undergraduate: "Prepare for your finals/Read your Bible"; medical: "Jesus Still Makes/House Calls"; commercial: "Find Help Fast/The Bible Pages"; economic: "Despite Inflation,/The Wages of Sin Are/Still the Same"; culinary: "The bread of life/Never gets stale"; obituary: "Jesus for/the REST of your life" ["rest" inside a drawing of a coffin]; and even a sort of *Consumer Reports* promise: "Satisfaction Guaranteed/Jesus." In each of these, the contrast serves to remind the reader of his relatively unenlightened state if bothered by uncooperative physicians, expensive insurance premiums, stressful examinations, or the like, and also to assert the superior wisdom of the sticker-affixer, to whom (presumably) these little things are no longer worrisome.

This sense of superiority is by far the most pervasive theme of religious bumper stickers. The examples in the fourth group all emphasize the joys of belief, stressing either the superiority of the religion or the superiority of the believer. Many stickers assert the attributes of the deity or the church, often in aggressively positive terms: "No one understands . . . /Like Jesus," "Go Jesus/He's Number One" [notice the neat shift of person addressed between the first and second lines of that one], "Every Day is CHRISTmas/With Jesus," "Beautiful Things Happen/When You Pray," and the ubiquitous "I [heart] God" or Jesus or My Church or whatever. A subgroup of this type emphasizes the power of God or Jesus, functioning simultaneously as a bumper-borne paean and a reminder to the less faithful: "GOD has everything/Under control," "If God Said It/It's Guaranteed," "Just for the *Record* /God's writing it all down," "Worthy to be Praised/JESUS CHRIST," "JESUS is the reason/For the season" [a Christmas model], "When God Speaks/E. F. Hutton Listens," "GOD is GREATER/Than Any Problem I have," and "When Satan Rocks Your Boat/JESUS is your Best Anchor."

Besides asserting the power and superiority of a particular concept of God, Christ, or religious faith, many legible automobiles serve the function of legible clothing by directly proclaiming the superiority of the sticker-affixer. This group of messages emphasizes not the love of or praise for a deity, but the love of and praise for the palpable superiority of the believer to other mere mortals: The most modest of these is "Christians aren't perfect/ . . . just forgiven." The relative humility here, however, is the exception rather than the rule. The more egotistical messages include those positing heavenly guidance: "God is my Pilot/I'm Only the Co-Pilot," "This is a God/Squad Car"; divine athleticism: "Christian Cowboys/Eternal Winners," "Be a hunk/If You Love Jesus/Fellowship of Christian Athletes"; certainty of membership in the elect: "Redeemed by Blood," "Follow Me/I'm Not Lost," "You'd Smile Too [happy face]/If you were going to heaven"; downright assertion of personal perfection: "I believe in miracles/I am one," "Jesus Put Me/All Together," "Jesus is the/reason for/my life," "Jesus Is My/Best Friend," "Christ Changed/My Life," and, in a marvelous example of the perils of clause placement, "I Accepted Jesus/He Forgave Me."

This last example, treading close as it does to the boundaries between intelligibility and unintelligibility, brings us to our last category and to the research and analysis that remain to be done: some religious bumper stickers just do not seem to make sense. For instance, "Christians Without Crosses/Are Swords Without Blades," obviously intends a metaphorical connection between Christians and swords, crosses and blades, yet the parallelism seems somewhat deficient on both the literal and the figurative levels. "W.O.W./The Word over the World" seems to assume a context of which we are ignorant—is it an allusion to a Bible verse, to the Woodmen of the World organization, or to some televangelist's catch phrase? "God Made Man/Smith and Wesson/Made Them Equal" suffers not only from a problem with pronoun number (what is the antecedent of "them"?) but also from an apparent implication that the work of the Lord was deficient until repaired by the invention of long-distance murder by firearm, yet exactly what we are to believe or do remains mysterious. And, finally, to close this list of hermeneutical horrors, what are we to make of "Not Only Cars Are/Recalled By Its Maker"? The mind reels.

Omitted from this survey, for reasons of time, were the flourishing genre of Spanish bumper stickers, as well as a small but significant number dealing with the "rapture" and "the mark of the beast." From even this brief and partial outline, however, several conclusions can be drawn. First, the bumper sticker takes numerous forms and fulfills numerous rhetorical purposes within the boundaries of its religious orientation: it may exhort, warn, praise, pray, self-congratulate, or baffle. Secondly, while the televangelists have left their marks on the numerous too-cute and cloyingly self-congratulatory samples (even hardened researchers such as ourselves long for the day when the small red heart no longer serves as a verb), good old-fashioned down-home images still abound. (Consider, for instance, the sticker drawn to look like a theater or football game ticket with the legend "ADMIT ONE" and below that the question, "At the PEARLY GATES/Will you have your TICKET?") Finally, the legible automobile seems here to stay, and we urge all of you to join in our continuing effort to amass a complete file of stickers.

Bibliography

Fussell, Paul. *Class.* New York: Ballantine, 1984.

Miss Ludell Ainsworth of the Spanish Bluff Road, Nacogdoches, in her slat bonnet (Courtesy of F. E. Abernethy)

17

The Sunbonnet as Folk Costume

★

Janet K. Jeffery

WHEN MY GREAT-GREAT GRANDMOTHER CHOSE TO WEAR HER sunbonnet, she was not only protecting her face from the steady beating of the sun and the whipping winds of the West, she was identifying herself as a working woman of the American frontier. As a symbol, the sunbonnet readily stamped her as a pioneer, just as the cowboy or western hat did her husband.

Clothing styles throughout the southern United States fall within three categories: elite, popular, or folk. Elite clothing is one-of-a-kind fashion, usually created for a member of the leisure class. Popular clothing can either be homemade or store-bought, but it is created and worn observing the current fashion dictates of Paris or New York.

Folk clothing, on the other hand, does not follow fashion. It is clothing dictated by its community's traditions, and it tends to remain static for decades, sometimes hundreds of years. It can, however, be a purchased, ready-made piece as well as a home-sewn garment (Yoder 309).

Folk costume identifies its wearer as a member of a certain community by placing it within an historical, regional, ethnic, or sectarian context. It also marks that person's place within that community by identifying that person's sex, age, social, and occupational status.

The sunbonnet places its traditional wearer on the nineteenth-century American frontier.

Women were wearing bonnets indoors and out as early as the Middle Ages. The Hindu word *banat,* which means woolen or broad cloth, may have inspired the old French *chapel du bonet,* or a hat made of *bonet,* a coarse cloth used for head coverings in medieval Europe (Skeat 67). However, the word "bonnet"

Mob Cap
1780–90

which evolved from *bonet* wasn't used to refer to women's and girls' head coverings until the end of the eighteenth century (Pickens 28).

In seventeenth- and eighteenth-century Colonial America, women of fashion typically wore caps which covered only their hair. The basic cap was a mobcap whose brim was a mere suggestion of ruffles or gathered frills; these brims were certainly not used to shade the face. Many headcoverings at this time were variations of mobcaps. Some had a ruffle made from the same fabric, others had two lappets hanging in the back, still others had both ruffles and the two lappets (Worrell, *Early American Costume* 55, 67, 69, 73). To protect their skin from the effects of the sun, Southern upper-class women carried parasols.

By the 1750s, toward the end of the Colonial Period, thousands of immigrants were leaving Ireland, England, and Germany for the United States. Once the American Revolution was over in 1783, the empty regions west of the Appalachians lured these emigrants through the Cumberland Gap to the western frontiers. The female settlers walking those trails wore what they called a bonnet, but it was still similar to the brimless mobcap popular during the American Revolution. They also they tied straw hats or bandanas on their heads (Worrell, *Early American Costume* 130).

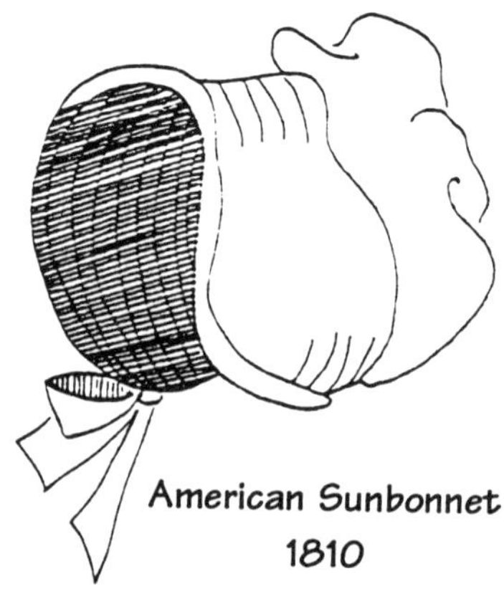

American Sunbonnet
1810

If our pioneer forebearers in the eighteenth century were

happily wearing non-protecting caps, where did the sunbonnet—this encapsulating bonnet that protected not only the hair but the face and upper shoulders as well—come from?

The American sunbonnet, part of a working costume, evolved in the lights of fireplaces and kerosene lamps. For scores of years, women exchanged patterns among themselves. No pattern company, no ladies' magazine documented printed instructions for their convenience and our edification. When posing for a portrait, a woman would remove her working clothes, posing for posterity in her very best. If she wore a bonnet at all, she chose as fashionable a chapeau as possible. Consequently, it is hard to say whether the American pioneer woman copied the work of French milliners or if, feeling a need for skin protection, she developed the sunbonnet coincidentally and in parallel.

Estelle Ausley Worrell has suggested that the American sunbonnet evolved from the mobcap. What Worrell characterized as a transition bonnet appeared between 1790 and 1800. The brim had flared and widened a bit and was like a mobcap in reverse (*Children's Costume in America*). It is just as likely that the fashionable leisure class first wore this brimmed bonnet. The frontier woman, recognizing its usefulness, copied the style. Using her homely materials, she transformed a fashionable Parisian straw bonnet into the American sunbonnet.

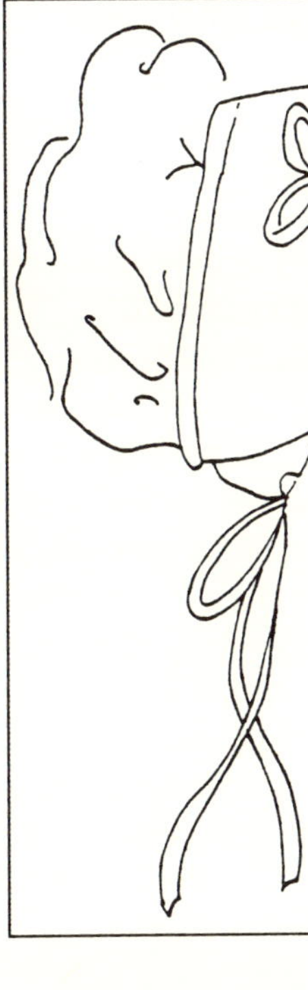
Cabriolet Bonnet 1810

In 1810, the Cabriolet bonnet, a headcovering suggesting the shape of a cabriolet carriage, whose cab had a forward or poke top, appeared on Parisian and New York streets (Pickens 28–29). It bears a striking similarity to Worrell's transition bonnet.

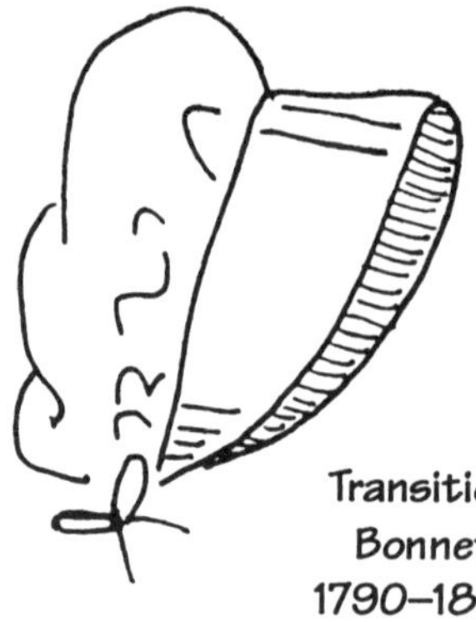

Transition Bonnet 1790–1800

By this same time, American women working in the fields or traveling on the emigrant trails were wearing the typical sunbonnet (Worrell, *Early American Costume* 130). At first white like the preceding mobcap, soon women were sewing bonnets in a variety of colors. The new American-made calico was popular, and the calico sunbonnet became strongly identified with frontier women.

Parisian milliners had no say in this bonnet's changing look. Frontier seamstresses themselves experimented with methods to make the very practical growing brim stand away from the face. They starched them and they quilted them. By the mid-nineteenth century, they were cutting up cracker or soap boxes and inserting cardboard panels to make slat bonnets. The cape in the back was long or short, depending upon the position of the neckline.

A variety of bonnets evolved and crossed this continent as emigrants fulfilled America's Manifest Destiny. Guidebooks advised women to travel with sturdy clothing, such as a calico dress without hoops and, of course, a sunbonnet. In the middle of the nineteenth century, the slat bonnet was popular on the western trails (*The Women* 28–29).

By the 1890s, sunbonnets began to cross into documented literature. Patterns began appearing in magazines. The Montgomery Ward catalog was offering ready-made bonnets for women and children (Mills 57). In the East, the bonnet appeared with bathing costumes. The sunbonnet continued to evolve in the twentieth century. Buttons were used to attach the cap to the brim and replace pulled gathers, contouring the bonnet to the head. The cape in back of many twentieth-century bonnets has all but disappeared. One recent variation which appeared during the 1980s is a bonnet which, once unfolded, can be worn as a clothespin apron.

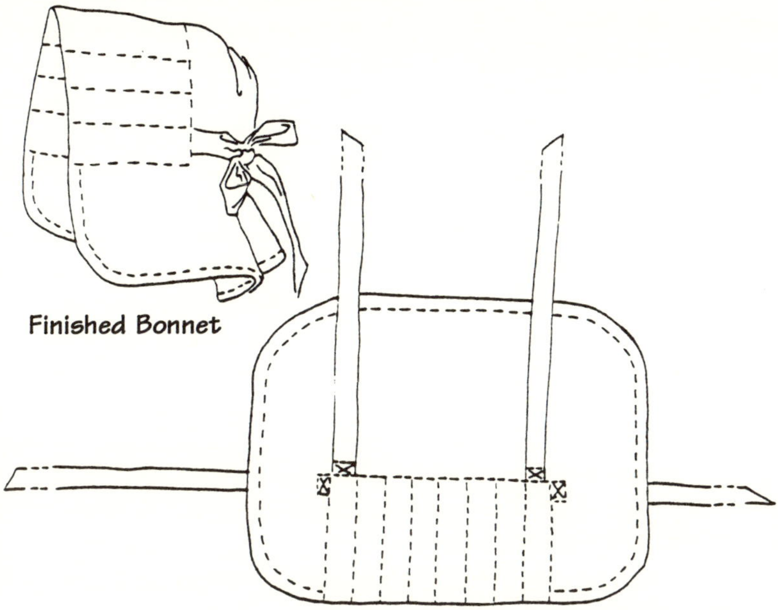

Finished Bonnet—Open View

Throughout the last two hundred years, sunbonnets have joyfully reflected the individuality of their makers. Even so, the sunbonnet traditionally has four basic parts: the crown, the brim, the ties, and, optionally, the cape hanging in the back.

The crown is the central piece, pulling together the other three parts. Its size and puffiness depend on the style. Normally, it is gathered on three sides and attaches either with stitches or buttons to the brim. The fourth side is joined to the cape.

It is the brim that gives the bonnet its basic style. Some brims begin at the back of the head and extend twelve inches to the front, reducing the crown to a minimum. Others begin halfway forward on the head and extend seven or eight inches over the eyes. The crown on this bonnet is naturally larger and puffier.

The brim is the part normally decorated, with ruffles made from the same fabric as the body being a favorite and inexpensive means to do so. Women also added eyelets, rickrack, and lace. They commonly continued the decorative motif onto the bottom edge of the cape. For a dressier bonnet, they might quilt or execute drawn work on the brim (Worrell, *Early American Costume* 54–56).

Depending on the bonnet's style, the ties (sometimes called strings) are sewn either to the brim or the crown. This element is purely functional. To be useful, a bonnet must stay secured by itself. A woman cannot work if she must constantly fiddle to hold her headgear in place.

The fourth part of the bonnet is the cape. Sometimes called a curtain, or bavolet, it hangs from the bottom of the crown over the neck. It protected the back of the neck in the days when suntan or burn was considered a scandal. The lower the neckline in the back, the longer the cape.

Sunbonnet styles fall into two basic categories: the poke bonnet and the slat bonnet.

The poke bonnet is named for the way the brim "poked" out from the crown over the face. Women used several different methods to stiffen the brim of the bonnet so that it would poke

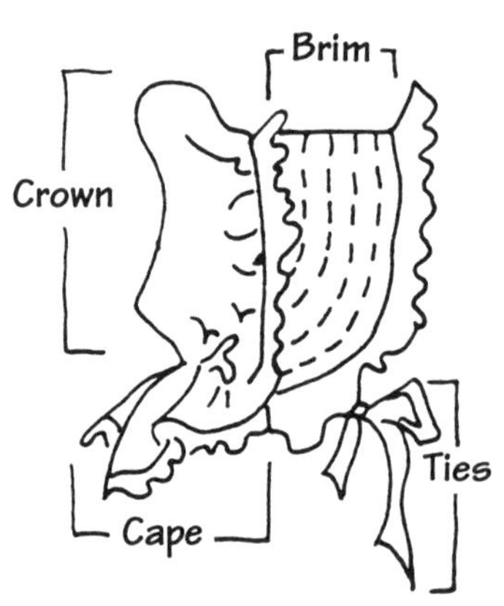

Poke Bonnet

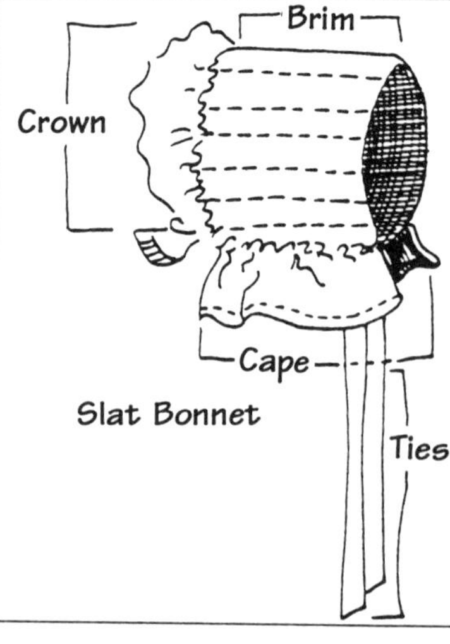

Slat Bonnet

out properly. Several layers of cloth might be sewn together or stiffened with crinoline, then stitched in various quilting designs, such as diamonds, squares, or lozenges. Some brims were simply starched heavily and ironed.

Slats of cardboard stiffening the brim give the slat bonnet its name. Sometimes called a slit bonnet, it was popular because it did not need starching. Women sewed lines of stitches parallel to one another; these formed horizontal casings at a right angle to the width of the brim. They then inserted strips of cardboard cut to fit the casings. On wash day, they could quickly remove the cardboard, wash and iron the bonnet, and finally return the slats to the brim (Mills 56).

Women used more than cardboard for stiffening. The museum collection at The Museum at Texas Tech University in Lubbock owns a bonnet stiffened with hickory slats (Mills 1988). In Arkansas, women stiffened their bonnet brims with cornshucks (Blair). The brim is edged with fabric, leaving the shucks uncovered. With this style, the brim is buttoned rather than sewn to the crown of the bonnet.

Many patterns, even those for the puffiest bonnets, can be opened up and laid flat for easy ironing.

The frugal life on the frontier dictated bonnet materials. Fabric had to be durable, easily obtained, and affordable. Depending upon the circumstances, it could be either homespun or factory spun. Once farmers quit growing and milling their own wheat, their wives had access to the cloth that sacked store-bought flour. Bonnets were normally sewn from cotton, muslin, calico, gingham, and sometimes finer fabrics such as silk, taffeta, and sateen. A bonnet could be any color, depending upon the whims of the maker and what she had on hand.

As she traveled on the emigrant trail or worked her Cross Timbers farm or High Plains ranch, our ancestress wore her bonnet for protection, to keep the wind out of her ears, the sun off her face, neck, and shoulders, and the dirt out of her hair.

The nineteenth century—when Thomas Jefferson's yeoman farmer was the backbone of the United States—was the heyday of the sunbonnet. Although the bonnet was most popular in the South, the Midwest, and Great Plains, no single American region could claim it. Rather, it stayed on the farms and followed the frontier. Once the frontier closed, the sunbonnet remained in rural pockets, especially throughout the South.

The sunbonnet has done more than protect of the heads of American farm women; it has been a useful tool in Texas politics. Just as Clayton Williams wore a cowboy hat to emphasize his connection with the Texas past in the 1990 race for governor, Ma Ferguson wore a sunbonnet during her 1924 campaign to remind the voters of her country roots (Paulissen 147).

A symbol of the white pioneering woman, the sunbonnet's very function was to preserve a woman's ethnic identity in an age when varying shades of skin color locked a person into certain social and economic strata. By contrast, black women preferred to wear turbans or bandanas.

Lillian Schlissel, discussing women on the westward journey, commented, ". . . in their steadfast clinging to ribbons and bows, to starched white aprons and petticoats, the women suggest that the frontier . . . threatened their sense of social role and sexual identity. . . . Precisely because work roles were blurred on the frontier, and because women were often called upon to do chores recognized as men's work, dress became a primary mode of asserting the delineation of the sexes" (85).

Adrietta Hixton wrote this about her journey westward: "While traveling, mother was particular about Louvina and me wearing sunbonnets and long mitts in order to protect our complexions, hair and hands. Much of the time I should like to have gone without that long bonnet poking out over my face, but mother pointed out to me some girls who did not wear bonnets and as I did not want to look as they did, I stuck to my bonnet growing used to it" (Schlissel 84).

Some bonnet styles—such as the Quaker bonnet, the Shaker bonnet, and the Dunker bonnet—identified women as members of a particular religious organization (Yoder 318). The American sunbonnet, however, was an occupational choice rather than a religious one.

Nineteenth-century Texas rancher Sally Skull, famous for wearing men's clothing, toting a sixshooter, and straddling her horse, still tied on "her slatted bonnet . . . her only bow to femininity when on the road" (Kilgore 59–71).

In *Gone With the Wind* Scarlett wore a straw bonnet to the Wilkes barbecue, and Rhett tempted her with a green, taffeta bonnet from Paris, but when the hard times came and she and her sisters worked in the cotton fields, they wore calico cloth sunbonnets.

A frontier woman liked to have a black bonnet in her wardrobe for funerals. And if she could not buy a good bonnet from a milliner, she could use her sunbonnet pattern and sew one in black taffeta or black calico. Black bonnets dominate the collection at The Museum at Texas Tech, probably because these bonnets, like fancy quilts, were set aside and rarely worn. Working bonnets, used until they fell apart, did not survive as well, leaving us with few museum pieces (Mills 1988).

Opal Harris Pittman of Bluff Dale, Texas, remembers a funeral the Harris family with its five girls attended in the early part of this century: "Mama took every one of our bonnets, and washed and ironed them so we'd be dressed for the funeral." But the Harris girls did not wear black bonnets to the funeral; their mother simply washed the ones they normally wore to school.

Because of their strong feminine identification and because they kept ordinary features hidden, sunbonnets could be coquettish. "In her [1913] autobiography," wrote Betty Mills in *Calico Chronicle,* "Mrs. [A. E.] Barr. . . described the white sunbonnets of the Texas girls as things of beauty; the very act of their removal communicated a pleasant surprise and revelation of unsuspected charm" (52).

When the sunbonnet was in its heyday, it protected females of every age from the sun and wind. Now, however, toward the end of the twentieth century, elderly women hoeing their gardens in small Texas towns are the principal wearers of the American sunbonnet. Popular fashion has not required head coverings since the 1960s, and the rest of the day's female population, save babies and little girls, are too sophisticated for such a head covering.

Like the quilt, the bonnet was the product of a true folk tradition. The pattern was normally copied from a neighbor's and adapted to one's own tastes, needs and materials at hand. A

Texas woman felt no shame in admiring a friend's bonnet, then asking to copy it. Women traced and traded patterns, cut and sewed fabric as they moved with the frontier across the continent.

Unlike the quilt, the sunbonnet has not enjoyed a resurgence of popularity or become a collector's item. Once their cultural horizons widened and economic standards improved, Texas women quickly switched from folk to popular styles. The generation of rural women born at the beginning of this century seems to be the last one willing to wear sunbonnets as they do their yard work. Bonnets sewed today appear in gift shops,

Mrs. F. A. Davenport of the Nash Community near Waxahachie, Texas, evokes rural American womanhood as she mows along her fence row in her slat sunbonnet. July 8, 1943. Photographer, Charles Brady. From the Texas Agricultural Extension Service Collection, Archives, Sterling C. Evans Library, Texas A&M University, College Station, Texas.

occasionally selling as decorative items for homes with a country motif. However much we honor our great-great grandmothers, we prefer to distance ourselves from the bonnets they wore. The sunbonnet is an article of clothing that all too well represents work that could break a body in two, fingernails ragged and black with dirt, and poverty that could push even the most devout believer to question the very nature of her universe.

Bibliography

Abbott, Shirley. *Womenfolks: Growing Up Down South.* New York: Ticknor & Fields, 1983.

Blair, Kay. Letter to the Author. 6 February 1984.

Kilgore, Dan. "Two Sixshooters and a Sunbonnet: The Story of Sally Skull." *Legendary Ladies of Texas.* Ed. Francis Edward Abernethy. Dallas: E-Heart Press, 1981.

Mills, Betty J. *Calico Chronicle.* Lubbock: Texas Tech Press, 1985.

Mills, Betty J. Personal interview. April 1988.

Paulissen, Maisie. "Pardon Me, Governor Ferguson." *Legendary Ladies of Texas.* Ed. Francis Edward Abernethy. Dallas: E-Heart Press, 1981

Pickens, Mary Brooks. *The Fashion Dictionary.* New York: Funk & Wagnalls, 1957, 1973.

Pittman, Opal Harris. Personal interview. December 1984.

Reiter, Jean Swallow. *The Women.* Alexandria, Va.: Time-Life Books, Inc., 1978

Schlissel, Lillian. *Women's Diaries of the Westward Journey.* New York: Schocken Books, 1982.

Skeat, Rev. Walter W., ed. *Etymological Dictionary of the English Language.* London: Oxford at the Clarendon Press, 1958.

Twain, Mark. *The Adventures of Huckleberry Finn.* New York: Bantom Books. 1884.

Worrell, Estelle Ansley. *Children's Costume in America 1607–1910.* New York: Charles Scribners & Sons, 1980.

———. *Early American Costume.* New York: Charles Scribners & Sons, 1975.

Yoder, Don. "Folk Costume." *Folklore and & Folklife, An Introduction.* Ed. Richard M. Dorson. Chicago: University of Chicago Press, 1972.

Note

Sketches by Janet Jeffery.

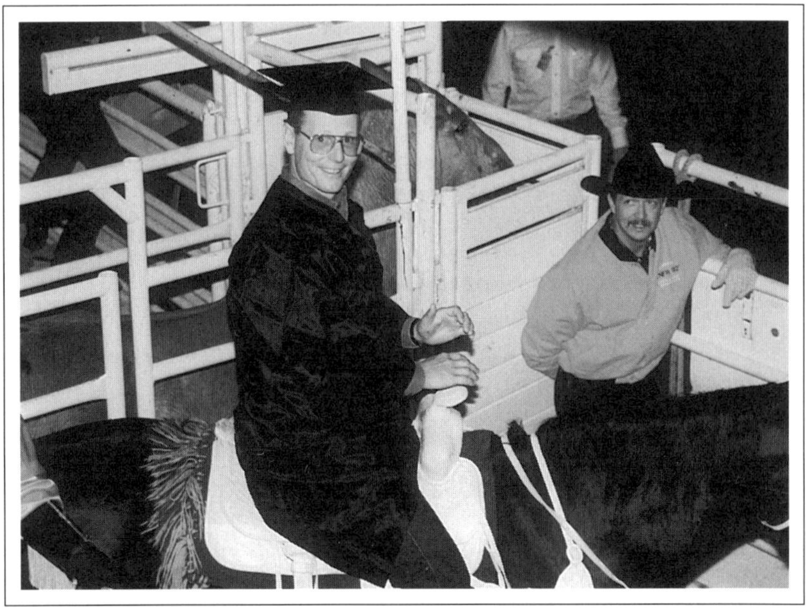

College cowboy Sonny Hansen, LaGrande, Oregon, wears a cap and gown during the grand entry at the 1992 College National Finals Rodeo to emphasize that rodeo has gone to college.

18

College Creates a New Breed of Cowboy

★

Sylvia Gann Mahoney

"I'M NOT A COWBOY; I JUST FOUND THE HAT" IS THE MESSAGE ON the bumper sticker. The hat might fool the general public, but a modern college rodeo cowboy can determine many things by looking at another cowboy's hat. He can tell the part of the country that the cowboy is from, the rodeo event that he enters, his age, and his financial status. He can look at a cowboy's clothes, his belt buckle, his horse trailer, and then listen to him talk, and he can learn more about him than he could get from a biography. He can also tell what type of cowboy this one is—whether he is a ranch cowboy, a rodeo cowboy, or the drugstore type.

He can also tell whether or not this is one of the new breed, the college cowboy. Since rodeo has been transplanted to the college campus, the college rodeo cowboy and cowgirl have added their own styles to the activity they call America's number one sport.

In collegiate rodeo the six men's events, the traditional rodeo events, offer a variety of challenges to a cowboy. In bareback bronc riding the cowboy attempts to ride a bucking horse with only one hand in a leather rigging around the horse. In saddle bronc riding, the cowboy uses a saddle. Steer wrestling adds a combination of elements. One man with his horse helps another man riding a horse to physically subdue a steer. Calf roping is a cowboy in partnership with his horse working to gain control of a calf. In team roping a man riding a horse ropes a steer's horns while another man riding a horse ropes the steer's heels. Bull riding, usually the public's favorite, is the easiest to understand and the most dangerous. It pits the cowboy against brute force.

The college cowgirls' events evolved as they invaded the cowboys' domain seeking equal status. Cowgirls started with the traditional women's event, barrel racing, a test of riding skills in a race against the clock. Cowboys often call these contestants "can chasers" and refer to a stubborn roping horse as "crazy as a barrel horse." Another college cowgirl event is goat tying. This event requires skills similar to a calf roper's skills. Riding a horse at break-neck speed, a cowgirl dismounts on the run, catches a tethered goat, throws it, and ties it like a calf roper ties his calf. College cowboys make light of the event by calling the goat tiers "nanny whammers." Pushing for equality, the cowgirls started breakaway roping. The cowgirl ropes a calf, then the rope breaks away from the saddle horn. Recently, college cowgirls crossed the gender barrier by competing as partners with men in the team roping. That is not done in professional rodeo. Roping has produced the highest compliment given to a cowgirl by a college rodeo cowboy, "She ropes like a man."

College rodeo is different from professional rodeo and from other college sports. College rodeo has teams, which is something that professional rodeo has been attempting to organize but has never found a formula that works. College rodeo is different from all other college sports in that anyone can compete at a college rodeo who is a full-time student and has a 2.0 or C grade average. Some universities enter as many as eighty contestants. The college rodeo team concept is different from other college teams, also. Before a rodeo starts, each rodeo coach chooses six men and three women to be the official rodeo teams, a men's team and a women's team. Only the points won by these designated students are counted as college team points. The points won by the other contestants who are not "on the team" are used to qualify them individually for the College National Finals Rodeo (CNFR). The top two teams in each of the eleven regions, both men's and women's, qualify for the CNFR. The top two individuals in each of the nine events in each region also qualify to compete at the CNFR.

College rodeo has some other unique differences. Universities and two-year colleges compete with one another. Also, all the contestants in a region compete at each of the ten

Each college designates three women and six men to collect points for team championships. Women compete in three all-women events: goat tying, break-away roping and barrel racing and one with men: team roping. Shown is the 1985 national champion team from Sul Ross State University. Tami Noble, left, was the first woman to win the average in team roping at the College National Finals Rodeo. Also shown, SRSU President Humphreys, Noble, Jacque Jenkins, Jinita Williams and Coach John Mahoney.

regional rodeos. For example, in the Southwest Region, of the eleven schools that compete, five are universities and six are two-year colleges. Approximately 270 contestants from these eleven schools compete at each of the ten regional rodeos. Another unique aspect is that the governing organization, the National Intercollegiate Rodeo Association (NIRA), is run by a twenty-two member national board of directors. Each region elects a regional student director and a regional faculty director (coach) who serve on the NIRA board, which governs the sport of college rodeo.

Hats, boots, spurs, buckle, and denim might be the public's idea of a typical cowboy, but for collegiates this type of outfit is for the ranch or the arena. In the arena, as required by rodeo rules, they dress in boots, a western hat, and a long sleeve shirt. Their shirts though are not the traditional pearl-butoned, closely fitted style with a yoke. They wear the oversized ones sold by Bugle Boy, Cavaracci, and other popular brands. On campus they wear college t-shirts, with starched Wranglers for guys and starched Rocky Mountains for girls.

The one article that remains universal to even the collegiates is the trophy buckle. The buckle itself is a trophy, much like the mounted antlered buck that a successful hunter displays. The belt buckle is a symbol that announces the status of the cowboy. The gold and silver of a professional national champion's Gist-brand buckle can be spotted across a restaurant, arena, airport, or dance floor. A Gist buckle is the Mercedes of

The cowboy's trophy buckle is even worn with a tuxedo at a wedding. Turtle Powell is dancing with his sister, Nena Powell Boettcher at her wedding in Alpine, Texas.

buckles. Once a Gist is won, other buckles are usually thrown in a drawer or sent home for display in the family glass-top coffee table.

The vests, required for college rodeo contestants, are as individual as the students. All must display the college name on the front and back, but each student often chooses his or her vest color and style. The vests reflect many interests, such as American history, ranch life, folk and Indian art. Vests are never yellow in the Southwest because cowboy superstition designates yellow as bringing bad luck. Yellow rain slickers are the only exception.

Along with the differences in vests are differences in dress for the various events. A bronc rider may have a feather in his hat; a roper never would. Ropers' hat bands also are usually simple black bands with a silver buckle. A rough-stock rider wears chaps that reflect his tastes in color, glamour, religion, or folk art. Ropers never wear chaps. Rough-stock riders frequently wear high-heeled boots. Timed event contestants usually wear the lower one-inch heeler Roper boot. The rough-stock rider and the roper both wear the new lace-up boot that harkens back to the old-time rancher's lace-up boot.

The collegiates' pickups and horse trailers indicate a variety of lifestyles. Their pickups, or as they call them, "trucks" or "rigs," go from plain to fancy, often with the traditional dog in the back. The dog is usually a blue-heeler, but rottweilers, spitzes, and other breeds are becoming more popular. The horse trailers span the spectrum from utilitarian to luxurious trailers that can carry five or six horses and have all the comforts of home, including television and running water. The trailers may sport commercial ads about their owners' horses, their preference in drink, or their religion. They also may advertise their owners' names, titles, and events.

Horses' names and contestants' nicknames signify a variety of cultural aspects. Their horses might have conventional names such as Paint, Roany, Black, and Yeller. Reflecting the Western and rodeo culture are Stetson, Gunnysack, and Jerkline. Others represent American's penchant for food: Popcorn, Iceman, and Beer. Nicknames for collegiates may indicate their home state, such as Gator (Mississippi) and Tater (Idaho). Others are

Rough stock riders wear chaps that reflect their preference in color, glamour, religion, or folk art named for western towns, Sheridan, Cheyenne, and Cody. One girl from Wyoming wanted a double name as is often used by Texans. Instead of just Cori, her roommates named her Cori Bob. One cowboy was named Round Bale, indicating his size. Others identify attitude, such as Tuff and Rodeo.

The attitude toward life for the collegiates basically holds true to the Old West ideals. A roper may loan his horse to another roper who might win the event, yet he will be the first to say to him, "You made a hell of a run." Hospitality abounds in the college rodeo world. Seldom does a cowboy or cowgirl lack for a bed anywhere he or she goes. Most have friends everywhere on the circuit. If a contestant's home is close, usually the parents have to pick their way across the floor in the morning to miss the sleeping rodeo kids.

Some college cowboys bring their superstitions to college. They would never take a fifty-cent piece if they were broke. Bad luck is sure to happen if a coin is picked up, unless it is heads-up. They would hold their hat all night rather than lay it on the bed. Then, they might be seen drawing a circle on the ground and spitting in it to hex another cowboy's run in the rodeo.

Humor is the way to handle most situations for the collegiates. Jokes are used to induct new kids into the group and to redirect a pretentious cowboy or cowgirl's attitude. If they cannot handle jokes, the others will, as they say, "hard-ass them until they learn how to take it." Humor is always abundant when cowboys and cowgirls party. One cowboy commented about partying at the notorious Crystal Bar in Alpine, Texas, "You have to clean your feet when you come *out* of there." Injuries often generate humor. One rodeo cowboy after a fist fight had a broken jaw and an eye swollen shut. He said, "If you think I look bad, you should have seen what I did to his hand." Another had two black eyes and a broken nose. When a comment was made to him about having a fight, he said, "Yep, he damn-sure knocked me out from under my hat."

Never admitting to pain is one of the unwritten laws of the code of the college cowboy. I saw a cowboy almost cut his thumb off while dallying (turning the rope around the saddle horn) in team roping. He rode over to another cowboy who had

College cowgirls are an independent breed. They arrive on campus with a dog, two or three horses, a horse trailer and a truck. Shown is Melanie Graf, Vernon, Texas.

not seen it happen. Calmly, he said, "Will you hold my horse? I think I cut my thumb off." Another one broke his leg in the bull riding at the College National Finals Rodeo. While on the stretcher going to the ambulance, he asked for a walking cast so that he could ride his second bull the next night. College cowboys perpetuate this stoicism. While judging a junior rodeo, one college cowboy bent over a kid lying in the arena who had just been bucked off a steer. Appearing to help him, he quietly, but sternly, said to him, "Get out of the arena, you little cry-baby."

College rodeo cowgirls and cowboys are as independent a breed as were the open range cowboys. Most arrive on campus for their freshman year with two or three horses, a dog, a horse trailer, and a pickup. Often, they have to travel twenty-four hours one way to a rodeo. As one said, "The rodeo is so far that I will have to change the oil in my truck twice before I get home again." When a rodeo kid calls, the first question that he or she is asked is usually, "Where are you?" When they leave, they usually say, "See you down the road."

The educated cowboys and cowgirls are adding their own working and dressing style to rodeo events. Yet their attitude toward life indicates a strong attachment to the traditional western ways. Most collegiates would say, "My door is open to you. I laugh at my problems, and I can take care of myself." With over two hundred colleges and universities fielding rodeo teams, this new breed is putting a new brand on an old American sport.

Endnote

All photographs are by Sylvia Mahoney.

COW POKES **By Ace Reid**

"Wul, we ain't got rain er grass, but we've got lots of grasshoppers...and to show our independence, we won't ask fer government assistance...we'll let them grasshoppers starve by themselves!

19

Laughing at the Clouds: Texas Drought Humor

★

Rana K. Williamson

TWO OLD MEN SAT ON THE FRONT PORCH ONE SWELTERING afternoon in 1953 discussing the drought. Rainfall in more than three-quarters of the state was well below normal, and dust-bowl conditions had returned to parts of the Panhandle. Despite the grim reports, one of the men gazed hopefully at thunderclouds off in the east and said, "Joe, looks like rain, don't you think?"

"Sam, long as you've lived in West Texas you ought to know better'n that."

"But Joe, just look at those big clouds over there."

"Hell, Sam, they're just empties coming back from Florida" ("Fine Wool" 33).

Nobody but fools and newcomers predict the weather in Texas. Since one of the earliest recorded Texas droughts resulted in the disappearance of the Antelope Creek Focus, a native culture on the Canadian River in the mid-fifteenth century, recurring droughts have driven settlers from the state and plagued the generations of those who stayed. To cope with such emergencies, Texans have developed a distinctive drought mentality characterized by wryly poking fun at themselves and by black, "gallows" humor.

The term "humor" describes a subjective and exclusive body of material. Jokes associated with given segments of society often fall flat for outsiders. Boundaries of understanding may be cultural, regional, professional, racial, sexual, or as in the case of drought, circumstantial, but humor peculiar to a particular group offers insight into its values and concerns (Mintz 17).

Tragedy or hardship frequently inspires gallows humor. Consider the story of the soldier who lost his hand in battle. A friend asked him about the injury. The soldier replied, "I decided to take the advice of the . . . Yellow Pages—'Let your fingers do the walking.'" To listeners who have not participated in battle or been wounded, the humor is grisly and difficult to appreciate (Ziv 55).

In much the same vein, people from outside Texas have trouble identifying the ironic reality in the story of the tourist who remarked to a native: "Awfully rainy weather, just like The Flood."

The cowboy frowned and asked, "The Flood?"

"You know," said the stranger, "The Flood, Noah, the Ark, Mount Ararat."

The cowboy shook his head, "Sorry friend, but I ain't seen the paper yet this morning" (House 7).

Drought anecdotes paint a grim picture of the state in all seasons, and jokes often describe the perils of land transactions during those dry times. In the summer and drought of 1954, an Englishman visited Texas to buy a ranch. The real estate salesman could see that what he had to offer did not impress his client. As he drove along a rutted, dusty lane, a roadrunner jumped out of the brush and sprinted along in front of the truck. "My word, what is that?" asked the visitor.

The agent, hoping to salvage the sale, replied matter of factly, "That's a bird of paradise."

"Then he's a beastly long way from home," the Briton shot back (Kelton interview).

The story does not reveal whether the Briton bought a piece of paradise or not, but one disgusted Texas farmer did manage to turn the real estate tables in his favor before quitting the state. As he and his family headed back East after years of battling the harsh West Texas climate, a neighbor saw their wagon, pulled by an old mare and a scrawny ox, and flagged them down. "What happened to your other horse?" he asked.

"The drought got so bad ole Dollar just couldn't take it and he up and died on me. So I traded a feller two sections of land for this here ox," the farmer answered.

"Sounds like a steep trade," the neighbor remarked.

"I'm satisfied," he replied. "I offered him one section, but when we sat down to make out the papers, I found out the damned old fool couldn't read, so I made out the deed myself and stuck him with both sections" (Chariton 37).

A northerner was persuaded to invest in Texas land after he grew tired of the snow and ice. In his new home, around the first of November, he asked a Mexican ranch hand, "Juan, have you ever seen snow here?"

"No señor," Juan answered, "but I have seen rain—twice."

Such unpredictable weather produced an attitude of resignation among natives. A "drouthed-out" stockman reported to the Pearly Gates and announced, "I'm Jasper Mulligan from Pecos County."

St. Peter consulted his book and said, "I'm awfully sorry, but with a record like this I'll have to send you down to Hell." Mulligan shrugged and said, "Well, at least that's some improvement" (Kelton, *The Time It Never Rained* 195).

Milligan's appraisal would probably have been echoed by a limping rancher working his sheep in a pen in 1951. A curious bystander asked, "How'd you get crippled, old timer?"

He replied, "Horse threw me out in the cedar brakes, broke my leg and run off."

Anxious to hear the rest of the story, the on-looker persisted. "How'd you get in to town?"

"Didn't. Crawled a mile or two and died."

"What do you mean you died? You're hobbling around here very much alive."

Slamming the gate behind the last skinny ewe, the man cocked an eye toward the burning sun, spat and asked, "You call this living?" ("It Is Worth It?" 41)

At times resignation turned to frustration and consternation. In the Thirties a Texas newspaperman couldn't decide if long-awaited rains that finally broke a drought but claimed several lives were good or bad. The headline he composed read, "Beneficial rains cause 10 deaths in West Texas." In the Fifties a father lamented, "I wish it would rain—not for my sake because I've seen it rain, but on account of my seven-year old boy" (House 6; Chariton 37).

Drought one-liners inspired ludicrous images. Texans claimed to live in the land of the five-inch rain—the drops were five inches apart. Their cows produced evaporated milk, and the chickens plucked themselves to escape the heat. A hen caught with her tail pointed toward a Panhandle dust storm had to lay the same egg half a dozen times. The crops were so bad the crows had to lie on their stomachs to steal corn. Pet ducks and frogs fell into buckets of water and drowned. An Odessa oil man needed water so badly for his drilling rig, that he offered to trade oil for water, barrel for barrel. A West Texas cowboy was struck by a drop of rain, and the shock was so great it took two buckets of sand to revive him (Chenoweth and Kelton 72; Chariton 35, 36, 39; House 10; Webb 73; Worcester).

Under such circumstances, many people turned to prayer. In 1889 a Coleman County stockman, beset by drought and a troubled economy, persuaded an elderly neighbor to lead them in prayer. As the men bowed their heads, the old gentleman attempted to intercede with God. "Oh, Lord, give us help; give us barrels of flour, barrels of sugar, barrels of coffee, barrels of chile pepper . . . .." At that point, a friend jabbed him in the ribs and whispered, "Jim, dry as it's been, that's a way to hell too much chile pepper" ("Just What's Needed, Lord" 48).

In a neighboring county the preacher suggested the community come together to pray for rain. A skeptic in his congregation said, "Go ahead if you want to, parson, but prayin' ain't gonna do you a bit of good unless the wind's outta the east" (House 6).

Different denominations suffered in different ways. In 1889 the *Taylor County News* reported a June so dry that "the fish in the creeks are carrying toadstools for parasols . . . [and the] Baptists and Campbellites are beginning to favor baptism by sprinkling, and they have quit turning their noses up at Presbyterians . . . " (Holden 109). One old-timer claimed things were so dry in his neck of the woods that the Baptists only sprinkled and the Methodists just used a damp cloth (Worcester).

And then there were those who didn't know exactly where to direct their prayers. Like many families on the Edwards Plateau in the 1950s, the Billy Allens of Kimble County listened to Henry Howell's farm and ranch program on radio WOAI, San Antonio, every morning at six o'clock. When the program was over, Billy would pick up his coffee and walk out to the yard, hoping to see some sign of rain. One morning his little son, Tom, followed his father outside. They stood silently for a few minutes, hands on their hips, staring up at the clear sky. Then

Tom solemnly asked, "Daddy, when are God and Henry Howell gonna let it rain?" (Allen).

Drought humor gained a visual dimension in the 1950s in the work of Texan cartoonist Ace Reid, who grew up in Wichita County in the 1930s. His father, an oil field worker and small ranch operator, waged a daily battle against triple enemies—drought, depression, and dustbowl. This struggle left indelible images in the younger Reid's mind and gave him the determination to make a better life for himself. He did not foresee, however, that the key to realizing that dream would be a combination of artistic ability and the one thing he hoped to escape, drought.

After returning from the South Pacific when World War II ended and attempting various business ventures, Reid's first cartoon appeared in the *National Quarter Horse Journal* in 1946. By 1951 his drawings appeared regularly in the *West Texas Livestock Weekly* just as the opening stages of the seven-year drought became apparent. Reid, a colorful folk figure in his own right, used his "Cowpokes" panel and the laconic ranch hands, Jake and Zeb, to depict the ironies and hardships of life in drought-stricken Texas (Erickson 31).

The theme proved so successful, Reid continued to use it long after the rains returned in 1957. In 1966 his cowpokes read a newspaper whose headlines proclaimed, "Drouth gets worse," "Cattle Prices Hit Bottom," and "Feed Yards Go Broke." Jake's comment, "Them people in that poverty area are livin' on $400 a year, that beats me by about $200." That same year, Jake visited a fortune teller and commented, "Madame, that blond sounds fine, but can't you be more definite about the cow market and the next rain?" (Reid, *Cowpokes Comin' Yore Way*)

His attitude ran true to form in 1974. With a spraying rig strapped to his back, Jake told Zeb, "Naw, I ain't trying' to kill my bitter weeds, it's so dry I'm going' down and spray my fish fer ticks!" In another panel he described drought conditions and blasted the myth of the land-rich Texan. "To think, all this ranch is mine, 15,000 acres of land, no grass, five miles of creek, and no water" (Reid, *Cowpokes Ride Again*).

In the spring of 1990, when areas around Sanderson and Dryden measured only two inches of rainfall in two years, the boys were shown on the loading dock of Bud's Feed Store. As

Jake dragged a feed sack into the truck he said, "Yeah, we jist got over one drought, now we're gittin' ready fer another one." That summer Jake surveyed his cattle and explained, "Now this is my welfare herd, they jist stand around and bawl for another handout" (McClure; Reid, "Cowpokes").

Reid's ability to find humor in events causing mental and financial depression and communicate it visually and verbally stemmed from his subtle perception of black humor's therapeutic value. Texan novelist Elmer Kelton displayed a similar understanding in *The Time It Never Rained,* a fictional account of the 1950s drought.

In the 1930s, Kelton, like Ace Reid, watched his father battle the nagging lack of rain, in his case on the McElroy ranch near Crane. The 1950s found Kelton working as a reporter and livestock editor for the *San Angelo Standard Times.* In *The Time It Never Rained* Kelton presents a portrait of the demoralizing effects of drought through the losing struggle of his main character, rancher Charlie Flagg (Kelton interview).

As Flagg and his neighbors suffer increasingly from the drought, a ranch hand, Lupe, dredges up a time-worn joke, in a vain effort to comfort his employer. "The time Old Noah built his Ark, we don't get but a quarter-inch here at Rio Seco." And when the braggart Rounder Pike assembled an audience, he related the unhappy fate of the San Angelo cow thief who turned himself in after he stole two heifers and lost eighty dollars on the deal (Kelton 114, 232).

In 1987, Kelton observed that the jokes circulating in the 1950s were a way of helping people get by a day at a time. Something had to offset the brutal conditions. Kelton remembered San Angelo dust storms that turned the sun into a muddy orange ball. He saw bawling cattle follow pickups through pastures as stockmen tossed government feed off the tailgates. And he recorded an exchange between a Big Spring banker and his client. "If it don't rain pretty soon, looks like I'm gonna have to rob a bank," said the executive.

"If it don't rain pretty soon," replied the rancher, "looks like I've already robbed a bank" (Chenoweth and Kelton 71–72).

Such self-deprecating cynicism, coupled with the western tradition of exaggeration, bred a large body of weather-related humor in Texas. It reflected the resiliency of spirit essential to facing life in a state where annual rainfall could drop below three inches in some areas. The Almighty designed Texas to be dry. Some folks found that out the hard way.

One afternoon in 1957, two Bandera men sweated over the chore of building a water-gap in a dry creek bed. Suddenly a clap of thunder sounded and pelting raindrops drove them to the shelter of a large cedar bush on the bank. No sooner had they reached its branches than a four foot wall of water roared across the spot where they had been standing. One man turned to the other and said, "By damn this Texas sure is a funny world, ain't it? It's either too 'nuff or too nuthin' in all the wrong places" (Hatfield 40).

Bibliography

Allen, Margaret. Interview with Rana K. Williamson, February 1991.

Bureau of Business Research. "1953—Year of the Drought." *Texas Business Review* 26, no. 7 (July 1953).

Chariton, Wallace O. *Texas Wit and Wisdom.* Plano, Texas: Wordware Publishing Inc., 1990.

Chenoweth, Dean and Elmer Kelton. "Texas Dry Humor." *Readers Digest*. March 1953.

Dunn, Roy Sylvan. "Drouths in Texas." *The Handbook of Texas.* Walter Prescott Webb, H. Bailey Carroll, Eldon Stephen Branda, eds. Austin: Texas State Historical Association, 1952.

Erickson, John R. *Ace Reid-Cowpoke*. Perryton, Texas: Maverick Books, 1984.

"Farms Dry Up Again—But Farmers Stay Put." *Business Week.* 22 May 1954.

"Fine Wool and Clippings." *Sheep and Goat Raiser.* April 1953.

Hatfield, Thomas M. "Drought and Texas Cities." *West Texas Historical Association Yearbook* 40 (October 1964).

Holden, William C. "West Texas Droughts." *Southwestern Historical Quarterly* 32 (October 1928).

House, Boyce. *I Give You Texas.* San Antonio: The Naylor Company, 1943.

"Is It Worth It?" *Sheep and Goat Raiser.* December 1951.

"Just What's Needed, Lord." *Sheep and Goat Raiser.* April 1954.

Kelton, Elmer. Interview with Rana K. Williamson, 14 November 1987.

———. *The Time It Never Rained.* New York: Doubleday, 1973.

Lowry, Robert L., *A Study of Droughts in Texas.* Austin: Texas Board of Water Engineers, 1959. Plates IX-XI, 17–18, 19.

McClure, Joe. "Western Drought—Trans-Pecos Region Suffering Deeply From Two Year Dry Spell." *San Angelo Standard Times.* 1 April 1990.

Mintz, Lawrence E. "American Humor and the Spirit of the Times." *It's A Funny Thing, Humour.* Anthony J. Chapman and Hugh C. Foot, eds. New York: Pergamon Press, 1977.

Reid, Ace. *Ace Reid's Cowpokes Comin' Yore Way.* Kerrville, Texas: Ace Reid Enterprises, Inc., 1966.

———. "Cowpokes." *San Marcos News.* 29 March 1990.

———. *Ace Reid's Cowpokes Ride Again.* Kerrville, Texas: Ace Reid Cowpokes, Inc. 1974.

Webb, Walter Prescott. "Billion Dollar Cure for Texas Drought." *Harper's.* December 1953.

Worcester, Don. Interview with Rana K. Williamson, October 1990.

Ziv, Avner. *Personality and Sense of Humor.* New York: Springer Publishing Company, 1984.

20

The Blues and Jives of Dr. Hepcat

Alan Govenar

"HEY THERE, CHAPPIE, 'LO CHICKS, YOU'VE LATCHED ONTO THE Rosewood Ramble with your music recorded. That's a cool deal that I'm going to wheel. So stand by while I pad your skull."

With this introduction in jive talk Lavada Durst, with the call name "Dr. Hepcat," began his show on KVET radio in Austin. He then proceeded to play Duke Ellington's "Things Ain't What They Used to Be," and for the next hour he treated listeners to the big band and rhythm-and-blues hits of the day until signing off with Ellington's "Deep Blues." Thus Lavada Durst's profession consisted of carrying both the linguistic and the musical traditions of black Texans through a large part of the twentieth century.

In the late 1940s Durst made jive talk the hallmark of his radio show, which was on the air from 10:30 to 11:30 P.M., Monday through Friday, and from 9:00 to 10:00 A.M. on Saturday. Durst was the first black disc jockey in Texas and began broadcasting in 1948. "John Connally was the principal owner of KVET," Durst remembers, "and he hired me because of my reputation as an announcer at baseball games in the Negro leagues for the Austin Black Senators and Austin Black Pioneers. Connally took the chance of integrating radio, and it was a big success for him and for me."

During his show Durst used jive talk to pique the interest of his listeners in making introductions to records, public service announcements, and commercials: "Jive talk was common on the street corners and byways in black communities at that time. It was the talk that hipsters young and old alike used to communicate with one another."

Jive talk was first popularized in its modern form by musicians in the 1920s. Based on a variety of African-American colloquialisms and folk speech, jive talk was used on the radio, in trade journals, magazines, and newspapers. In the *New York Amsterdam News,* managing editor Dan Burley wrote in his column "Back Door Stuff" that jive talk was a by-product of Swing jazz that "first saw its light of day within the Savoy (ballroom) where it had myriad variations and countless definitions started by musicians playing" and was quickly adopted by dancers and fans.

Burley devoted several columns in the *Amsterdam News* to jive talk, and in 1944 he published his own book on the subject, entitled *Dan Burley's Original Handbook of Harlem Jive.* In this book Burley provided numerous examples of dialogues in slang with translations, followed by a full glossary called "The Jiver's Bible."

By all accounts jive talk was widespread among African-American musicians of the Swing era in the 1930s and 1940s, although its usage was clearly not limited to New York, and its etymology was probably rooted in the folk speech of earlier periods (Brown, Conrad, Dalby, Gold, Taylor). According to Lavada Durst, jive talk was common across the United States: "It was a lingo, a jargon, a way to say something to your friends without outsiders knowing what it was you were saying." Durst, however, was unaware of Dan Burley's column or book on the subject.

In 1953 Durst published his own booklet entitled *The Jives of Dr. Hepcat,* in which he provided a fourteen-page description of how to use jive, followed by a glossary of terms: "It was based on what I heard and was geared toward my listening audience, although I had trouble distributing it. I couldn't do it. I didn't know how. At that time it was selling for fifty cents, which was big money then. It was sold around Central Texas in drugstores and groceries. There were only two record shops in Austin, and none of them were black."

Durst was ultimately unsuccessful at marketing *The Jives of Dr. Hepcat* and at establishing himself commercially as a "jive talk" aficionado. Despite these limitations, however, he continued to work part-time as a disc jockey at KVET for approximately fifteen years, but also kept a day job as a recreation leader at Rosewood Recreation Park in East Austin. "I was athletic supervisor," he says; "I taught boys and girls how to play softball, baseball, and tennis, and also promoted musical shows that were held in the gym (which was known as Doris Miller Auditorium, named after the black hero of Pearl Harbor). There were teen hops and adult dances. I promoted the big bands, including T-Bone Walker (My cousin Lonnie Polk was T-Bone's valet.), Ray Charles, BB King, Ella Fitzgerald, Ruth Brown, Sam Cooke, Charles Brown, Nat King Cole, Duke Ellington, and Coleman Hawkins. Just name them and I can claim them."

In addition to his multi-faceted work as disc jockey and jive linguist in the Austin African-American community, Durst was an active bearer of black music traditions. Born in Austin, January 9, 1913, he learned to play the piano as a child and emulated the traditional styles he heard growing up. "I was self-taught," he recalls; "I used to slip across the street to the church house and one-finger that piano. I had heard Meade Lux Lewis and

Lavada Durst, Dr. Hepcat, at the piano (Courtesy Alan Govenar)

Pete Johnson on record and around Austin I heard a lot of piano players, Baby Dotson, Black Tank, and Boots Walton."

In 1933 Durst met the legendary Robert Shaw, who was then living in Austin. "Robert was a master of barrelhouse blues who played that Sugarland [Texas] style of fast piano," Durst says, "combining blues with ragtime and stride." From Shaw, Durst learned the rudiments of what is now referred to as the Texas barrelhouse piano style. Over the years, Durst has carried on and elaborated this tradition, although his audience has changed: "When I was young I used to play at house-rent parties, barbecues, and Saturday night suppers, and then after I became a disc jockey I would make appearances with different bands. I played some with Johnny Simmons, who passed some time ago, but was one of the best musicians in this area of Texas. As a novelty I'd take over the piano for a few numbers and his band would kind of back me up."

In the early 1950s Durst met the legendary Don Robey: "He had already started Peacock Records, and he'd contact all the black disc jockeys. He came to Austin promoting records, and I told him about my playing and about a local spiritual group called the Bells of Joy which Robey later recorded." Durst claims to have written a song for the Bells of Joy called "Let's Talk About Jesus," which became their first big hit. Unfortunately, Durst was never credited and never received payment or royalties: "I was too ignorant to put down that I was the author because I was a blues singer," he says. "At that time people were stifled by tradition. Blues and spiritual songs didn't mix. Of course, I found out later that these old traditions didn't hold much water."

In 1953 and 1954 Durst recorded two sides for the Peacock label himself. His recordings included "Hattie Green" and "I Cried All Night" and featured Durst on piano backed by studio musicians playing guitar, tenor saxophone, trumpet, and drums. About these sessions, Durst says, "I had some idea of what to expect. I had already recorded 'Hattie Green' and 'Hepcat's Boogie' around 1949, 1950, for Fred Caldwell, the program director at KVET" *(Down South Blues)*. Caldwell owned the Austin-based Uptown label, but Durst never got any royalties. "I was hoodwinked into that," Durst states. "Caldwell later got fired at KVET and was replaced by Bill Deeson. So, when Robey came along I was ready to record again, but it didn't turn out much better. I made the record, but it never went anywhere on the charts, and I didn't get anything out of that other than the fifty or so dollars I got paid after the recording session."

In the late 1950s Durst became manager of "The Chariottes," an Austin-based spiritual group comprised of six black women: "They recorded some songs for Robey using my lyrics. One of their better known numbers was 'Step by Step,' which was eventually made into sheet music. You can still find it in churches today, but I got no money for that either."

During the late 1960s Durst's interests changed. He became more involved in his church and in 1965 was ordained a minister at the Mt. Olive Baptist Church in Austin. He held this position until 1972, when he was named Associate Minister at the Olivet Baptist Church, where he still works today.

Durst stopped playing the piano between 1965 and 1975. "If you belonged to the church," he says, "and you were a Christian then you were not supposed to play blues. But my values were set straight by Dr. Wicks, pastor of the Olivet Baptist Church, who said, 'Gifts are God given and it's no harm to pursue your God given gift.' So I started playing again and soon I was contacted by different arts groups and started playing for them and at festivals, but I refused to play in bars or nightclubs."

In the early 1980s Documentary Arts, a non-profit organization in Dallas, recorded Durst as part of a compilation entitled "Deep Ellum Blues" that was released in 1986. In 1987 Tary Owens assembled the "Texas Blues Reunion" and later issued a compilation album called *Texas Piano Professors* on his Catfish label (#1002) which featured Durst with Erbie Bowser, T. D. Bell, and Grey Ghost.

The songs in Durst's repertory are mostly traditional and usually feature renditions of his earlier recordings, "Hattie Green," "I Cried All Night," and "Hepcat's Boogie," accompanied by others that he learned as a young man, such as "How Long," "Piggly Wiggly," "Evil Woman," "Staggerlee," and "Black Gal" (Rowe, Szilagyi, Simond). Some of his songs are original, including "I Need My Baby," a slow tempo blues, and "Lookin' Back" and "I Believe I'm On My Way," which are essentially talking blues that recount Durst's early years and the house-rent parties of his youth. In his playing Durst combines elements of barrelhouse and boogie woogie with improvisatory talking blues and jive. "My left hand was influenced by the solid bass that I heard on the records of Albert Ammons, Meade Lux Lewis, and Pinetop Smith," Durst says, "but my right hand goes crazy with those Sugarland riffs that I learned from Robert Shaw. I like to finger the piano lightly. I tickle the keys and make it up as I go along."

Endnote

Editor: A barrelhouse was exactly that—a barn or shed lined with barrels of beer and whiskey, cleared at one end for a piano and cleared in the middle for dancing, and with a convenient back door leading to the "ladies" stalls. "Barrelhouse" as applied to music is a generic term. Barrelhouse music is loud and driving and in the black traditions of blues and ragtime. The bass was heavy, sometimes eight-to-the-bar boogie, sometimes the steady stomp of the stride, a long-step dance, almost in march time. The treble jazzed around the tune line with as much variation as the player could muster. The piano is the center of barrelhouse music, but when guitars, basses, horns, reeds, and drums are available, a whole band plays barrelhouse. As Robert Shaw says of his style of piano barrelhouse: "When you listen to what I'm playing you got to see in your mind all them gals out there swinging their butts and getting the mens excited. Otherwise you ain't got the music rightly understood. I could sit there and throw my hands down and make them gals do anything. I told them when to shake it, and when to hold it back. That's what this music is for. . ." (Robert Shaw. "Texas Barrelhouse Piano." Almanac Records #10, by Mack McCormick).

Bibliography

Brown, Claude. "The Language of Soul." *Rappin' and Stylin' Out: Communication in Urban Black America.* Thomas Kochman, ed. Urbana: University of Illinois Press, 1972. 134–40.

Conrad, Earl, ed. *Dan Burley's Original Handbook of Harlem Jive.* New York: Dan Burley, 1944.

Dalby, David. "The African Element in English." *Rappin' and Stylin' Out: Communication in Urban Black America.* Thomas Kochman, ed. Urbana: University of Illinois Press, 1972. 170–88.

Down South Blues 1949–1961. Uptown recording: African Folk Society Lp 3428.

Durst, Lavada. Personal interviews. 1983 through 1992.

———. *The Jives of Dr. Hepcat.* Austin: 1953. Dallas: Documentary Arts, 1989.

Gold, Robert S. *Jazz Talk.* New York: The Bobbs-Merrill Co., 1975.

Rowe, Mike. "The Jives of Dr. Hep Cat." *Blues Unlimited* March/April 1978: 4–7.

Simond, Ada. "Dr. Hep Cat Uses Insights of Disc Jockey to Aid Ministry." *Austin American-Statesman* 5 August 1984: B14.

Szilagyi, Pete. "Doctor of the Air Waves." *Free And Easy* No. 9, January/February 1975.

Taylor, Clyde. "The Language of Hip: From Africa to What's Happening Now." *First World* 1 (January/February,1977): 25–32.

Texas Piano Professors. Catfish 1002.

Figure 1 San Marcos City Cemetery

21

Motorcycles and Majorettes: Grave Markers for Youth in Central Texas

Rollo K. Newsom

SOME YEARS AGO I BECAME AWARE OF A GRAVE MARKER IN A CITY cemetery in San Marcos that I thought was out of the ordinary. The back side of this fourteen-year-old male's marker had the word "LATER" (presumably a contraction of "See you later, alligator") and a motorcycle carved into the stone. The front side was quite traditional, except for two quails carved into the bottom edge of the stone. His nickname, "BUBBA" was on the footstone (Fig. 1).

Later I happened upon a striking marker for a thirty-two-year-old male in the Centerpoint Cemetery. The marker was over six feet tall and the east face was, except for its size, fairly traditional. It had traditional symbols, a book (the Bible?) at the top, stairs leading through the gates of heaven, the deceased's picture, and vital statistics. The other faces of the marker were not so traditional. The south face said,

> MY HEART IS A
> MELODY
> BEATING A TEMPO
> YET UNBROKEN
> AND MY MIND IS A
> BIRD ON THE WING
> A SERAPH WITH
> A GOLDEN NOTE,
> THOUGHT, BUT STILL
> UNSPOKEN
>
> by Stacy

The poem was written by the deceased, Stacy. The west face (Fig. 2) showed a pyramid with the words "THE 13th FLOOR ELEVATORS," an Austin rock band of the sixties, and "Lead Guitar 1965–1970," Stacy's position in the band. The north face said,

Figure 2 Centerpoint Cemetery

BLESSED WITH
THE MAGIC OF
MUSIC
THE WRITTEN
WORD
AN EYE FOR
BEAUTY
AND A LOVING
HEART

These two markers led me to begin to notice the ages of persons whose markers were in some way peculiar or distinctive. Then I noticed what I now believe to be a general practice: it seems to me that we mark the graves of adolescents and young adults in ways that are different from the ways we mark the graves of other people, especially the very young and the very old.

Perhaps experience has taught us to expect a substantial loss of life among the very young and among middle-aged and older adults. Mortality statistics would certainly lead to that conclusion. But neither the statistics nor our experiences would suggest that we should expect adolescents or young adults to die. I believe that we have a special feeling for those who die in their prime, in their youth. It is often unexpected, and it upsets our sense of order, our sense of justice. It seems inappropriate, an insult to the fitness of things. In addition to the grief we feel at the loss of any loved one, we feel an added injustice when the deceased is young. It is this additional feeling of a disordered world that leads us to mark the graves of adolescents or young adults in special ways that are different from the ways we mark the graves of those who die in the fullness of their time.

Sometimes the distinction among grave markers is principally in size. A marker for a thirty-year-old male in the Blanco Cemetery is at least nine feet tall and is by far the largest and most noticeable marker in the cemetery. Another marker for a twenty-four-year-old female in the same cemetery is not by itself notable. It is just over waist high, but it is in a family plot and is approximately three times as large as the marker for her parents and other relatives who lived a more normal life span.

The Fredericksburg Catholic Cemetery contains a marker for a twelve-year-old male that is topped with a large and elaborate statue of an angel. This marker is notable in itself, but it is made even more so by the other very modest and traditional nearby markers in the family plot. In Fischer there is a relatively conventional marker for an eleven-year-old female that includes an epitaph:

> DARLING VERA, SHE HAS LEFT US
> LEFT US, YES, FOR EVERMORE
> BUT WE HOPE TO MEET OUR LOVED ONE
> ON THAT BRIGHT AND HAPPY SHORE.

None of this is really exceptional, neither the symbols nor the epitaph on this marker, but the size of Vera's marker is at least three times the size of the markers for nearby relatives who died at more "appropriate," advanced ages.

If the size of markers for some young people does not catch the eye, then the nature of the marker itself might, as with the one for a twenty-six-year-old male in the Port Lavaca cemetery. Even in Port Lavaca it is unusual to mark a grave with a large concrete fish and or to use a real anchor and welded chain as a footstone (Fig. 3). Neither is it common to have an anchor styled to resemble a cross (or vice versa) as is the case on a Port Lavaca grave for a twenty-three-year-old male (Fig. 4). In the Lockhart City Cemetery is a large (head high), half-egg-shaped marker for a nineteen-year-old male. This marker has what appears to be a lightning bolt carved into the face of the stone and a small painted stone decoration that reads, "DEATH IS ONLY A MEMORY OF LIFE." Neither the form of the stone nor its message is clear to me, but the marker is large and distinctive, and definitely demands the viewer's attention.

Sometimes, it is not so much the marker itself, as it is the decorations that catch the eye. For example, in Boerne there is a grave for an eight-year-old male whose stone is pretty but not remarkable. What is remarkable are two large ornamental cedar trees flanking the marker that catch the eye and make this grave site the first thing one notices upon entering the cemetery. A marker for a nineteen-year-old male in the Lockhart Cemetery

Figure 3 Port Lavaca City Cemetery

Figure 4 Port Lavaca City Cemetery

is very traditional. It does have his nickname carved into the stone and a small wooden cross, but it also has a large foot stone that reads:

> I AM A PET ROCK.
> MY NAME IS IRVIN.
> I BELONG TO JIM MADDOX.

It strikes me as exceedingly unlikely that we would decorate an older person's grave with a pet rock. I do not think we would even think of it, but here it seems touching, moving, even appropriate.

More often, the graves of the young are distinguished by the carvings that adorn their stones. One twenty-one-year-old male's marker displayed his picture in his Boy Scout uniform, flanked by the U.S. flag and the flag of his scout troop, Troop 104 of the Alamo Area Council (Fig 5). The use of elaborate epitaphs was declining by the 1930s, but his read:

> PRESERVE TO ME THE LOVE, THE JOYS
> THAT RING MY WORK ABOUT
> AND HELP ME LEAD MY GIRLS AND BOYS,
> DEAR LORD, TILL SCHOOL IS OUT.

The heart-shaped marker is popular for teenage girls and young women. One marker in New Braunfels has the

Figure 5 New Braunfels Cemetery

traditional picture, but here the picture has a cover that can be closed (Fig. 6). Below the picture is the parental epitaph:

GOOD NIGHT PUNKINS, PLEASANT DREAMS
LOVE YOU, SEE YOU TOMORROW
MOM DAD
GOD BE WITH US ALWAYS, 'YOU NEEDED ME'

Nicknames, such as "PUNKINS" here, appear frequently on youth grave markers. In Blanco, "Robbie" is carved into the gravestone along with the figures of Robbie as a baseball player and a football player, complete with uniform numbers (Fig. 7). A New Braunfels twenty-two-year-old male has an eighteen-wheeler carved into his stone marker (Fig. 8). A Lockhart stone shows a marker for a twenty-four-year-old male decorated with well used boots and an oil derrick carved into the stone (Fig. 9). A Lockhart stone for a twenty-one-year-old male displays a dirt

Figure 6 New Braunfels Cemetery

Figure 7 Blanco Cemetery

Figure 8 New Braunfels Cemetery

Figure 9 Lockhart City Cemetery

bike (Fig. 10). Nearby, another twenty-one-year-old male's stone shows a touring bike.

In the Port Lavaca Cemetery there is a very pretty, traditional marker for a twenty-two-year-old female, with a picture of a shrimp boat in a setting with a beach, birds, and sunrise or sunset (Fig. 11). Was she a shrimper? Was she an artist, with the carving depicting a picture she painted? We do know that she was a young woman and that someone did something very unusual on her grave marker. Also very unusual and in the same cemetery is a fourteen-year-old male's marker that is a granite slab covering the entire grave with a long prose epitaph. Carved near the bottom edge is an upside-down skateboard and an automobile. In the Edna Cemetery is a marker for a twenty-two-year-old male with a Ford Bronco carved into the stone. The bottom left of this marker has some sort of derrick-like industrial structure (Fig. 12).

The generations that reached their majority in the 1930s might have anticipated high maternal mortality, but by the

Figure 10 Lockhart City Cemetery

Figure 11 Port Lavaca City Cemetery

Figure 12 Edna City Cemetery

1990s we most emphatically do not expect the deaths of young mothers. We might, then, respond to the extraordinary with an extraordinary grave marker such as the one in Shiner Cemetery for a twenty-three-year-old mother. It has the names of her three children carved into the stone and a picture of her with the girls on the bottom left.

A long single grave stone in the Boerne City Cemetery marks the resting place of an eighteen-year-old boy and girl who died on the same day, presumably together, and were buried side by side (Fig. 13). A heart with a dove is centered over each grave, and the connecting stone contains a heart with "T + R," for Timothy and Renee. A carved drum majorette and the words "MY SISTER" grace her end of the stone. A football player, backfield number "31," and the words "OUR BROTHER" are carved in his end of the stone. The figures are facing each other, just as the carved doves are flying toward each other, drawing the two sides of the marker together into one unified gravestone. Both sides have small dolls resting on the foundation stone. Additionally, under Timothy's side a football helmet holds flowers; a

Figure 13 Boerne City Cemetery

small majorette statue stands under Renee's end of the stone. Their epitaphs were on each side of the initialed heart and were inclusive of both young people.

THE ROAD OF LIFE	THEY FELL ASLEEP
AHEAD THEM LAY	IN THIS LIFE OF GRIEF
WHEN GOD ABOVE CALLED	AND WOKE TO A WONDROUS
THEM HOME TO STAY	LIFE OF PEACE

This one marker illustrates much of my argument. If this couple had been married and older, or single and younger, even if killed together, I doubt that they would have been given such a personalized marker. If married they might have shared a marker, but not the symbolic linking "T + R" or the other symbols of youth. Neither the majorette nor football figures nor the interrelated epitaphs would be fitting for any but the young. These deaths violate our romantic notions of right and order, and hence we, with the markers, violate the expected and create extraordinary memorials.

Another way we distinguish the gravemarkers of young people is with grave decorations that are more distinctive than those used for graves of the elders. A stone in Lockhart has a thirty-year-old male's actual boots, bronzed and permanently attached to the base of the marker. His nickname was "Whispering Slim," and the bronzed boots are being used to hold flowers (Fig 14). More bronzed boots were found integrated into a marker in the Edna City Cemetery, along with the nickname "Felark," a photograph, and at the top right corner a western style hat carved from the stone (Fig. 15).

As previously observed, epitaphs seem to have been decreasing in popularity throughout most of this century. However, they seem to continue to appear on youth markers with extraordinary frequency. Consider the many examples in the preceding illustrations. We would expect to find epitaphs on older grave markers, and we do find many, like the one from 1916 for nineteen-year-old Hilda that says,

SLEEP LOVED ONE ON THE LOWLY BED
FOR THE BLESSED ARE EARLY DEAD

Figure 14 Lockhart City Cemetery

Figure 15 Edna City Cemetery

Clearly not an appropriate sentiment for an older person and not a modern sentiment either.

From the 1950s we have a fifteen-year-old male's epitaph that reads:

> DEAREST CHILD THOU HAST LEFT US
> AND THY LOSS WE DEEPLY FEEL
> 'TIS THE LORD THAT HAS BEREFT US
> OF ONE WE LOVED SO WELL.

Moving into the 1980s, a marker for a seventeen-year-old female reads:

> SHE BROUGHT JOY
> TO EVERYONE SHE MET
> HER BEAUTIFUL WAYS
> WE CANNOT FORGET.

The epitaph "KAYLA'S EYES" appears on the back of a heart-shaped teenager's marker and reads:

> ON A BEAUTIFUL DAY
> IF YOU LOOK TO THE SKIES
> YOU'LL WITNESS THE BEAUTY
> OF KAYLA'S BLUE EYES
>
> IF YOU LOOK AT THE STARS
> ON A CRYSTAL CLEAR NIGHT
> YOU'LL SEE LITTLE KAYLA'S EYES
> TWINKLING BRIGHT

Another heart-shaped marker, this time for a young mother in the Lockhart City Cemetery, includes an epitaph that reads, "LOVING MOTHER OF DESTINY." I do not know what that means, but I feel that it has something to do with her age. She was just twenty-one.

An epitaph for one youth suggests a short but hard life. From Lockhart the epitaph for a twenty-seven-year-old male reads "LIFE IS TOUGH, THEN YOU DIE." Would anyone have put that on the marker for a man who died at, say, eighty-seven or seventy-seven or even forty-seven? Perhaps life for this young man was tough and perhaps cruel as well, but think how bitter the person who survived must be to leave that message on his grave marker.

Death to young people is such a distortion of the expected that even when the deceased is unknown we may memorialize them with a very distinctive marker, such as the one in Fredericksburg that reads:

> Here lies the murdered body
> Of a young girl found near
> Fredericksburg, Sept. 20, 1927.
> Laid to rest with Christian
> Ceremonies Sept. 30, 1927
> Erected by Boy Scouts of Am.

The young who die in military service deserve special attention. We are all familiar with the highly stylized and rather austere markers used for those who have served in the military. These have remained remarkably the same since the Civil War. But for some military deaths, particularly young ones, we carve distinguishing messages and symbols such as the Air Force, Navy, and Marine symbols that can been seen on several markers in the Luling City Cemetery. The marker for a twenty-one-year-old sailor reads "I, LIKE MANY OTHERS DIED TO SAVE DEMOCRACY FOR YOU." One sailor who "DIED MAY 20, 1943 IN A PLANE CRASH SOME WHERE IN THE PACIFIC" has his picture in uniform on the left side and a picture of his B17 on the right side (Fig 16). In the Blanco Cemetery is a marker from World War I, for brothers, two young men age twenty-two and twenty-three with only one day's difference in their death days. Their marker displays crossed American flags and the epitaph:

> THEY HAVE THE SOLDIERS RECOMPENSE
> THEIRS IS A PATRIOTS GRAVE
> WHERE CALM IN DEATHS REPOSE
> OUR NOBLES TRUE AND BRAVE

Figure 16 Luling City Cemetery

Figure 17 Fredericksburg Catholic Cemetery

A WW II memorial for twin brothers who were buried at sea in 1945 is quite large and is placed between their parents, where it substantially dwarfs the parents' markers (Fig 17).

I have not gathered the kinds of records that would permit the computation of statistical probabilities of the patterns shown in these figures. Hence these are not conclusions or findings in a scientific sense. They are observations which I believe illustrate the tradition that we mark the graves of adolescents and young adults in ways that are different from the ways we mark the graves of other people.

NOTES

The title of this article was inspired by Carol Edison's article, "Motorcycles, Guitars, and Bucking Broncos: Twentieth-Century Gravestones in Southern Idaho" in *Idaho Folklife: Homesteads to Headstones* edited by Louie W. Attebery (Salt Lake City, University of Utah Press, 1985).

All of the photographs were taken by the author between September 1991 and February 1992, using a Nikon FG set on "program" and Kodacolor 64 film. Special thanks to the Media Services division of the Alkek Library of Southwest Texas State University for photographic reproduction services. The photographs are from twenty-one different cemeteries in central Texas (if central Texas is considered to be on or close to a line drawn from Fredericksburg on the west to Port Lavaca on the east). Particular cemeteries were selected because they were convenient to me or because I was there anyway.

Texas folklorists have not neglected the study of Texas grave markers. The use and meaning of seashell grave markers has been described by Sara Clark in "The Decoration of Graves in Central Texas with Seashells," p. 33–43 in *Diamond Bessie and the Shepherds,* ed. by Wilson Hudson, PTFS XXXVI (Austin: Encino Press, 1972) and by Terry Jordan in his "The Roses So Red and the Lilies So fair: Southern Folk Cemeteries in Texas," *Southwestern Historical Quarterly* 83:32 (1980), p. 227–58, and in *Texas Graveyards: A Cultural Legacy* (Austin: The University of Texas, 1982).

Mexican-American grave decorations have been analyzed by Lynn Gosnell and Suzanne Gott, "San Fernando Cemetery: 'Decorations of Love and Loss in a Mexican-American Community,'" *Cemeteries & Gravemarkers: Voices of American Culture,* Richard E. Meyer, ed., (Ann

Arbor: UMI Research Press, 1989) 217–236; by Beverly Kremenak-Pecotte, "At Rest: Folk Art in Texas Cemeteries," *Folk Art in Texas,* Francis Edward Abernethy, ed., PTFS XLV (Dallas: Southern Methodist University Press, 1985) 52–63; by Dorothy Jean Michael, "Grave Decoration," *Backwoods to Border,* Mody Boatright, Donald Day, eds., PTFS XVIII (Dallas: Southern Methodist University Press, 1943), 129–36; and by Anita Pitchford, "The Material Culture of the Traditional East Texas Graveyard," *Southern Folklore Quarterly* 43 (1979), 277–90; and John O. West, "Folk Grave Decoration along the Rio Grande," *Folk Art in Texas,* Francis Edward Abernethy, ed. PTFS XLV (Dallas: Southern Methodist University Press, 1985), 46–51.

22

Singing People Are Happy People: A Brief Look at Convention Gospel Music

★

Richard J. Mason

CONVENTION GOSPEL MUSIC AND COMMUNITY GOSPEL SINGING are two variations of an American heritage that dates to colonial New England. Although many proponents claim that jazz is the only unique American contribution to music, community gospel singing and gospel singing conventions weaken the sanctity of this claim. Gospel singings speak to the nature of rural folklife where individuals re-enact the process of community through artistic folk expression. They sing religious hymns and reaffirm warm bonds of social support through the informal festival of a picnic among neighbors. "All day singing and dinner on the grounds" still stimulates thoughts of a cozier time in rural America when society's embrace was much more cohesive and humane than today's urban business relationships.

Gospel music was the main venue for creative folk expression in rural Southern agricultural communities during the late nineteenth and early twentieth centuries. Evangelistic singing masters toured rural America teaching musical fundamentals to young audiences and providing them the opportunity for self-education and artistic expression. Modern academics have lugubriously labeled this singing genre the seven-shape-note tradition of church hymnody but fortunately spared the rural folk such onerous titles. Ask a convention participant for a label and you'll hear: "Singing people are happy people."

It is impossible to explore the myriad manifestations of community singings in a single paper, which is unfortunate since this folk-art form attracts less scholarly attention than it deserves. Outside George Pullen Jackson's *White Spirituals in the*

Southern Uplands, a classic work now five decades old, folklorists, historians and other intellectual flavors of the academy have produced little beyond an occasional article. The Texas Folklore Society fortunately has witnessed at least two of these presentations in the last twenty years, one by Francis Abernethy, another by Everett Gillis. In 1987, grants from the American Association of State and Local History and Ruby M. Mason underwrote a series of interviews with singing school teachers, convention singers, and employees of songbook publishing companies in Texas, Alabama, and Tennessee. Those interviews provided most of the information for this discussion.

One can contend that community singing and its more formal cousin, convention gospel music, constitute the first instance of mass musical participation in American popular culture. If we view American vernacular music in this century, technological advancements such as radio, recordings, and taped cassettes provide mass folk participation in specific musical genres such as rock 'n' roll or country-and-western music. Characteristic too are the large urban crowds at concerts in which spectators undergo a communal musical mass experience which, to old-timers, is as exciting as an afternoon in traffic.

Gospel music generated a similar experience, although the nature of mass participation differed because of the impediments of rural life before rural electrification. Instead of purchasing the latest albums or cassettes, community singers bought convention books. Rather than passive entertainment at the hands of musical specialists, community singers in Valley Mills, Becton, Bradford, Indian Creek, Gilmer, or Throckmorton gathered on appropriate weekends and actively created their music from those same convention books. And, instead of lusting after the latest release of George Strait, the Rolling Stones, or Guns and Roses, rural community singers joyously awaited songs written by Albert Brumley, Joe Roper, or Virgil Stamps. They were there on the same page in each new convention book, as right as rain and as constant as summertime 'skeeters in Southeast Texas.

In the homogenizing confinement of rural Southern culture, community singing was a hopeful piece of enlightenment.

Singings tended to be interdenominational: "There are no denominations in heaven," singers say, although in the next breath they will tell you it is not likely that there are any fiddle players there either.

The first Texas community singing using the seven-shape-note tradition reportedly occurred in the latter part of December, 1879. Itinerant teachers representing the A. J. Showalter Company of Dalton, Georgia—including company founder A. J. Showalter himself—ventured west to Giddings, Texas, and conducted a rural music school that lasted for several weeks. At least two individuals from that first school learned enough to continue on as teachers of the seven-shape-note method and were employed subsequently by the Showalter company. The seven-shape-note tradition had arrived in Texas.

Showalter employees carried their founder's zeal for bringing musical education to rural people. The company's primary contribution to seven-shape-note gospel music involved codifying older standards of musical education into simple rudiments which were conveyed to young students in structured singing schools that used these new rudiments for shape-note instruction.

Shape-notes are a musical notation system which reduce the tones of the scale to specific shapes such as circles, trapezoids, or squares. The shapes represent relationships between the root note "do" and the subsequent notes of the melody. It is an alternative form of notation to the more formal method of musical education which conveys the tonal relationships of sound through positions on lines and spaces. Shape-notes are easier on the eyes and less confusing for the minds of neophyte singers.

Published transcriptions of shape-note music employ a compromise with formal musical education today and place the shapes on lines and spaces. Still, shape-notes provide an advantage in vocal music for those who have attended rural singing schools because shape-notes readily accommodate differences in human vocal range. This is done through the movable "do" system which simplifies transposing melody to different keys. As Julie Andrews sings: "When you know the note to sing, you can sing most anything."

Similarly, shape-note music enables singers to move the root note—or key—up or down a notch or two to fit individual vocal ranges because the shapes easily convey the relationship between the root note and subsequent melody. Although the same process can be done using lines and spaces, it engenders a greater challenge because of the combination of sharps, flats, and other changes in position necessary to communicate different keys in the lines and spaces method of musical notation.

The seven-shape-note tradition is a nineteenth-century evolution from the original fasola, or four-note solmization, which developed in colonial America. The four-note form exists today as Sacred Harp, and the Sacred Harp tunebook has remained relatively unchanged since the 1840s. The seven-shape-note tradition, in contrast, became a dynamic vehicle for gospel songwriters in the late nineteenth century and attracted a growing body of new compositions, which demonstrated greater musical sophistication than their fasola cousins. Seven-shape-note songbooks exhibited the musical versatility which appealed to young attendees at singing schools and were responsible, therefore, for the growing popularity of the seven-shape-note tradition.

While community singings are relatively unstructured, convention gospel singings display formal organization. Generally, a convention is a gathering of participants from several communities. Conventions occur on the county, regional, and state levels. In 1936, as community gospel music approached its peak popularity, singers from several southern states gathered at the behest of the songbook publishers to stage the first national gospel singing convention in Birmingham, Alabama. The national convention continues to this day, rotating among various small towns in the South. National conventions were staged at Plainview, Texas, in 1968 and Stephenville, Texas, in 1987.

A convention president operates the singing in a formal but sensitive manner. Individuals are called from the audience to lead the class or congregation. They choose the song and the piano player, and they lead the singing. Convention presidents make sincere efforts to allow all who want to lead the opportunity to do so during the gathering, which operates Saturday afternoon and evening and reconvenes on Sunday.

Convention singing relies on newly-published convention books which participants purchase to take home to their own communities. In fact, without the support of the songbook publishers, convention singing could not have achieved its widespread popularity. In the early conventions, quartets demonstrated the musical ideals of harmonic gospel singing. While many quartets were informal family or friendship arrangements, songbook publishers asked the better groups to represent their companies. While skillfully demonstrating the art form in its ideal, quartets were good practical advertising for songbook publishers. Stamps-Baxter Music and Printing Company in Dallas had a dozen quartets on the road in the 1930s. After World War II, the Stamps Quartet Music Company was represented by more than thirty in the South. In Georgia, Alabama, and Mississippi, quartets aligned themselves with the aggressive Texas music companies.

The other prominent twentieth-century songbook publishing enterprise includes Vaughn Music Company in Tennessee, which originated the trend of using multiple quartets as company representatives in 1910. During the latter part of the twentieth century other songbook publishers of varying sizes have been active, the most notable of which is the Tennessee Music and Printing Company in Cleveland, Tennessee. It is not uncommon in convention gospel music to find an individual who compiles songs, adds a few original compositions, and self-publishes smaller books.

It is important to recognize the formal structures through which gospel music grew in popularity. The music and the ability to sing the music was spread through the rural singing-school tradition which relied on the personal industry of itinerant music teachers. Singing schools using the seven-shape-note system spread rapidly in Alabama, Georgia, and Virginia after 1900; became common in East Texas during the World War I era; drifted into Oklahoma in the early 1920s; and roared into West Texas as that decade came to a close.

In Alabama, local churches hosted annual community singing schools, rotating among denominations. This pattern held true for Texas, although in western regions of the state the community itself put up singing school funding, frequently through an auction of local baked goods.

Singing school teachers became skilled at bidding up prices for the food supplied by the community. They were resourceful, too. When one auction bogged down, a singing school teacher, recognizing his precarious financial situation and facing the gnawing pangs of hunger, carefully studied his agricultural audience and asked, "Well, does anybody have a chicken?"

A typical ten-day singing school began at nine o'clock in the morning and lasted until three or four o'clock in the afternoon. Teachers reviewed musical rudiments. If an individual worked hard, he could master the scale and direct a song at the end of the two-week session. Meanwhile, there was daily practice from the new convention books which the teacher provided. At the end of the session, the community was invited to witness the class debut. Rough-edged farm children, painfully shy, were transformed into heavenly harmonic singers, at least in the eyes of their parents.

The next year, the itinerant teacher returned again to provide more advanced classes. "When we left the community, we left them with something they could use," one singing school teacher said. The practical result was that churches developed choirs, and the overall level of musical competence improved.

The story of twentieth-century community gospel music basically revolves around the success of Stamps-Baxter Music and Printing Company in Dallas, Texas. The company was founded in 1924 by V. O. Stamps, who subsequently entered into a partnership with J. R. Baxter, a former employee of A. J. Showalter. Baxter handled the business end of the operation out of his Chattanooga, Tennessee, office. Virgil Stamps, a gifted, charismatic promoter, took care of all outside affairs and was responsible for the company west of the

V. O. Stamps

J. R. "Pap" Baxter, Jr.

Clarice H. "Ma" Baxter

Mississippi River. In the early 1930s, Luther G. Presley opened a third office in Pangburn, Arkansas.

Innovation characterized the company's operation. V. O. Stamps attracted the major songwriters to his company, lined up the best quartets, and hired the most gifted musical instructors to conduct the music schools. V. O. approached Albert Brumley, author of "I'll Fly Away," furnished him a car, and paid him to produce four songs annually for Stamps-Baxter songbooks. Gifted singers worked in the Stamps printing plant during the day and sang with quartets at nights, on radio programs, or in weekend conventions. Employees also taught in the company's normal school, which offered advanced musical instruction.

V. O.'s typically Texan goal was to develop the largest gospel-music publishing company in the world. While most publishing companies produced one songbook a year, Stamps-Baxter published two convention books annually, beginning in the early 1930s. Printing presses ran day and night in Dallas, and in 1940, Stamps-Baxter generated published music at the rate of a song a day. Sales of convention books alone exceeded 150,000 copies every six months. Despite investments in modern automated printing equipment, the company achieved debt-free status in 1939.

A major factor in the spread of gospel music's popularity lay with new technology. Radio became the secret. Previously, if Virgil Stamps wanted to reach people in Mineral Wells or Austin, he took his quartet there. Through radio, it was possible to reach both audiences simultaneously. The big break occurred during the Texas Centennial celebration. A series of radio studios in glass booths were erected in hexagonal shape at the fair grounds. Rural folk were fascinated. They had heard radio broadcasts but had never seen one in action. Stamps-Baxter Quartets performed several live broadcasts at the state fair, and KRLD in Dallas, impressed with the reception, decided to try a noonday program in the fall of 1936.

V. O. Stamps was an excellent motivator. At the end of most songs, his soothing bass voice asked KRLD listeners: "Folks, do you like this music? If you do, you've got to write this station a letter. Tell them you've got to have this kind of music."

Within a week, KRLD was deluged with mail. It is still possible to find copies of a photograph showing V. O. Stamps seated at a desk behind a mountain of mail. The KRLD broadcasts, sponsored by American Beauty Flower, became noontime staples in Texas. Eventually, live gospel singing expanded into the morning hours at 6:15 and occupied a ten o'clock evening slot. At noon, you could walk down any street in Texas communities within broadcast range of KRLD and hear the Stamps-Quartet singing "Give the World a Smile Each Day."

In 1938, the Stamps-Baxter singing normals in Dallas had become so popular that V. O. decided to host an "All-Night Singing" at the end of the three-week class session in June. KRLD carried the first broadcast, which was held in the Cotton Bowl. At midnight, FCC limitations were lifted. KRLD turned up the wattage, and the broadcast went international. Soon, V. O. and his quartet were traveling to Del Rio and providing wire recordings to radio station XERA for national broadcast. XERA, like other "X" radio stations, usually operated across the border from the United States and was free from FCC regulation. In America the FCC licensing system regulated radio stations to specific markets by restricting the wattage and broadcast reach of a particular transmitter. The outlaw "X" stations ignored such limitations and consequently could be heard across the United States and as far away as ships at sea.

In 1937, V. O. Stamps asked listeners to send a list of their ten favorite radio songs with a dollar bill. He promised the first 1,500 a book—*Favorite Radio Songs*—with their name stamped in gold on the cover. The Stamps-Baxter Music and Publishing Company received 5,000 lists within the first week. These supplied the votes determining which songs to include in the new book. *Favorite Radio Songs* sold hundreds of thousands of copies and became the company's first major special publication.

The startling success of V. O. Stamps' foray into radio promotion attracted interest across the United States. In fact, the president of Sterling Insurance Company in Chicago, Illinois, soon called V. O. seeking a partnership arrangement. Sterling and Stamps-Baxter entered into an agreement to market special gospel songbooks. Each book sold for a dollar. Stamps-Baxter received sixty cents; the insurance company got the other forty cents. The insurance company was permitted access to the mailing list in exchange for operating the staff that handled the mailings. In their first joint venture, this new enterprise sold 800,000 books within a few weeks. Listeners as far away as California purchased books. Then, a few weeks later, each purchaser received a flyer in the mail offering a special on life insurance.

Once Virgil Stamps understood the significance of radio as a tool for reaching mass audiences, he worked to create his own radio station which would broadcast the healing, soothing, and educational harmonies of gospel music. Mr. Stamps was a shrewd entrepreneur. In 1939, Stamps-Baxter employees canvassed Dallas businesses seeking advertising support for the proposed radio station. When the Federal Communications Commission approved the station's license in 1940, the Stamps-Baxter Music Company already had program sponsors signed to contract. But on August 19, 1940, one week before the papers were to be signed that formally awarded the station license from the government, Virgil O. Stamps died unexpectedly. Stamps' calm bass voice had entreated thousands to "keep on keeping on" during the Depression. At the age of forty-seven, "the man with a million friends" fell victim to a heart attack.

When V. O. died, no one else in Stamps-Baxter was willing to pursue his dream of a gospel-music radio station. In the aftermath, Gordon McClendon bought the station, which he named KLIF, and thus took the first concrete steps toward developing modern radio formats. McClendon pioneered the Top Forty concept in musical programming.

Interests changed after World War II. The singing school declined in popularity as people moved to urban centers. Convention gospel music was, after all, a phenomenon of rural America. Meanwhile, quartets discovered they no longer needed sponsorship from songbook publishers and achieved popularity on their own as entertainment acts. The Statesmen Quartet added flourishes which entertained new audiences—exuberant singing, arm waving, hand clapping, and electrifying performances. This was alien behavior for traditional convention quartets. But the new behavior attracted interest. The Statesmen became so popular that subsequent gospel quartets imitated their style.

In fact, quartets like J. D. Sumner and the Blackwoods became so successful financially that they purchased the Stamps-Quartet Music Company in 1962. Similarly the Blackwoods and the Statesmen purchased the James D. Vaughn Music Company in 1964. The publishing end of the companies declined rapidly

The Stamps-Baxter Quartet of the 1960s L to R: Dwight Brock, piano; Bert Carroll, baritone; Wilford Roach, tenor; Charles Collier, tenor; Clyde Roach, bass; Jack Taylor, organ

after the purchase, and rights to the Vaughn company were sold subsequently to the Church of God.

Similarly, Zondervan, a religious publishing company in Michigan, purchased the Stamps-Baxter Music and Printing Company and eventually moved the operation to Michigan. Today, the seven-shape-note tradition of gospel singing has become an isolated niche inside the greater market of gospel music. While a national convention for gospel quartets attracts thousands of devotees and participants from across the United States during the course of a week, the National Singing Convention draws less than a thousand for a weekend meeting somewhere in the South.

The trend parallels musical expression in modern America. Music has evolved from a communal folk activity in which individuals actively participate, into a genre that supports individual musical specialists who reach mass audiences through technological means such as radio and recordings. Convention gospel music and community singings still occur in Mineral

The Neches Valley Singing Convention at Woodville, Texas, 1976

Wells, Brownfield, Seymour, Stephenville, and dozens of small Texas towns. Thanks to good highways and automobiles, participants can travel a couple hundred miles or more in a weekend to attend such gatherings. They sing new songs and old, visit warmly with one another, and re-enact a folk tradition now two centuries old. It is a stable audience but one that ages every year. And every year there are fewer in attendance. From our vantage point on the small end of the twentieth century, Gordon McClendon and his Top Forty format was the direction of the future; V. O. Stamps the highwater mark of the past.

Contributors

Tom Breedlove grew up in South Texas and worked as a petroleum geologist until retirement. He is now engaged in playing cowboy in Fayette County with a registered herd of canners and packers.

Bill Brett was once honestly employed as postmaster at Hull, Texas, in the Big Thicket. He worked in the oil fields and ranched and farmed before he took up writing. Since then he has published numerous books of short stories and the award-winning novel, *The Stolen Steers.* He is a much traveled lecturer about Big Thicket lore and can tell you more about hogs than is necessary for your survival.

Phyllis Bridges has been a member of the English faculty at Texas Woman's University since 1972. She has also served as Dean of the Graduate School, Assistant to the President, and interim Vice President for Academic Affairs. In 1990 she served as chairman of the Southwest American Culture Association and the Australian Literature Section of the South Central Modern Language Association. Presently she is a member of the board of the Australian and American Fiction and Film Foundation.

Mark Busby, a native of Ennis, Texas, is the Director of the Center for the Study of the Southwest at Southwest Texas State University. Formerly on the English faculty at Texas A&M, he is the author of *Ralph Ellison* (1991), *Lanford Wilson* (1987), and *Preston Jones* (1983); the coeditor of *The Frontier Experience and the American Dream* (1989); and contributing editor to *Taking Stock: A Larry McMurtry Casebook* (1989).

George Ewing, born 1923, is a fifth generation Texan who grew up in the Lower Rio Grande Valley and Corpus Christi. After studying and teaching electronics and radar during WWII, he took a bachelor's degree in Bible, carpentered, and preached for a few years before finishing graduate degrees (M.A., '52, Ph.D., '62) in American literature from the University of Texas, writing theses on the frontier preacher in Texas and the verse of the Temperance Movement, the latter published as *The Well-Tempered Lyre.* During his thirty-seven years teaching at Abilene Christian University, he has written a few articles, hymns, book reviews, and poems, drawn publishable doodles, and given ten gallons of blood to the local blood bank.

ALAN GOVENAR is the President of Documentary Arts in Dallas, which he founded in 1985 as a non-profit corporation to broaden public knowledge and appreciation of the arts of different cultures in all media. Dr. Govenar is the author of several books, including *Stoney Knows How, Meeting the Blues, The Life and Poems of Osceola Mays,* and *The Early Years of Rhythm and Blues: Focus on Houston*.

RICHARD GRAHAM is a musician and anthropology student at Rutgers University, researching the cultural dimensions of the central African Diaspora. In between classes and recording for MuWorks in N.Y.C., he indulges a third passion for writing, contributing to a number of journals, academic and otherwise.

LONGINO "LONNIE" GUERRERO is a long-time singer, musician, and composer in Austin. In 1983, when he was sixty-six, he was inducted into the Tejano Music Hall of Fame. He was employed by the East Austin Chicano Economic Development Corporation.

RICHARD HOLLAND was born in Montague County Texas in 1941, the great-grandson of pioneers to the area. He attended the University of Texas for most of the 1960s, eventually receiving three degrees: BA in English (1965), MA in History (1967), and Masters of Library Science (1970). Beginning in 1971 he became Social Sciences Bibliographer in the University of Texas Library. After seventeen years there, Holland moved to the library (now the Albert B. Alkek Library) at Southwest Texas State University, where he became the library's first Special Collections librarian and the founding curator of the Southwestern Writers Collection. Holland is a member of the board of the Book Club of Texas and is editor of the Club's "New Texas Fiction" series.

JANET K. JEFFERY graduated from the University of Texas in Austin with a B.S. in Art History in 1967. A member of the Texas Folklore Society since 1983, she has presented two papers to the Society, the first on Glen Rose moonshine and the other on Texas sunbonnets. She is a technical writer and produces computer documentation for a software development firm in Austin, Texas. In June, 1991, she returned to the University of Texas as a part-time student to study creative writing.

AL LOWMAN of Stringtown is a long-time member and past president of the Texas Folklore Society. His contributions have appeared in several of the Society's annuals over the last decade. He is also a fellow of the Texas State Historical Association and a notorious bibliophile. Having spent twenty-one years on the staff of a half-way house for military retirees in downtown San Antonio, he now directs research for the advancement office at Southwest Texas State University and devotes the remainder of his energy to writing a bibliography of Carl Hertzog, the noted El Paso book designer and printer.

SYLVIA GANN MAHONEY, a native Texan, crossed the line into New Mexico and spent forty years in Lea County where she earned her A.A. at New Mexico Junior College, Hobbs, and her B.A. in English and M.A. at Eastern New Mexico University, Portales. She taught English for five years at Hobbs High School, then she taught English for ten years at New Mexico Junior College. She also was the NMJC rodeo coach and helped found the Lea County Cowboy Hall of Fame and Western Heritage Center and worked as its executive director for ten years. She now teaches English at Quanah High School and lives in Vernon, Texas, with her husband John Mahoney, who is the rodeo coach at Vernon Regional Junior College. She does freelance writing and photography. She has a daughter and a son and five grandchildren.

RICHARD J. MASON is self-employed as a communications consultant in Lubbock, Texas, providing editorial and graphic design services to a broadbased clientele. He previously spent a decade conducting oral histories and gathering historical materials for the Southwest Collection at Texas Tech University and is formerly director for the Nita Stewart Haley Memorial Library in Midland. He has had historical articles published in *Journal of the West*, the *West Texas Historical Association Yearbook* and the *Permian Historical Society Annual*. In addition he has had articles and photographs published in a variety of media including *USA Today* and *Texas Highways* magazine. He conducted research into community singing across the South while employed at Texas Tech.

PATRICK MULLEN is a transplanted Texan living in Ohio, reversing the usual rustbelt to sunbelt migration pattern. He teaches folklore and American literature at Ohio State University and has expanded his field research area from the Gulf Coast of Texas to Ohio and the Blue Ridge Mountains of Virginia and North Carolina. His latest book is *Listening to Old Voices: Folklore, Life Stories, and the Elderly.*

ROLLO K. NEWSOM was born in Sweetwater, and has lived in Texas all his life except for three years in the U.S. Marine Corps and two years teaching in Tennessee. He has earned degrees from NTSU and UT Austin and has been a member of TFS since 1982. Trained as a demographer/sociologist he spent most of his career in university administration. Returning to full time teaching in 1990 he now teaches a course in Texas folklore in the Sociology Department at Southwest Texas State University and is convinced that the only really good job on the college campus is plain old full professor.

NOLAN PORTERFIELD, despite having grown up in West Texas, retains an abiding affection for the state, reflected in both fiction and non-fiction he has published over the past twenty-five years. His biography of Jimmie Rodgers, "the father of country music," won the ASCAP award, and his liner notes for the Smithsonian reissue of *Jimmie Rodgers on Record* earned a Grammy nomination in 1988. A graduate of Texas Tech (B.A., M.A.) and the University of Iowa (Ph.D.), he teaches creative writing at Southeast Missouri State University.

FERNANDO GARZA QUIRÓS was born in Monterrey, Mexico in 1931. His first Alma Mater was Monterrey Tech (ITESM), where he studied for a CPA; his second Alma Mater was Tulane University, where he got a Masters Degree in Business Administration; and at the Universidad Nacional Autónoma de México, where he got his Bachelor in Psychology. He now works as a professor and private consultant. He has numerous publications, the most recent being "Etcétera," an essay on religious practices in northern Mexico.

JOYCE ROACH holds both B.F.A. and M.A. from TCU and is a member and past president of the Texas Folklore Society. Joyce is a three time Spur Award winner for *The Cowgirls,* best book of nonfiction in 1978, "A High Toned Woman," best short nonfiction for 1988, and "Just As I Am," best short fiction for 1990. She co-authored *Eats: A Folk History of Texas Foods* with Ernestine Sewell, which won the non-fiction book prize from T.I.L., and most recently edited *This Place of Memory: A Texas Perspective,* published by UNT Press. Joyce is an instructor in English at TCU, and helps with the family business in Keller, Texas.

JEAN GRANBERRY SCHNITZ was born in Spur, Texas, October 11, 1931. She received her B.S. degree from Texas College of Arts and Industries, now Texas A&I University, in 1952 (summa cum laude). She has been a legal secretary for more than fifteen years, after having been a teacher of home economics and general science. She has been married to Lew Schnitz for thirty-eight years and has three sons and one grandson. She is now and has been involved with numerous professional, social, and civic activities including being Past President of Nueces County Legal Secretaries Association and serving on various boards and commissions, including Texas A&I Alumni Association Board of

Directors. She has performed at the Texas Folklife Festival for the past ten years.

ERNEST B. SPECK, a native of Llano County, is a former president of the Texas Folklore Society, and edited *Mody Boatright, Folklorist* for the Society. He is the author of a number of articles in the Society publications, and has read papers at a good many meetings. After some forty years of teaching in four states, he is now Professor Emeritus of English at Sul Ross State University in Alpine, where he resides.

PAUL CLOIS STONE, a native of Coryell County, Texas, has worked as a journalist, congressional aid, film maker, and cowboy. He is a graduate of Harvard University and received a doctorate in western American history from Yale in 1993. He specializes in the history of folkloristics, anthropology, and western American culture.

JULIA WHITSITT is an associate professor of English at Lander College in Greenwood, South Carolina. She taught for thirteen years at Texas Tech University and has published studies in Victorian and modern poetry. She continues to collect bumper stickers in South Carolina.

RANA K. WILLIAMSON, a native of Junction, Texas, received a B.A. in journalism from Southwest Texas State University in 1986 and an M.A. in history in 1990. She is currently working toward a Ph.D. in history at Texas Christian University in Ft. Worth. Her research in drought humor began while completing a study of the political and economic impact of the seven-year drought of the 1950s for her master's thesis. Williamson will expand this work for her dissertation.

Index

Abernethy, Francis, 177, 268
Abilene, Texas, 60, 167, 168, 169
Abrahams, Roger, 179
Adams, Mrs. Frank, 88
Adams, Kate, 28
Adventures of a Ballad Hunter, 32, 39, 42–46
African folklore, 131–137
Afro-American folklore, 177–180, 185–194, 239–240
Alamo Cenotaph, 24
Albek (Albert B.) Library, 10
Albright, J. F. "Bliss," 73
Alexander the Great, xii
Aley, Texas, 147, 152, 157
Alice, Texas, 169–170
Alpine, Texas, 224, 227
Amarillo, Texas, 98, 166
American Anthropologist, 23
American Association of State and Local History, 268
American Beauty Flower, 274
American Folklore Society, 47–63
American Original: The Life of J. Frank Dobie (An), 4, 14, 26
Ammons, Albert, 244
Anderson County, Texas, 75
Andrews, Julie, 269
antebellum conditions in Texas, 32, 36, 38
Antelope Creek Focus, 231
AntiShyster, 96
Apache Gold and Yaqui Silver, 67
Apache Indians, 90, 93
"Arkansas Traveler," 164
Arrington, Cap, 89
Assadourian, Norma, 28
Athens, Texas, 151
Attal, W. C., Jr., 7
Augustin, J. J., 54
Austin American-Statesman, 7
Austin Black Pioneers, 239
Austin Black Senators, 239
Austin, Stephen F., 25, 36, 141
Austin, Texas, 50, 151, 197, 239–243, 247, 274

Baker, LaVern, 177
Baldwin, James, 177
banat, 209
Bandelier, Adolph, 58
Bandera, Texas, 237
Barbeau, C. Marium, 50
Barker Texas History Center, 3, 5, 28, 151
Barraza, Erasmo, 25
Barry County, Missouri, 159–160
Barry, Phillips, 50
Baxter, J. R., 272–277; photo, 273
Baylor County, Texas, 166
Baylor University, 4, 28
Bean, Judge Roy, 25
Beaty, Dan, 198
Beaumont, Texas, 176
Becktold Bindery, 76, 79
Becton, Texas, 268
Bedichek, Lillian, 18
Bedichek, Roy, 16–19, 27, 45
Beeville, Texas, 171
Bell, Hesketh J., 137
Bell, T. D., 243
Bells of Joy, 242

Beloved, 187
Benavides, Texas, 119
Benedict, Carl Peters, 78, 79
Benedict, H. Y., 78
Benedict, Ruth, 59, 60
Berlandier, Luis, 125
Bierce, Ambrose, 95
Big Bend, 91
Big Spring, Texas, 236
Billings, Harold, 28
Bird Life of Texas (The), 5–7
Birmingham, Alabama, 270
"Black Gal," 243
black music traditions, 241–244
Blanco Cemetery, 249, 254, 263; photo, 255
Bluff Dale, Texas, 217
Boas, Franz, 50, 52–56, 58–59, 62; photo, 51
Boatright, Mody, 17, 19, 79–82, 88, 94
Bob More, Man and Bird Man, 9
Boerne City Cemetery, 250, 259; photo, 259
Boettcher, Nena, photo, 224
Bolton, Herbert E., 55, 56
"Bonaparte's Retreat," 163
bonet, 209–210
Book Club of Texas, 68, 75
Boone, Elmer, 79
border radio, 274–275
Borglum, Gutzon, 24
Bosque County, Texas, 37–38, 41
Bosque River, 36
bottle trees, 132–138; photos, 130, 132, 133, 134
Bourke, John G., 58–59
Bowie, Jim, 25
Bowser, Ernie, 243
Bradford, Texas, 268
Brady, Haldeen, 82, 83
Brammer, Billy Lee, 11
Brill, Captain Son, 175–176, 178–190, 192–193
Brown, Charles, 241
Brown, Ruth, 241
Brownfield, Texas, 278
Brumley, Albert, 268, 273
Bruni oil field, 115, 119
Built in Texas, 109
bumper stickers; religious, 201–207; secular, 221
Burch, Ethel, 59
Burley, Dan, 240
Burt, Addie, 131–132
Bush, George, 99
Bustamante, Dr. Jorge A., 124
Byrd, Jim, 147

Cabriolet bonnet, 211
Calamity Jane, 92
Caldwell, Fred, 242
Calendar of Twelve Travelers Through the Pass of the North (A), 83
Calico Chronicle, 217
Cambridge University, 26, 78
Canadian River, 231
Captain Bill McDonald, Texas Ranger: A Story of Frontier Reform, 154
Carleton, Don, 28
Carlton Press, 155
Carroll, H. Bailey, 78
Carter, Jr., 175–176, 178–181, 183–193
Caruthers, Buddy, 141
Casey, Ellen, 90
Cassidy, Ina Sizer, 69
Cassville, Missouri, 159
Castile, Lady, 88
Catfish Records, 243
"Cathedral Hill March," 163
Caxton Club, 26
Cedar Creek Dam and Reservoir, 147, 150, 151, 157
Centerpoint Cemetery, 247; photo, 248
chapel du bonet, 209
Chariotes (The), 243
Charles, Ray, 177, 241
Chattanooga, Tennessee, 272
Chauvel, 125
Chicago, Illinois, 275
Chicago World's Fair, 62

"Choked Goose," 163
Christian fundamentalism, 201–207
Church of God, 277
Citizens Against Lawyer
Monopolies, 96
Ciudad Juarez, Mexico, 124
Civil War, 160, 263
Class, 202
Cleaver, Eldridge, 177
Cleveland, Tennessee, 271
Clower, Jerry, 120
Cochran, Johnny, 40
Code of the West, 87
Coker, Willie Belle, 5, 6, 8, 9, 27, 28
Cokesbury Book Store, 73
Cole, Nat King, 241
Coleman County, Texas, 234
College National Finals Rodeo, 222, 223, 229
College of Mines and Metallurgy, 67, 69
Coltrane, John, 177
Columbia University, 19
Comanche County, Texas, 160, 166
Conkle, Virginia, 18
Connally, John, 239
Cooke, Sam, 241
Coppini, Pompeo, 24
Corner Forever Texas (A), 5, 27
Corpus Christi, Texas, 171
Coronado's Children, 15, 16, 67
Cortez, Santos, 47
Country Gentlemen, 57
Cow People, 8, 12
cowboy music, 45
cowboys, 31, 44, 45, 221, 222
cowgirls, 222–229; photos, 228
"Cowpokes," 230, 235
Cox, Mayme W., 60
Cox, Mike, 7
Crabb, Bob, 88
Crabb, Mrs., 88
Crane, Ed, 68
Crane, Texas, 236
Cross, Paulette, 190, 192–194
Crow (Indian) Agency, 23
Cushing, Frank Hamilton, 58

Daisetta, Texas, 139, 141, 143
Dallas Morning News, 96, 149, 152
Dallas, Texas, 60, 81, 96, 157, 243, 271, 273–275
Dalton, Georgia, 269
Dan Burley's Original Handbook of Harlem Jive, 240
Daniels, Mrs. Victor, 91
Darden, Getro, 115, 120
Dash, Julie, 137
Davenport, Mrs. F. A., photo, 218
Day, Donald, 75
de Zavala, Adina, 60
"Deep Blues," 239
"Deep Ellum Blues," 243
Deeson, Bill, 243
Del Rio, Texas, 274
Depression, 110, 115, 136, 275
Desdemona, Texas, 160
"Devil's Dream," 163
Dial, Don, 28
Dial, Thornton, 137
Dickerson, Judge, 149
"Dixie," 163
"Dixie Fried," 177
Doan, D. F., 24
Doan's Crossing, 24, 25
Dobie, Bertha, 5–9, 11–16, 26, 28
Dobie, Dudley, 28
Dobie, J. Frank; and American Folklore Society, 47–62; and Bill Wittliff, 8, 9; books, *Apache Gold and Yaqui Silver,* 67, *Bob More, Man and Bird Man,* 9, *A Corner Forever Texas,* 5, 27, *Coronado's Children,* 15, 16, 67, *Cow People,* 8, 12, *Legends of Texas,* 12, 55, 56, 61, 62, *Out of the Old Rock,* 12, *Prefaces,* 12, *Some Part of Myself,* 12, 14, 19, 47, *Tales of Old Time Texas,* 8, 11, 12, 13, *Tongues of the Monte,* 67, *Vaquero of the Brush Country,* 15; conflict with UT, 4;

Dobie, J. Frank *(Continued)*
correspondence, Benedict, Ruth, 60, Bedichek, Roy, 16–18, 45, Boas, Franz, 52, 53, 55, 56, 59, Bolton, Herbert E., 55, 56, Dobie, Bertha, 14, 15, Goddard, Pliny E., 56, Hertzog, Carl, 68, 71–79, Kittredge, George Lyman, 58, Reicherd, Gladys, 61, Roberts, Dr. Warren, 5; corrido on, 197–200; death, 5; diaries, 19–21; Dobie Room, 5, 6; edits Range Life Series, 68–79; estate, 6, 7; folklore revelation, 47; heads TFS, 48–62; market for, 3; papers, 3–28; research files, 22–25; speeches and lectures, 25–26, 57–58; wills, 26, 27; photos, 29, 48
Dobie, Uncle Jim, 15, 47
Documentary Arts, 243
Doris Miller Auditorium, 241
Dorsey, James Owen, 58
Dotson, Baby, 241
Douglas, C. L., 154
Drager, Bertha, 155
"Drinkin' Wine Spo-Dee-O-Dee," 177
Driskill Hotel, 197
Drought, Ethel, 59
drought humor, 231–237
Dryden, Texas, 235
Dugger, Ronnie, 18
dulcimer, 159–173
"Durang's Hornpipe," 163
Durst, Lavada, 239–244
"Dusty Miller," 164
Duval County, Texas, 115
Dyak shaman, viii, xx

Eagle Pass, Texas, 24
East Texas State University, 147
Eastland County, Texas, 160
Edna Cemetery, 256, 260; photo, 258, 261
Edwards Plateau, 234
"Eighth of January," 164
El Capote, 124
El Colegio de la Frontera, 124
"El Corrido de J. Frank Dobie," 197–200
El Paso Public Library, 67
El Paso Salt War, 154
El Paso, Texas, 66, 67, 69, 72, 82, 124
Ellington, Duke, 177, 239, 241
Emmanuel College, 17
Encino Press, 7–9, 83
English, Jake, 24
Espinosa, Aurelio M., 50
Eureka Springs, Arkansas, 132

Famous Texas Feuds, 154
Faulk, J. J., 154
Faulk, John Henry, 16–18, 120
Favorite Radio Songs, 275
Federal Communications Commission, 274, 275
Fehrenbach, T. R., 32
Fenley, Edie, 89
Ferguson, Ma, 216
Fewkes, J. Walter, 50, 58
Fields, William, 40
Fischer, Texas, 250
"Fisher's Hornpipe," 160, 163, 171
Fishtrap, Texas, 141
Fitzgerald, Ella, 241
Flagg, Charlie, 236
Folksongs of the Mexican Border, 61
Ford Foundation, 169
Ford, Henry, 169
Ford, "Rip," 155
Forney, Texas, 98
Fosdick, Stella, 93
Fowler, O. S., 43, 44
Fredericksburg Catholic Cemetery, 250; photo, 264
Fredericksburg, Texas, 263
Freer, Texas, 115, 116, 119, 120
Fussell, Paul, 202

Gaddis, Isabel, 28
Gaddis, John, 147

gamelan music, xv–xx
Garrett, Becky, 82
Garrett, Elihu, 149, 152
Gay Place (The), 11
"Giant Song (The)," 164
Gib Morgan: Minstrel of the Oil Fields, 79–81
Giddings, Texas, 269
Gila Valley (Arizona), 91
Gilliam, Franklin, 28
Gillis, Everett, 268
Gilmer, Texas, 268
"Give the World a Smile Each Day," 274
Glenn, Hubert, 132, 133
"Glide Waltz," 163
Gluckstadt, Denmark, 54
Goddard, Pliny Earle, 50, 53, 56–59
Golden Gems of Thought, 43
Goliad County, Texas, 25
Gone With the Wind, 217
gospel music, 267–278
Government Wells oil field, 115
Graf, Melanie, photo, 228
Granberry, Bill, 171
Granberry, Lena Belle Scudder, 169
Grant, Lyman, 16
grave markers, 247–265; photos, 246, 251–259, 261, 264
Graves, John, 10, 11
Greenhaw, Arthur, 147, 151
Greenhaw, John, 147, 151–153, 155, 156
Grey Ghost, 243
Guerra, Dora, 28
Guerrero, Longino, 197, 198; photo, 199
Guinness Book of Records, 117
Gulf Coast, 190
Guns and Roses, 268

Hacker, Andrew, 194
Haley, J. Evetts, 21, 27, 83
Hall, Sam, 147
Hamburg, Germany, 54
Hamer, Marcelle, 79, 81
Hamilton, Sir John, 95
Hammons, David, 137
Handman, M. S., 59
Hanna, Bob, 45
Hardcastle, L. R., 116
Hardesty, Robert, 10
Hardin, John Wesley, 90
Harrell, Adele, 88
Harrison, Ken, 137
Harrison, R. C., 60
Harry Ransom Humanities Research Center, 3, 5, 10, 27, 28
Harvard University, 48
"Hattie Green," 242
Hawkins, Coleman, 241
Hebronville, Texas, 118
Hellums, "Blackie," 116–118
Help Arrest Legal Tyranny, 96
Henderson, Alice Stillwell, 91
Henderson County Historical Society, 151
Henderson County, Texas, 147, 148, 151–154
"Hepcat, Dr.," 239–241; photo, 241
"Hepcat's Boogie," 242, 243
Hertzog, Carl, 67–83; photo, 68
Hewett, Edgar, 58
Hill, Maggie, 147, 149, 158
History of Henderson County, Texas, 154
hot dogs, 140–146
hog hunters, 139–146; photos, 140, 142
Hogtown, Texas, 160, 163
Holland, Sol, 89
Holmes, William H., 58
Houston Bar Association, 99
Houston, Sam, 26
Houston, Texas, 99
"How Long," 243
Howell, Henry, 234, 235
Hudson, W. H., 13, 19, 83
Huisinger, Edward, 59
Humphreys, SRSU President, photo, 223
Humphries family, 148–152, 155–157

Humphries, Jim, 148, 157
Humphries, Willie, 151
Hurd, C. W., 88
Hussein, Saddam, 98, 99

"I Believe I'm On My Way," 244
"I Cried All Night," 242, 243
"I Need My Baby," 243
I'll Die Before I'll Run, 154
"I'll Fly Away," 273
Illinois State Historical Society, 26
Indian Creek, Texas, 268
Indiana University, 190
Indonesia, ix–xxii
Indonesian folklore, ix–xxii
Indonesian puppetry, xvi–xvii
Institute of Americanism, 83

J. D. Sumner and the Blackwoods, 276
J. J. Little and Ives, 155
Jackson, George Pullen, 267
Jamaican folklore, 54
"Java March," 163
Javanese dance and drama, vx
Jenkins, Jacque, photo, 223
Jennings, Mrs. W. E., 78
"Jenny Lind Polka," 164
Jim Hogg County, Texas, 115
Jim Wells County, Texas, 119
jive talk, 239–241
Jives of Dr. Hepcat (The), 240
"Johnny's Gone for a Soldier," 166
Johns, W. A., 155
Johnson, Pete, 247
Johnson, Robert, 177
Johnson City, Texas, 132, 133
Jordon, Jim, 136
Journal of American Folklore, 50–61
Journal of Mammalogy, 23

Kandu, 135
Keats, John, 95
Keefer-Boatright, Elizabeth, 69
Keeth, Kent, 28
Keillor, Garrison, 112
Keithley, Lee, 15
Kelton, Elmer, 236
Kennedy, John, 197
Kerouac, Jack, 177
Kidder, A. V., 53
Kilgore, Texas, 78
Kimble County, Texas, 234
Kincaid, Edgar, 5–8, 13, 18
King, B. B., 241
King, Larry L., 10, 11
King, Martin Luther, 184
Kingsville, Texas, 171
Kittredge, George, 48, 58
Klasner, Lily, 90, 94
KLIF, 276
KRLD, 274
Kroeber, Alfred L., 50
KVET, 239, 240, 242, 243

La Gloria oil field, 118
"La Tragedie del Presidente Kennedy," 197
Lake Woebegon, 112
Lamar Tech University, 177
Laredo, Texas, 124, 128
"Laughing Cotillion," 164
lawyer jokes, 96–103
Le Blanc, Rene, 28
Lea, Tom, 7, 67, 69–71, 74–77, 80, 83
Lea, Tom, Sr., 76
Leach, Sally, 28
Leadbelly, 177
"Leather Britches," 164
Lee, Columbus Addison, 159–162, 164–167, 169, 171–173; photo, 161
Lee, Cora, 166
Lee, Jean, 11
Lee, Miller, 159, 160
Lee, Nancy Wheeler, 159, 160
Lee, Permelia Caroline, 160, 164, 166, 167
Lee, Russell, 11
Legends of Texas, 12, 55, 56, 61, 62
"Let's Talk About Jesus," 242
Letters of Roy Bedichek, 16

Lewis, Barney, 70, 79
Lewis, Jerry Lee, 177
Lewis, Meade Lux, 241, 244
Lilly, Ben, 79
Lincoln County, New Mexico, 90
"Listen to the Mockingbird," 163
Little Britches, 92
Live Oak County, Texas, 27
"Livvie," 136
Lockhart City Cemetery, 250, 251, 254, 260, 262; photos, 256, 257, 261
Lomax family, 31–36, 38, 42, 43
Lomax, James, 32–36, 38, 39, 41; photo, 35
Lomax, John Avery; and TFS, 48, 81; birth, 34; character, 31, 42; education, 40, 41, 43, 44; family background, 32–34; influences, 38, 39, 42–45; interest in Texas and cowboys, 31, 44; religion, 42, 43; West paper on, 197
Lomax, John, Jr., 197
Lomax, Mary, 40, 41
Lomax, Richard, 33, 41
Lomax, Susan Frances Cooper, 34, 42; photo, 35
Lomax, Tillman, 32
"Lonesome Dove," 11
Lonesome Valley, Arizona, 93
"Lookin' Back," 244
los mojados, 123
Lottinville, Savoie, 13
Lowman, Al, 28, 78–80
Lubbock, Texas, 60, 171, 201
Luling City Cemetery, 263; photo, 264

McCauley, J. E., 73–78
McClendon, Gordon, 276, 278
McCoy, Dorothy Abbott, 119
McCracken, Harold, 13, 14
McDonald, W. J. "Bill," 153–156; photo, 153
McNelly, L. H., 155
Mahan, 147, 148, 152, 153
Mahoney, John, photo, 223
Mailer, Norman, 177
Marcus, Stanley, 68, 73
Martin, Howdy, 148
Martin, James, 133
Mason, Ruby M., 268
Massachusetts Institute of Technology, 50
Matamoros, Mexico, 124, 126
Meador, Newton, 160
Mears, Bill, 10, 28
Meek, J. W. "Dub," 115–118
Memphis, Tennessee, 134
Meridian Blade, 40
Meridian, Texas, 36, 37
Mexican folklore, 15
Mills, Betty, 217
Mineral Wells, Texas, 274, 277
minkisi, 134, 135
"Mississippi Sawyer," 163
mobcap, 210, 211; illustration, 210
Mobeetie, Texas, 89
Modern Language Association, 59
Monaghan, Jim 157
"Money Musk," 171
Montaigne, 95
Montgomery Ward catalog, 212
Morris, G. B., 166
Morrison, Toni, 187
Mt. Olive Baptist Church, 243
"Mountain Hornpipe," 163
Mulligan, Jasper, 233
Murdock, Arietta, 93
The Mustangs, 13
My Rambles as East Texas Cowboy, Hunter, Fisherman, Tie-Cutter, 68, 70–73, 79

Nash Community, 218
National Geographic, 57
National Intercollegiate Rodeo Association, 223
National Quarter Horse Journal, 235
National Science Foundation, 100
National Singing Convention, 277
Natural History, 57

New Braunfels Cemetery, 253, 254; photos, 253–255
New Mexico Folklore Society, 82
New York Amsterdam News, 240
Newell, William Wells, 62
Nichols, Ed, 41, 45
nkisi nkandu, 135
Noble, Tami, photo, 223
Northwestern University, 26
Nugent, Mary, 90

Obeah, 137
Oberholser, Harry, 6
Odessa, Texas, 78, 234
Oglethorpe, James, 95
Ogowe River, 135
oil boom town conditions, 115–120
Oil, Mud & Guts, 119
Oklahoma A&M University, 53
Olds, A. W., 153
Olivet Baptist Church, 243
Ompung, xi
Orton, Esther Scudder, 166, 169
Out of the Old Rock, 12
"Over the Waves," 163
Owens, Jack, 132
Owens, Tary, 243
Owens, William, 16, 18
Oxford, Mississippi, 131

Paducah, Texas, 166, 167
Paine, Albert Bigelow, 154, 155
Painter, Theophilus, 4
Palestine, Texas, 75
Pangburn, Arkansas, 273
Panza, Sancho, 15, 17
Paredes, Americo, 197, 198
Parker, Charlie, 177
Parsons, Elsie Clews, 50, 53, 54, 58
pato, 123–129; photos, 122, 125, 127
Patterson, Jennifer, 28
Patterson, Jim, 147, 148, 152, 155, 156
Patterson, Paul, 88
Payne, L. W., 48, 81, 82
Peabody, Charles, 52, 53
Peacock Records, 242
Pearce, J. E., 59
Pearsall, Texas, 116
Pecos County, Texas, 233
"Peekaboo Hornpipe," 163
Peleliu Landing, 80
Penguins (The), 177
Perkins, Carl, 177
Perry, George Sessions, 4
Petter, Rudolphe, 23
Phillips, Sam, 177
phrenology, 43
"Piggly Wiggly," 243
Pike, Rounder, 236
Pittman, Opal Harris, 217
Plainview, Texas, 270
pogie fishing, 176, 180, 182, 187
poke bonnet, 214, 215; illustration, 214
Pontotoc, Mississippi, 132
Pony Tracks, 13
Port Lavaca City Cemetery, 250–252, 256; photos, 251, 252, 257
Powell, John Wesley, 58
Powell, Turtle, photo, 224
Prefaces, 12
Premont, Texas, 118, 119
Presley, Luther G., 273
Prohibition, 126, 128
Putnam, Edward K., 50

Quevedo, Francisco, 95
Quigley, Elise, 132

rabbit and lion story, 185–188, 192
race relations in folklore fieldwork, 175–195
Ramayana, xiv
Ranch Romance, 12
Rancho Los Olmos, 47, 59
Randado oil field, 115
Range Life Series, 68, 73–78
Ransom, Harry, 4, 5, 9, 27
Ratchford, Fannie, 60, 77
Ratcliff, "No-Eared Joe," 115–120
Rattlesnakes, 22
"Red Wing," 163

Redwine, Cassie, 88
Reicherd, Gladys, 59–61
Reid, Ace, 235, 236; cartoon, 230
Remington, Frederick, 13
Reynosa, Mexico, 128
Rhea County, Tennessee, 160
Rhodes, Eugene Manlove, 87, 94
Rhodes, John, 148, 155
Richards, Ann, 11
Rio Grande, 123, 124, 126–129
Rios, Frank, 197, 198
Roberts, Warren, 5, 9, 27, 28
Robey, Don, 242, 243
"Rochester Schottische," 164
rodeo, 221–229; photo, 226
Rogers, Will, 97
Rolling Stones (The), 268
Roosevelt, Teddy, 163
Roper, Joe, 268
Rose of Cimmaron, 92
Rough Rider Weekly, 93
Russell, Charles M., 5, 82

Sabine Pass, Texas, 175, 180
Sacred Harp, 270
Saint Peter, 101–103, 233
San Angelo Standard Times, 236
San Angelo, Texas, 236
San Antonio, Texas, 9, 15, 24, 60, 81, 234
San Diego, Texas, 119
San Marcos, Texas, 4, 10, 27, 78, 247
San Rafael de las Peladas, 127
Sanderson, Texas, 235
Santa Fe, New Mexico, 57
Sapir, Edward, 50
Sarepta, Miss, 132
Saturday Evening Post, 23
Schnitz, Jean Granberry, photo, 173
Schwarzkopf, Norman, 124
Schweitzer, Albert, 135
Scott, Fate, 147, 150
Scott, Louis Steven, 147, 148, 151, 158
Scott, Pampa, 150–153
Scudder, Dora Lee, 160–173; photo, 167
Scudder, William Lee, 166–168, 171
Seay, James, 137
Sedalia, Missouri, 160
Sedillo, Mela, 69
Selvon, Samuel, 137
Seven Sisters oil field, 115
Seymour, Texas, 166, 278
Shakespeare, William, 95, 96
shape-note musical system, 269, 270, 277
Shaw, Robert, 242, 244
Shiner Cemetery, 259
Showalter Co. (A. J.), 269, 272
Shrake, Bud, 10
Shuffler, R. Henderson, 78
"Significance of the Frontier in American History (The)," 153
Simmons, Johnny, 242
Simpson County, Mississippi, 136
Skolfield, Elizabeth, 53
Skull, Sally, 90, 91, 216
slat bonnet, 214; illustration, 214
Slaton, Texas, 168, 171
Smith, C. R., 82
Smith, Henry Nash, 17, 21
Smith, Pinetop, 244
Smith, T. P., 118, 119
"Soldier's Joy," 164
Some Part of Myself, 12, 14, 19, 47
Sonnichsen, Charles Leland, 67, 154
Soucek, Art, 81
Southern Agriculturist, 12
Southern Methodist University Press, 9, 75, 77
Southwest Gallery, 7
Southwest Library Association, 57
Southwest Review (The), 21
Southwest Texas State University, 4, 10, 14, 16, 28
Southwestern University, 4, 28
Southwestern Writers Collection, 2, 4, 10, 11, 19, 27, 28
Sparks, John, 147, 150, 151, 153
Speck, Ernest B., 86

"Staggerlee," 243
Stamps-Baxter Music and Printing Co., 271–277
Stamps Quartet Music Co., 271, 276
Stamps, Virgil, 268–276; photo, 272
Starr, Belle, 92, 93
State House Press, 155
Statesman Quartet, 276
Stephenville, Texas, 270, 278
"Step by Step," 243
"Steppin' Over the Line," 160
Stetson, John B., Jr., 54
Stevens, Bob, 147
Stevens, Mr. and Mrs. Lewis, 93
Stevenson, Matilda Coxe, 58
Stillwater, Oklahoma, 59
"Story Tellers I Have Known," 12
Stove-Up Cowboy's Story (A), 73–78; illustration, 74
Strait, George, 268
Straw, Nat, 23
Sugarland, Texas 242, 244
Sul Ross State University, 223
Sullivan, Maud Durlin, 67
sunbonnets, 209–219; photos, 208, 218; illustrations, 210–214
Sutton-Taylor feud, 154
Swanton, John Reed, 50

Tales of Old Time Texas, 8, 11, 12, 13
Tank, Black, 241
Taylor, Albert, 143–146
Taylor, Bowen, 139, 141, 142
Taylor County News, 234
Taylor, Hubert, 143–146
Taylor, Jack, 143–145
Taylor, R. E., 141, 142
Tejano Music Hall of Fame, 197
Ten Texas Feuds, 154
Tenderfoot Kid on Gyp Water (A), 78, 79
Tennessee Music and Printing Co., 271
Terry, Sonny, 177
Texas A&M University, 4, 28
"Texas Blues Reunion," 243
Texas Centennial, 274
Texas Folklife Festival, 172
Texas Folklore Society; 12, 28; and American Folklore Society, 48–62; and J. Frank Dobie, 47–48, 52–57, 59–60, 62; Publications, 56–58, 62, 68–83, 172, 177, 197, 268
Texas Observer (The), 18
Texas Panhandle, 88, 99, 203, 234
Texas Piano Professors, 243
Texas Rangers, 150–155
Texas State Historical Association, 3, 78
Texas Tech University Museum, 215, 217
Texas Western College, 82
"Things Ain't What They Used to Be," 239
13th Floor Elevators (The), 247
"Thomas Heywood: The Golden Age," 20
Thompson, Robert Farris, 135
Thompson, Stith, 48, 50, 60, 81
Thorp, Jack, 197
Throckmorton, Texas, 268
Tilley, "Red," 117
Time It Never Rained (The), 236
Tinkle, Lon, 4, 14, 26, 27, 47
Todd, Connie, 28
Tombstone, Arizona, 90
Toney, Bill, 126
Tongues of the Monte, 67
Town and Gown Club, 16
Transition bonnet, illustration, 212
Treasure Island, 107
"Turkey in the Straw," 163
Turner, Decherd, 10
Turner, Frederick Jackson, 153
Tuscavalalalavoo," 165, 166
Twain, Mark, 62, 154
Tylor, Ronald, 190–195

Universal Bookbindery, 81
University Interscholastic League, 16
University of California at Berkeley, 8, 55

University of Chicago, 59
University of Oklahoma Press, 13
University of Texas at Austin, 3–5, 10, 22, 24, 27, 47, 77, 78, 177
University of Texas at San Antonio, 4, 28
University of Texas Rare Book Collection, 77
University of Texas Press, 55
University of Wisconsin, 21
Uptown Records, 242
Uvalde, Texas, 89

Valley Mills, Texas, 268
Vaquero of the Brush Country (The), 15
Vaughn Music Co., 271, 276, 277
Vernon, Texas, 228
Villa, Pancho, 25
Vivion, Lafayette, 24, 25
Voice of the Coyote (The), 13
Vos, Nelvin, 103

Walden Pond, 20
Walker, T-Bone, 241
Wallace, Bigfoot, 27
Walton, Boots, 242
Wardlaw, Frank, 19
Warren, Harry, 20
"Washington's March," 163, 169
Waxahachie, Texas, 218
weather in Texas, 231–237
Webb County, Texas, 119
Webb, Walter Prescott, 4, 17–19, 36, 37, 154
"Wednesday Night Waltz," 163
Weeks, Polk, 155, 156
Weldon, Ida Lee, 160, 167
Welty, Eudora, 136, 137
West, John O., 197
West Texas Livestock Weekly, 235
Wheeler, Mrs., 89
White Spirituals in the Southern Uplands, 267, 268
Wichita County, Texas, 235
Wicks, Dr., 243
Wild West Weekly, 93
"Wild Woman of the Navidad (The)," 8
Wilkinson, Joe, 147, 148, 154–157
Wilkinson, Walter, 147, 153
Williams, Clayton, 216
Williams, Jinita, photo, 223
Wilson, Woodrow, 95
Wittliff, Bill, 7–11, 14, 15, 20, 22, 26, 28, 83
Wittliff Dobie Collection, 8, 9, 11–15, 20- 28
Wittliff, Sally, 8, 9, 11, 14
WOAI, 234
"Wobble Wheels Hornpipe," 163
Works Progress Administration, 23
"World Folk-Lore Congress," 62
World War II, 235, 265, 271, 276
Worrell, Estelle Ausley, 211
Wright, Sol, 68, 70, 72, 73

XERA, 274

"Yankee Doodle," 163

Zondervan Publishing Co., 277